Productivity Revisited

Productivity Revisited

Shifting Paradigms in Analysis and Policy

Ana Paula Cusolito and William F. Maloney

WORLD BANK GROUP

Contents

Boxes

Figures

Tables

Preface

Productivity accounts for half of the differences in GDP per capita across countries. Identifying policies to stimulate it is thus critical to alleviating poverty and fulfilling the rising aspirations of global citizens. Yet productivity growth has slowed globally in recent decades, and the lagging productivity performance in developing countries constitutes a major barrier to convergence with advanced-economy levels of income.

The World Bank Productivity Project seeks to bring frontier thinking on the measurement and determinants of productivity, grounded in the developing-country context, to global policy makers. Each volume in the series explores a different aspect of the topic through dialogue with academics and policy makers and through sponsored empirical work in our client countries. The Productivity Project is an initiative of the Vice Presidency for Equitable Growth, Finance, and Institutions.

The current volume, *Productivity Revisited*, takes stock of recent advances in what it refers to as the "second wave" of productivity analysis, which calls into question much previous research in this area. At the same time, these new approaches provide a new set of tools for navigating the debates surrounding the productivity slowdown and convergence. The work here extends this analysis using international and developing-country data sets and delineates how the findings imply important corresponding shifts in recommendations for productivity policy.

This volume is dedicated to the memory of Jan Walliser (1969–2018), former Vice President of the World Bank Group's Equitable Growth, Finance, and Institutions Practice Group.

William F. Maloney
Chief Economist
Equitable Growth, Finance, and Institutions Practice Group
World Bank Group

Other Titles in the World Bank Productivity Project

The Innovation Paradox: Developing-Country Capabilities and the Unrealized Promise of Technological Catch-Up. 2017. Xavier Cirera and William F. Maloney. Washington, DC: World Bank.

All books in the World Bank Productivity Project are available free at https://openknowledge.worldbank.org/handle/10986/30560.

Acknowledgments

This volume was written by Ana Paula Cusolito (Senior Economist, World Bank Finance, Competitiveness, and Innovation Global Practice) and William F. Maloney (Chief Economist, World Bank Equitable Growth, Finance, and Institutions Practice Group).

The authors thank Ceyla Pazarbasioglu (Vice President, Equitable Growth, Finance, and Institutions Practice Group); Jan Walliser (former Vice President, Equitable Growth, Finance, and Institutions Practice Group); Akihiko Nishio (Director, Strategy and Operations, Equitable Growth, Finance, and Institutions Practice Group); Najy Benhassine (Director, Finance, Competitiveness, and Innovation Global Practice); Paulo G. Correa (Practice Manager, Finance, Competitiveness, and Innovation Global Practice); Catherine Masinde (Practice Manager, Macroeconomics, Trade, and Investment Global Practice); and Jose Ernesto López Córdova (Practice Manager, Finance, Competitiveness, and Innovation Global Practice) for their support.

The work builds on a combination of analytical work by the authors from a series of background papers carried out under the umbrella of the Equitable Growth, Finance, and Institutions Productivity Project. The authors thank Francisco Buera (Washington University in St. Louis), Joel David (University of Southern California), Jan De Loecker (Katholieke Universiteit Leuven and Princeton University), Marcela Eslava (Universidad de los Andes, Colombia), Alvaro García Marín (Universidad de los Andes, Chile), John Haltiwanger (University of Maryland), Pravin Krishna (Johns Hopkins University), Giordano Mion (University of Sussex), Carlos Molina (Massachusetts Institute of Technology), Rafael Prado Proença (Harvard University), Diego Restuccia (University of Toronto), Richard Rogerson (Princeton University), Martin Rotemberg (New York University), Melissa Rubio (University of Gothenberg), Chad Syverson (University of Chicago), Heiwai Tang (Johns Hopkins University), Venky Venkateswaran (Federal Reserve Bank of Minneapolis), and T. Kirk White (U.S. Census Bureau's Center for Economic Studies).

For their contributions, we also thank our World Bank colleagues: Paulo G. Correa, Tatiana Didier, Roberto Fattal, Ana Margarida Fernandes, Leonardo Iacovone, Daniel Lederman, Norman Loayza, Hibret Maemir, Ha Minh Nguyen, Jorge Pena, Daniel Rogger, Luis Sanchez, Joana Silva, and Gabriel Zaourak. Further, we would like to thank Xavier Cirera, Jose Ernesto López Córdova, and Andrei Mikhnev for providing specific inputs for the policy chapter.

We acknowledge invaluable comments from the peer reviewers of this project: Otaviano Canuto (World Bank), Mary C. Hallward-Driemeier (World Bank), Jan De Loecker (Katholieke Universiteit Leuven and Princeton University), and Chad Syverson (University of Chicago), as well as other World Bank colleagues, including Najy Benhassine, César Calderón, Francesca de Nicola, Mark Dutz, Ivailo V. Izvorski, Aart Kraay, Pablo Saavedra, and Sudhir Shetty.

We thank speakers at the World Bank Productivity Conference, who shared frontier knowledge with us and therefore helped us shape the storyline for this book. Speakers included Ufuk Akcigit (University of Chicago), Andrew Bernard (Dartmouth College), Nick Bloom (Stanford University), Jan De Loecker (Katholieke Universiteit Leuven and Princeton University), Romain Duval (International Monetary Fund), Marcela Eslava (Universidad de los Andes, Colombia), Keith Owen Fuglie (U.S. Department of Agriculture), Pinelopi Koujianou Goldberg (Yale University and World Bank Group), John Haltiwanger (University of Maryland), Chang-Tai Hsieh (University of Chicago), Joseph Kaboski (University of Notre Dame), Marc Melitz (Harvard University), Diego Restuccia (University of Toronto), Richard Rogerson (Princeton University), Mark Rosenzweig (Yale University), Esteban Rossi-Hansberg (Princeton University), Chad Syverson (University of Chicago), and Jo Van Biesebroeck (Katholieke Universiteit Leuven). Clearly, they bear no responsibility for the final product, and all interpretations and errors are our own. We also thank Filippo di Mauro (National University of Singapore) for helpful discussions, and we acknowledge fruitful interactions and collaborations with the Competitiveness Network (CompNet).

Production of the volume was managed by Aziz Gökdemir, Michael Harrup, and Susan Mandel of the World Bank's Editorial Production team; Patricia Katayama, of the Development Economics unit, was the acquisitions editor. Nancy Morrison edited the volume.

Abstract

Abbreviations

AI	artificial intelligence
CNP	Mexican National Productivity Commission
ECA	Eastern Europe and Central Asia
GDP	gross domestic product
GVC	global value chain
HS	Harmonized System
ICT	information and communication technology
IPUMS	Integrated Public Use Microdata Series
IT	information technology
LAC	Latin American and the Caribbean
MENA	Middle East and North Africa
NPS	National Productivity System
OECD	Organisation for Economic Co-operation and Development
OLS	ordinary least squares
PER	Public Expenditure Review
P-PER	Productivity Public Expenditure Review
QI	quality infrastructure
R&D	research and development
SAR	South Asia
SSA	Sub-Saharan Africa
STI	Science, Technology, and Innovation
TFP	total factor productivity
TFPQ	physical total factor productivity
TFPR	revenue total factor productivity

Executive Summary: The Elusive Promise of Productivity

The growth of *productivity*—the efficiency with which societies combine their people, resources, and tools—is the main driver of the development process. The appreciation of the central role of productivity enjoys a long and distinguished pedigree. Paul Krugman's oft-repeated quip that "productivity isn't everything, but, in the long run, it is almost everything" (Krugman 1994) echoes the earlier reflections of the medieval Arab social theorist Ibn Khaldun (1332–1406), who argued even more portentously in his *Muqaddimah* (1377) that "civilization and its well-being as well as business prosperity, depend on productivity."

Sustained increases in productivity are critical not only to the average denizen of civilization but also to lifting those who share least in its benefits. Long-term increases in earnings in industry or agriculture—the source of employment and livelihoods for many of the poor—can be achieved only by increasing worker or farmer productivity. Workers will leave informal self-employment only if earnings in the formal sector merit the shift. Hence, the route to generating good jobs transits directly and inexorably through a sustained agenda to raise productivity. In addition, productivity-driven cost reductions reduce the prices of key products consumed by the poor and thereby increase household purchasing power, helping poorer households get more for less. New technologies reduce the cost and improve the efficiency and efficacy of service delivery in all social spheres. Raising global productivity growth is thus arguably the pivotal element of an integrated strategy to generate jobs—and good jobs—and reduce poverty.

The Twin Productivity Puzzles

The central role of productivity has gained renewed salience in current policy debates for two reasons. First, the global productivity engine that powered the advanced world to prosperity has slowed, threatening to reduce the rate at which all countries grow and with which global poverty is reduced. This slowdown in productivity[1] is occurring despite spectacular advances in computing power and a host of derivative technologies: the promise of rapid advances through science and technology seems out of sync with observed slower growth in productivity.

Second, the hoped-for natural convergence of follower countries in the developing world to the global frontier remains elusive, and many countries remain seemingly trapped at low- or middle-income levels. Both dimensions must be resolved to lift global productivity growth rates and reduce poverty.

The Global Productivity Slowdown

There is little consensus as to what has slowed the productivity engine. One school of thought argues that declining economic dynamism—the "churn" in the economy, in the form of job reallocation, firm turnover, and entrepreneurial activity—is responsible for the slump, possibly driven by an increase in regulation or distortions, which are gunking up the growth machinery. Poor regulation and anticompetitive practices are documented to exert a powerful drag on total factor productivity, although to explain the common trends across the diverse member countries of the Organisation for Economic Co-operation and Development would require attributing the slowdown to a type of coordination in driving policies that is not readily apparent. Furthermore, this volume does not find such a decline in churn for a small sample of developing countries. Another view argues that the global financial crisis financially constrained many firms; for those firms that depended more on outside financing, productivity had more trouble bouncing back. Again, the work in this volume confirms that in developing countries finance is generally more constrained, absolutely restricting investments in innovation and productivity. These are, in some sense, manageable issues from a policy point of view: regulation can be improved and the effects of the crisis should dissipate with time.

However, a more profound concern is that the fundamental fuel of growth, technological progress, may be drying up and that while eye-catching advances are appearing almost daily, they do not seem to add up to much in the productivity data, as Robert Solow (1987) noted, raising questions about how truly transformative they are. Furthermore, generating even these apparently lesser ideas is growing harder. Since 1950, the number of researchers needed to generate a unit of total factor productivity has steadily increased (Bloom et al. 2017). Some pessimists, like Robert Gordon (2015, 2017), argue that the best fruits of the tree of knowledge have already been picked. The new harvests are shinier, but far less nourishing to the process of growth.

More optimistic observers see the advent of artificial intelligence, DNA sequencing and cell analysis, high-powered computing, and web connectivity, to name a few, as constituting an entirely new set of tools for discovery or "reinventing inventing" that potentially multiply the productivity of the new processes for generating ideas. As Mokyr (2013, 2014) summarizes, "We ain't seen nothing yet." Furthermore, both the scope and the efficiency of that effort are increasing. The number of global researchers has doubled since 1995, with the largest contribution from developing countries, and information and communication technology facilitates collaboration across great distances. Like the fragmentation of production of goods in global value chains, a new globalization of research effort is evolving in which different research tasks are distributed to countries where they can be done most cheaply.

Some of the resolution of Solow's paradox likely resides in measurement issues. Syverson (2016, 2017) suggests that it is unlikely that the missing productivity can be accounted for by mismeasurement of information and communication technologies or web-related products. However, it is also true that in general, diffusion of technologies takes decades and occurs in multifaceted ways, some of them hard to measure—or even detect at first. Some technologies, like artificial intelligence, require substantial complementary investments in nontangible assets that, on the books, statistically depress productivity today but will appear as growth spikes in the future.

Though the pessimist's viewpoint cannot be discarded out of hand, there is something incongruous about the simultaneous concerns in civilization's discourse that innovation-driven productivity growth is a thing of the past, on the one hand, and on the other, that progress in robotics and artificial intelligence will displace masses of workers through productivity gains. There is evidence of the latter effect in the hollowing out of assembly jobs in the advanced economies thought to be due to automation. As this volume shows, to date there is little evidence of this effect in the developing world. In fact, robots per capita and the share of the labor force in assembly work seem positively correlated.

In sum, there is no accepted view yet on either the sources of the global productivity slowdown, or whether the causes are the same across groups of countries. This volume does not find a pronounced fall in dynamism, increase in industrial concentration, or shift toward lower productivity services in the follower countries that are considered important in the advanced economies.

The Weakness of Economic Convergence

The lack of impact on developing country labor markets may point to a second area of concern prompting new work on productivity: the continued failure of economic convergence. The average person in an advanced economy produces in just over nine days what the average person in the lowest-income countries produces in an entire year (Restuccia 2013). Even were productivity to come to a halt in advanced economies, the potential contribution to raising global productivity and reducing poverty by achieving convergence through technological catch-up is immense.

Yet despite early theoretical arguments for a natural force of convergence among the now frontier countries, it has proven statistically elusive. With some important exceptions, the gap has widened, leading to a "Great Divergence" among nations over the past few centuries (see, among others, Pritchett 1997). This lack of convergence prompted an examination of what the previous volume in this series called the *innovation paradox*. The gains from adopting and using existing technologies, products, processes, and management techniques from abroad are thought to be vast: the radiation of ideas, technologies, products, and processes to developing countries represents a positive externality of truly historic proportions. Yet countries and firms do not seem to exploit these potential gains (Comin and Mestieri 2018). Cirera and Maloney's (2017) focus on missing complementarities—in financial markets, in firm capabilities, and in the business climate—that lower the return to technology adoption offers one possible piece of this second productivity puzzle, but it is far from an exhaustive explanation.

In sum, there is no consensus on the first puzzle of the global productivity slowdown, and the second puzzle remains a long-standing analytical challenge that goes to the core of the World Bank's mandate.

Second-Wave Productivity Analysis

While the literature has not offered a definitive explanation for why the productivity engine has not regained its previous momentum, or why followers are so slow in catching up to the leaders, it has, over the last 20 years, dramatically increased our understanding of the underlying mechanisms and dynamics. More profoundly, it has revolutionized the conceptual and analytical techniques for analyzing productivity and its determinants.

This study pulls together the underlying shifts in paradigm and measurement and terms them the "second wave" of productivity analysis. This new wave has been facilitated by three critical evolutions. First, the access to detailed and high-quality firm-level data has improved greatly in some economies. Second, partly aided by this availability, an academic literature has emerged that critically revisits many established approaches, in particular, the estimation of firm production functions, and from there, the identification and measurement of the drivers of productivity growth. Third, the quantification of human capital or "capabilities" relevant to productivity improvements, in terms of both managerial skills and, more fundamentally, necessary psychological characteristics, has permitted a tentative opening of the black box of the role of entrepreneurship in productivity gains.

This volume employs manufacturing production firm-level data for a variety of developing economies—including Chile; China; Colombia; Ethiopia; India; Indonesia; Malaysia; Mexico; Taiwan, China; Thailand; and Romania—to forward this analytical agenda and ground it in the developing-country reality. The extensive empirical work and conceptual synthesis presented in this volume offers new guidance for productivity analysis and dictates a corresponding shift in how to approach productivity policy in several areas.

1. Employing the new wave of productivity diagnostics and analytics is essential to sound policy design and evaluation.

Many of the approaches commonly used in productivity diagnostics and analysis rest on weak conceptual foundations or use databases that lack key variables. They can lead to *identification problems*—an inability to distinguish among different potential drivers—and potentially erroneous policy prescriptions, mistakes in the inferences of welfare implications and distributional effects from policy reforms, and in the end, an inability to prioritize the policy reform agenda and make it more effective. To mention a few issues:

- *The most commonly used measure of productivity, which is revenue total factor productivity (TFPR, or more commonly written, just TFP), is a flawed diagnostic of efficiency; hence many analyses relating it to market failures or policy reforms are correspondingly unreliable.* TFPR backs out physical quantity measures by deflating firm revenues by *industry*-level price indexes. However, these measures are contaminated by residual firm-level price effects that capture firm-specific input costs, product quality, and market power considerations, all of which may be correlated with policy changes as much as efficiency is.
- *Productivity analysis that does not account for market structure and power may lead to false inferences about the impact of structural reforms and the channels through which they work.* As an example, the evidence from Chile and India presented here shows that the impact of trade liberalization on productivity can vary greatly depending on the structure of input and output markets. More generally, as De Loecker (2017) stresses, the study of productivity and market structure needs to be treated in an integrated fashion.
- *The commonly used metric of dispersion of TFPR proposed by Hsieh and Klenow (2009) is not a reliable measure of distortions in an economy or barriers to an efficient reallocation of factor resources between firms and sectors.* Conceptually, it depends on assumptions that are shown to be unsupported by the data. Moreover, dispersion can be driven by technological and quality differences, investment risk, adjustment costs, and markups. New evidence presented here shows that half of dispersion can be explained by markups and technological differences and thus are not related to misallocation at all. Empirically, inferences about misallocation of factors of production prove highly sensitive to how data are processed, rendering cross-country comparisons unreliable. Indeed, just using the raw U.S. data to calculate dispersion instead of the Census-cleaned data reverses the relationship between the calculated "gains from reallocation" and GDP, showing that the most advanced economies have the most to gain from reallocation.

- *Entrepreneurs cannot be assumed to be similar in human capital, including basic numeracy, managerial and technical skills, or psychological traits.* Traditionally, economics has shied away from opening the black box of the entrepreneur—the individual who on the ground actually combines factors of production or decides to launch a firm. However, the recent research on management quality and on culture, and an emerging psychological literature on the characteristics of successful entrepreneurs, suggest that these dimensions are almost in a definitional sense central to understanding productivity differences.

2. Productivity policy needs to be comprehensive and integrate all three components of productivity growth.

Aggregate physical total factor productivity (efficiency) growth can be decomposed into three components or margins: the reallocation of resources from low-productivity firms to high-productivity firms (the "*between*" component); increases in productivity within existing firms due to technology adoption, innovation, and better managerial skills (the "*within*" component); and entry of high-productivity and exit of low-productivity firms (the "*selection*" component).

The new productivity decompositions presented in this volume confirm that productivity growth occurs across all three margins. However, the within-firm margin is relatively more important than the reallocation of the between-firm margin in four out of six country cases, explaining roughly half or more of efficiency growth in these economies. Thus, the evidence suggests reweighting the policy focus toward firm upgrading.

This said, all three components are inextricably linked. On the one hand, barriers to reallocation of resources driven by distortions—such as trade barriers, poor regulation, or overbearing state-owned-enterprises that impede reallocation—can discourage innovation by existing firms and entry by potentially innovative firms. Thus, policy needs to go beyond standard static analysis and take into consideration dynamic effects. On the other hand, without innovative firms introducing new products and processes, even the cleanest economic system will cease to reap gains from reallocation, making understanding how firms upgrade and where new firms come from as important as eliminating distortions.

3. Policy needs to work on improving both the operating environment and human capital and firm capabilities, two essential and complementary ingredients that cut across all components.

Driving productivity across all three margins in a complementary way are both the operating environment and a range of types of human capital: numeracy, personality, managerial and organization skills, and technological capabilities, as well as firm organizational capabilities. Though policy approaches often weigh one significantly more than the other, productivity growth requires progress on both fronts.

Operating environment. Recent work confirms that competition policy and the reduction of distortions work on productivity through the reallocation channel by facilitating the transfer of resources to more productive firms; through the within-firm channel by stimulating incumbents to invest in productivity-enhancing innovation; and through the entry and exit channel by facilitating the entry of more productive firms and the exit of less productive ones. Hence, opening markets to international trade, exposing state-owned industries to competition, and reducing their ability to prevent the emergence of competitors are over the long term of central importance— subject to the caveat above that the actual impact of these policies may depend substantially on market structure.

Human capital. However, though the overall system may be crystalline— undistorted and with all market failures resolved—if there are no entrepreneurs with the necessary human capital to take advantage of it, there will be no growth. The centrality of this point and the need for better measurement of human capital is highlighted in the World Bank's recently launched Human Capital Project, which seeks to better measure and demonstrate the critical contribution to development of a wide range of skills. This volume documents that the vast majority of the self-employed in the developing world have limited numeracy and literacy skills, which leads to the non-productivity-increasing churning seen in much of the developing world. If the managers inside firms or incipient start-ups lack the managerial capabilities to recognize or respond to new technological opportunities or domestic and foreign competition, there will be no impetus to upgrade their firms or enter the market, and no arbitraging of the technology gap between the advanced and follower countries. The evidence presented here and elsewhere on immigrants makes this case. Some kind of human capital—whether world experience, business training, risk appetite, or tolerance or openness to seeing the viability of a project—permitted them to thrive in the same imperfect business climate and institutional setup in which locals did not. Attracting foreign direct investment is an initial way of transferring technology and driving reallocation, but over the longer term, the enhancement of human capital along several dimensions—managerial capabilities, technological literacy, capabilities in risk evaluation—becomes central for both within-firm performance upgrading and new firm entry.

The two factors, operating environment and human capital, interact importantly. On the one hand, the volume shows that even among the educated in developing countries, entrepreneurship rates are extremely low given the potential arbitrage of technologies to the developing world, perhaps reflecting the absence of these higher-order skills, but also perhaps reflecting a difficult operating environment that makes it unprofitable to start a business. On the other hand, recent work and evidence here suggest that response to policies to increase competition, such as trade liberalization, depends on firms' ability to develop a strategy to meet the competition—the capability to diversify into other products or upgrade to a different market. This, in turn, depends on higher-level firm capabilities that rest on core managerial competencies that developing countries lack.

4. Beyond efficiency: Policy needs to adopt a broader view of value creation in the modern firm.

The firm is the main creator of value added and the ultimate driver of growth. However, the work in this volume confirms and extends recent findings that firm performance or profitability depends on a broader set of firm drivers than efficiency.

Raising product quality. The prices of many products—women's shoes, cars, or even fruit—can vary vastly, and much of that variation reflects differences in quality. Raising quality may actually lower efficiency—because more labor or more expensive inputs are required to produce higher quality—but increase product differentiation and raise overall profits. These findings again suggest the need to model the demand side carefully when analyzing productivity. There is also a role for standard firm-upgrading policies, such as extension services, but also a specific focus on meeting international quality standards and then specialized research and development.

Expanding product demand. Relatedly, evidence from developing countries presented in this volume confirms recent advanced-economy findings that for firm profitability and growth, efficiency concerns are important at market entry, but over the life cycle of firms, cultivating a demand base is more important. Thus, the findings suggest the need to reweight business support services toward helping firms build a large customer base. Policies to support firm growth should therefore focus on scaling up demand, mainly through innovative solutions that reduce buyer-seller transaction costs due to searching, matching, and informational frictions. Examples of those policies include digital platform development or connection, business intermediation, and links to global value chains. Reducing matching costs has been highlighted as a major objective of export promotion agencies to facilitate access to foreign markets.

Clearly, *market power* raises markups and profitability, although, as the volume discusses, the long-term implications for technology adoption and growth are theoretically ambiguous and empirically vary by context.

5. Creating experimental societies: Productivity policy needs to encourage risk taking and experimentation.

Increasing productivity is fundamentally about placing bets under uncertainty—that a new product will become popular, that a new technology will provide a competitive edge, that an idea incarnated in a new firm is a good one and will generate enough business to survive and grow. The volume provides a simple framework of entrepreneurship as experimentation that integrates both considerations of operational environment and a variety of types of human capital.

From the former point of view, minimizing policies that exacerbate risk, such as erratic fiscal or exchange rate policies, is central, as is the establishment of institutions, such as universities or public research institutions that underwrite exploration and technological transfer, financial sectors to diversify risk, and government institutions to enhance and protect the value of profitable ideas, such as research and development (R&D) subsidies or patents.

On the human capital side, it requires individuals who, psychologically, are open to new ideas, can tolerate risk, and are driven to achieve results. Furthermore, these entrepreneurs need the particular human capital and exposure to the technological frontier to identify new products and new techniques to improve efficiency or quality and new markets to enter, and to evaluate and then manage the corresponding risks. They need to develop the capabilities to incorporate information and adjust plans accordingly: that is, to learn.

6. Raising government productivity is critical to raising overall productivity.

Government plays a key role in what can be called the National Productivity System (NPS) by setting the right framework of economic incentives, eliminating distortions, and resolving a broad set of potential market failures or distortions across areas ranging from infrastructure to innovation to education. Like firms, governments make policy under uncertainty, in this case, about which market failures or distortions are most important to address, and what the likely impact of any policy is likely to be. Also, like firms, governments differ in the productivity and quality of output. This "output" can be measured along at least four dimensions: the rationale and design of policy, the efficacy of implementation, the coherence of policies across the actors in the NPS, and policy consistency and predictability over time.

In the same way that the volume documents that firms in follower countries tend to have lower efficiency and produce lower-quality products, it presents evidence that the same is true of public organizations, also with important consequences: bureaucratic effectiveness declines with distance from the frontier precisely as the number of missing markets, distortions, and market failures that need to be redressed become larger. Thus, on the one hand, given finite resources, including the government's attention span (or bandwidth) and capacity, governments need to identify some rough ranking of the policy space to prioritize productivity policies based on the likelihood that they will have a large impact. On the other hand, increasingly the productivity of government allows taking on more of these tasks, and doing them better and in more coordinated ways, and thus improving the operational context and human capital essential to driving productivity growth.

Second-wave analytics are critical for ordering policy priorities. The limited productivity of the public sector dictates improving the ability of governments to identify truly critical failures in the NPS, and then design and implement feasible policies to remedy them. In undertaking this task, policy makers need to quantify the importance of a given market failure or distortion and weigh it against others. The second-wave analysis discussed in this volume has increased the uncertainty around the impacts of some traditionally recommended policies and made the analysis to identify critical policy areas more demanding. As this volume details, this analysis also requires a "second generation" of more detailed firm-level data on prices, marginal costs, intangible assets, quality, and management. Hence an effort at the global and country level to collect such data is necessary.

Governments need to engage in disciplined experimentation. As with the rest of society, in the absence of all the desired information on diagnostics and policies, governments must also become more experimental in searching for the appropriate solutions. Such experimentation requires nimbleness in adjusting to lessons learned and flexibility in measuring performance, including a tolerance for failure. Continuous well-designed evaluation of implemented policies, both as rapid follow up and as sophisticated program evaluation, is a central feature of every relevant government strategy to deal with a problem, as it both reveals information on what interventions work and develops a performance and accountability mindset. It also requires anticorruption policies to permit distinguishing corruption from simply a well-placed but unfortunate bet, and thereby freeing functionaries to take risks. This, along with a recent literature stressing the importance of giving well-intentioned and capable bureaucrats the autonomy to experiment (Rasul and Rogger 2018), points to new paths to rejuvenating the developmental state.

On the other side of the table, the experimentation also needs to be balanced against the fourth dimension of quality government: the consistency of policy over time for firms. Frequent policy reversals or changes in priorities with alternations of administrations adds to firms' uncertainty about the operational environment and discourages investments that could enhance productivity. Furthermore, productivity systems frequently show evidence of undisciplined experimentation over many years that leads to fragmentation of programs and duplication of mandates in many different ministries, without evaluation of the efficacy of the programs or their best location within the system.

Both consistency over time and the third dimension—coherence of policies across the NPS—can be partly mitigated by overarching productivity councils that span administrations, have legitimacy and weight within the public debate, and oversee the overall functioning of the various parts of the system. In the realm of innovation policy, the World Bank's Public Expenditure Reviews for Science, Technology, and Innovation offer a first step by generating a map of government programs and documenting the flow of resources among them. These can be enhanced to take a broader view of government productivity programs that can incorporate all three margins of productivity growth and other dimensions more explicitly. Not only would they reveal the implicit costs of tax write-offs or subsidies for R&D in existing firms, but they could map the competitive structure that those firms face, or the degree of regulatory uncertainty in the system.

Industrial policies need to be integrated into broader productivity policy. While much of the global productivity discussion in this volume focuses on improving managerial, technological, or innovation capabilities or removing distortions across the productivity system, industry-specific externalities—local industry-level knowledge spillovers, input-output links, and labor pooling, for instance—feature prominently in the literature on growth and trade and have been used to justify government support for particular sectors.

Such policies can be thought of in the context of policy ranking by the degree of certainty surrounding the market failure and the likelihood of implementing policy that can make a positive difference. Such targeted policies are arguably not more prone to poor execution than, for example, infrastructure or education; the real problem is that such industry-related externalities have proved extremely difficult to document and quantify, let alone permit a ranking of goods by their potential for productivity growth. Furthermore, the vast heterogeneity in levels of productivity and quality documented in this volume within identical products across different contexts raises concern that these within-product differences portend differences in magnitudes of spillovers in different contexts as well. That is, just because a good might have externalities does not imply that it automatically will; rather, *how* a good is produced is potentially more important than *what* is produced. This volume offers a framework for understanding the roots of this heterogeneity and how to address it.

Concluding Remarks

In sum, the tremendous effort behind advancing the second wave of productivity analysis suggests that Ibn Kaldun's assertion of productivity's centrality to societal progress is widely shared. This volume has extended this new literature, anchored it in the reality of the developing world, and sketched out how it implies a corresponding shift in policy approach. To date, however, the impact of the new analysis has been less to definitively answer central questions in productivity growth than to reopen many debates. Settling those debates will require greater investment in industrial surveys that collect not only firm-level prices, but also measures of quality, market power, investments in intangible assets, and technology and managerial capabilities across all sectors of the economy, including services. Similarly, efforts to understand the drivers of productive entrepreneurship must continue. This volume pulls together the first set of analytical and policy lessons from second-wave thinking to date, but also aspires to lay out the broad outlines of this ambitious analytical agenda going forward.

Note

1. This slowdown was characterized by a decline in labor productivity growth rates from 2.7 percent during the 1999–2006 period to 1.5 percent in 2015, and from 0.9 percent to −0.3 percent for total factor productivity for the same periods.

References

Bloom, N., C. I. Jones, J. Van Reenen, and M. Webb. 2017. "Are Ideas Getting Harder to Find?" NBER Working Paper 23782, National Bureau of Economic Research, Cambridge, MA.

Cirera, X., and W. Maloney. 2017. *The Innovation Paradox: Developing-Country Capabilities and the Unrealized Promise of Technological Catch-Up.* Washington, DC: World Bank Group.

Comin, D., and M. Mestieri. 2018. "If Technology Has Arrived Everywhere, Why Has Income Diverged?" *American Economic Journal: Macroeconomics* 10 (3): 137–78.

De Loecker, J. 2017. "Productivity Analysis Using Micro Data. Where Do We Stand?" Background paper for *Productivity Revisited,* World Bank, Washington, DC.

Gordon, R. 2015. "Secular Stagnation: A Supply-Side View." *American Economic Review* 105 (5): 54–59.

———. 2017. *The Rise and Fall of American Growth: The U.S. Standard of Living since the Civil War.* Princeton, NJ: Princeton University Press.

Hsieh, C. T., and P. J. Klenow. 2009. "Misallocation and Manufacturing TFP in China and India." *Quarterly Journal of Economics* 124 (4): 1403–48.

Khaldun, I. 1377. *The* Muqaddimah: *An Introduction to History.* Princeton, NJ: Princeton University Press. 2015 edition.

Krugman, P. R. 1994. *The Age of Diminished Expectations: U.S. Economic Policy in the 1990s.* Cambridge, MA: MIT Press.

Lederman, D., and W. Maloney. 2012. *Does What You Export Matter? In Search of Empirical Guidance for Industrial Policies.* Latin America Development Forum. Washington, DC: World Bank.

Mokyr, J. 2013. "Is Technological Progress a Thing of the Past?" Vox CEPR Policy Portal, September 8. https://voxeu.org/article/technological-progress-thing-past.

———. 2014. "Secular Stagnation? Not in Your Life." In *Secular Stagnation: Facts, Causes and Cures,* edited by C. Teulings and R. Baldwin. VOX EU.

Pritchett, L. 1997. "Divergence, Big Time." *Journal of Economic Perspectives* 11 (3-Summer): 3–17.

Rasul, I., and D. Rogger. 2018. "Management of Bureaucrats and Public Service Delivery: Evidence from the Nigerian Civil Service." *Economic Journal* 128 (608): 413–46.

Restuccia, D. 2013. "Factor Misallocation and Development." In *The New Palgrave Dictionary of Economics,* online edition, edited by Steven N. Durlauf and Lawrence E. Blume. Basingstoke, U.K.: Palgrave Macmillan.

Solow, Robert M. 1987. "We'd Better Watch Out." *New York Times Book Review,* July 12, 36.

Syverson, C. 2016. "Has a Worldwide Productivity Slowdown Started?" Background paper for *Productivity Revisited,* World Bank, Washington, DC.

———. 2017. "Challenges to Mismeasurement Explanations for the U.S. Productivity Slowdown." *Journal of Economic Perspectives* 31 (2): 165–86.

1. The Elusive Promise of Productivity

Productivity—the efficiency with which societies combine their people, resources, and tools—is the central driver of the development process. The appreciation of the central role of productivity enjoys a long and distinguished pedigree. Paul Krugman's oft-repeated quip that "productivity isn't everything, but, in the long run, it is almost everything" (Krugman 1994) echoes the earlier reflections of medieval Arab social theorist Ibn Khaldun (1332–1406), who argued even more portentously in his *Muqaddimah* (1377) that "civilization and its well-being as well as business prosperity depend on productivity."

Sustained increases in productivity are critical not only to the average denizen of civilization but to those who share least in its benefits. Long-term incremental improvements in earnings in industry or agriculture—the source of employment and livelihoods for many of the poor—can be achieved only by increasing worker or farmer productivity.[1] Workers will leave informal self-employment only if earnings in the formal sector merit it. Hence, the route to generating good jobs transits directly and inexorably through the productivity reform agenda. In addition, productivity-driven cost reductions reduce the prices of key products consumed by the poor and thereby increase household purchasing power, helping poorer households get more for less. New technologies reduce the cost and improve the efficacy of service delivery in all social spheres. Raising global productivity is thus arguably the pivotal element of an integrated strategy to generate jobs—and good jobs—and reduce poverty.

The Twin Productivity Puzzles

The central role of productivity has gained renewed salience in current policy debates for two reasons. First, the global productivity engine appears to have stalled. The recent productivity slowdown in advanced economies and, to a lesser extent, follower countries threatens to reduce the rate at which all countries are pulled ahead and global poverty is alleviated. This slowdown is occurring despite spectacular advances in computing power and a host of derivative technologies: the promise of rapid advance in science and technology seems out of sync with observed slower growth in productivity.

Second, the hoped-for natural convergence of follower countries in the developed world to the global frontier has not materialized, and many countries remain seemingly trapped at low- or middle-income levels. Both pieces of this puzzle must be resolved to raise global productivity growth rates.

As this chapter documents, there is no consensus on why the engine of productivity growth has not regained its previous power, or why followers are so slow in catching up to the leaders. However, over the past few decades, the analytical frameworks through which these phenomena are viewed and their roots are analyzed have experienced major shifts, both conceptually and empirically, dramatically increasing our understanding of the functioning of the underlying mechanisms and dynamics.

This volume pulls together the underlying shifts in paradigm and measurement and terms them the "second wave" of productivity analysis. This new wave has been facilitated by three critical evolutions. First, the access to detailed and high-quality firm-level data has increased across the world. Second, partly aided by this availability, an academic literature has emerged that is critically revisiting many established approaches, in particular, the estimation of firm production functions, and from there, the identification and measurement of the drivers of productivity growth.[2] Third, the quantification of human capital or "capabilities" relevant to productivity improvements, in terms of both managerial skills, and more fundamentally, psychological characteristics, has permitted a tentative opening of the black box of entrepreneurship, the central driver of productivity over the long run.

Each of these developments has important implications for how to think about the challenge of raising productivity and for the corresponding policies that are advanced. The relaxing of the assumptions of perfect competition and identical firms allows researchers to reintroduce questions of market structure into productivity analysis and reopen long-standing questions about the impacts of trade liberalization and competition on innovation and productivity growth. The focus on product quality and the evolution of product demand moves thinking about productivity beyond the unique focus on efficiency as a determinant of firm performance. An appreciation for the role of risk in all dimensions augments the customary discussion of distortions in the business climate. The realization of the broad spectrum of capabilities required to start and run modern firms dictates a reconsideration of the importance of human capital relative to the environment in which it operates.

These and other themes will be recurring leitmotifs across this volume, which synthesizes and extends this literature and provides new evidence to ground it in the developing-country reality. In particular, to illustrate the power of these approaches, the volume employs firm-level data sets from several representative follower countries that collect the variables needed to permit second-wave analysis.

The Current Productivity Conjuncture

Global labor productivity growth is showing signs of life after a 10-year period of stagnation.[3] Labor productivity—the additional output per worker—is projected to grow at 2.3 percent in 2018, up from 2.0 percent in 2017 and 1.4 percent in 2016, the Conference Board projects.[4] Despite this positive news, the projected rates remain substantially below the precrisis (2000–07) rates of 3.0 percent per year, and most of the recovery is driven by the advanced economies.

In the United States, aggregate labor productivity growth averaged only 1.3 percent per year from 2005 to 2015, less than half the average annual growth rate of 2.8 percent sustained over 1995–2004. Similarly sized decelerations have occurred in 28 of 29 other countries for which the Organisation for Economic Co-operation and Development (OECD) has compiled productivity growth data, as shown in panel a of figure 1.1. The unweighted average annual labor productivity growth rate across these countries was 2.3 percent from 1995 to 2004, but only 1.1 percent from 2005 to 2014.[5]

What Are the Drivers behind the Decline?

Panel b of figure 1.1 comes to the same conclusion, presenting a smoothed view over time for a broader set of countries. While developing countries had a larger productivity "bounce" from 2000 to the start of the global financial crisis, they too experienced downturns after 2007, leading to a significant slowdown in aggregate world labor productivity. These trends, if permanent, are hugely consequential. The worldwide drop of 0.8 percent per year in average labor productivity growth that occurred after 2006, and was sustained for 10 years, lowered gross world product in 2017 by about $8.3 trillion—or $1,100 per person—compared with the level it would have been in the absence of the decline (Syverson 2016).

Labor productivity growth has two sources: capital deepening (increases in the amount of capital used by workers) and growth in total factor productivity (TFP). The latter is the traditional measure of efficiency that captures the portion of output not explained by intermediate inputs, labor, and capital.[6] In general, comparable data on these inputs are difficult to find; hence labor productivity, simply economic output divided by labor, is used as a rough proxy. However, for the OECD member countries, where the necessary data are available, for 18 of the 30 countries shown in figure 1.1, slower growth in TFP appears to have been the principal driver of the overall labor productivity slowdown. Figure 1.2 shows the breakdown of average deceleration in labor productivity across these countries, which fell from 2.1 percent per year over 1995–2004 to only 1.0 percent annually over 2005–14. The OECD further splits capital deepening into two subcomponents: the part related to information and communication technology (ICT) capital, and the part tied to all other types of capital.

FIGURE 1.1 **The Rate of Growth of Output per Worker Has Been Falling in Both Industrial and Developing Countries for Decades**

a. Average annual labor productivity growth for 30 OECD countries, 1995–2004 and 2005–14

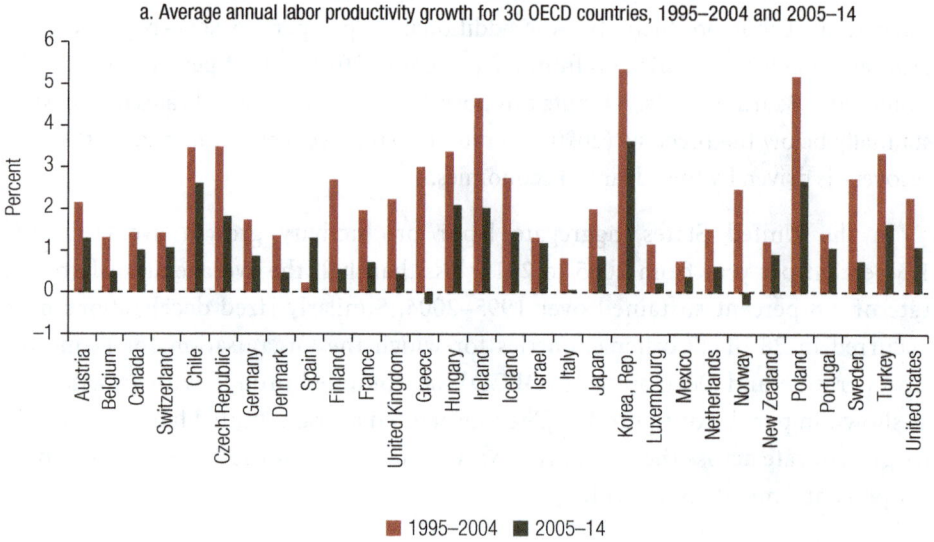

■ 1995–2004 ■ 2005–14

b. Smoothed average annual labor productivity growth by region, 1970–2015

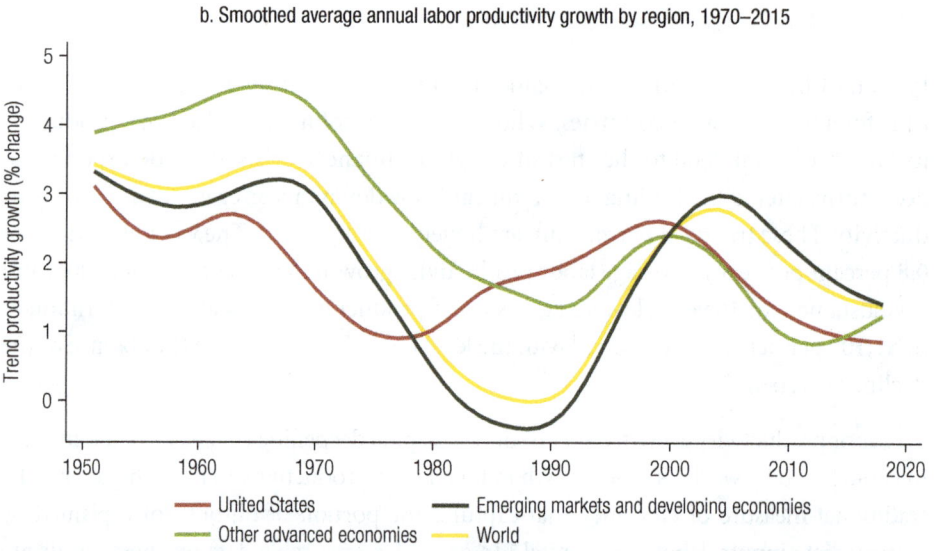

— United States   — Emerging markets and developing economies
— Other advanced economies   — World

Sources: Syverson 2016 (panel a); Conference Board, Total Economy Data Base, 2018 (panel b).
Note: Panel b plots the trend in the unweighted average rate of labor productivity growth across countries for four country groups between 1950 and 2018. Trends are obtained using a Hodrick-Prescott filter with smoothing parameter 100.

The total change in labor productivity growth is the sum of three components: the change in TFP growth, changes in ICT capital deepening, and changes in non-ICT capital deepening. Most of the 1995–2004 to 2005–14 labor productivity growth slowdown—about 0.9 percentage point of the total 1.1 percentage point drop—reflects a reduction in TFP growth. Though not discernable from the figure, this overwhelming contribution of TFP growth to movements in labor productivity holds

FIGURE 1.2 Decomposition of the Slowdown in Labor Productivity Growth into Two Components: Total Factor Productivity and Capital Deepening

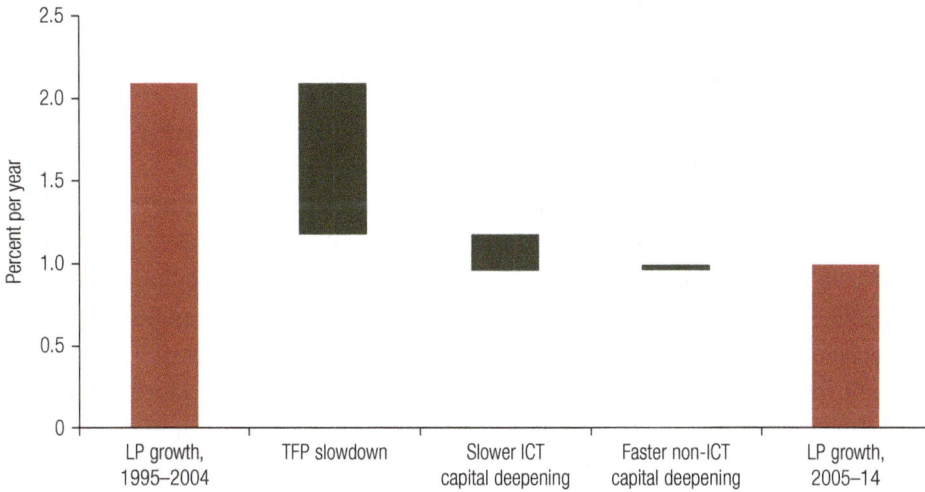

Source: Syverson 2016.

Note: ICT = information and communication technology; LP = labor productivity; TFP = total factor productivity.

when measured at annual frequency as well, with a correlation between the two measures of 0.95. Overall, the ties between labor productivity and capital deepening are substantially smaller.[7]

Hence, as suggested in the introduction, improvements in labor productivity, and thus worker remuneration over the long run, appear to be largely a function of TFP growth. The roots of this global (TFP) decline are thus of first-order importance. However, there is little consensus on what they are, whether they are common to both the advanced and developing countries, or to what extent, and how, they can be remedied.

Recent work for the United States (including Davis and Haltiwanger 2014 and Decker et al. 2015) has definitively established a moderation in U.S. business dynamism: the "churn" in the economy—job reallocations, firm turnover, and entrepreneurial activity—has been declining for some time, including in what are thought by many to be vibrant sectors, like ICT.[8] If this decline is driven by increased rigidities or uncertainty that prevent firms from adjusting to shocks or investing (Bloom 2007; Bloom, Bond, and Van Reenen 2007; Gorodnichenko and Ng 2017), it can be reversed with reforms, consistent application of policy, and time. Similarly, the global financial crisis financially constrained many firms. Productivity in firms that depended more on outside financing had more trouble bouncing back, as documented by Duval, Hong, and Timmer (2017). This setback is unlikely to be permanent. Another explanation emphasizes the role of technological change and fragmentation and internationalization of production in making firms' boundaries more permeable and changing how firms respond to shocks (Doms, Jarmin, and Klimek 2004; Foster, Haltiwanger, and Krizan 2006).

As chapter 4 suggests, new World Bank evidence based on the use of firm-level census data for six developing countries (Chile, China, Colombia, Ethiopia, Indonesia, and Mexico) since 1997 suggests some signs of declining business dynamism for some indicators for some economies—but if real, this decline is far less pronounced than that in the United States and does not appear to be generalizable.

However, the evidence suggests understanding productivity dynamics requires a longer historical view. The slowdown is not a new phenomenon or concern. Cette, Fernald, and Mojon (2016) find that the global slowdown started before the onset of the Great Recession, so it is not purely a result of cyclical factors; Baumol and McLennan (1985), Wolff (1985), and Fischer (1988) document a slowdown in the 1970s and 1980s; and Phelps (2013) asserts that America's peak years of productivity gains ran from the 1820s to the 1960s! Figure 1.3 presents Bureau of Labor Statistics estimates of TFP over the past 119 years for the United States and documents that, in fact, productivity growth swings are very long. It might be that the bunching of innovations from the two world wars propelled the U.S. economy through the 1970s, but their contribution played out by the 1990s. Viewed at this historical scale, the impacts of crisis, increased uncertainty, or increased rigidities seem almost conjunctural. The overriding question is why productivity growth since 1973 has been roughly half that from 1919 to 1973—or, put differently, what drives these 50-year productivity booms? The pace of invention and diffusion of new technologies would seem to be the primary candidate.

FIGURE 1.3 **The United States Experienced Long Swings in Productivity Growth**
(Growth in U.S. total factor productivity, 1899–2018)

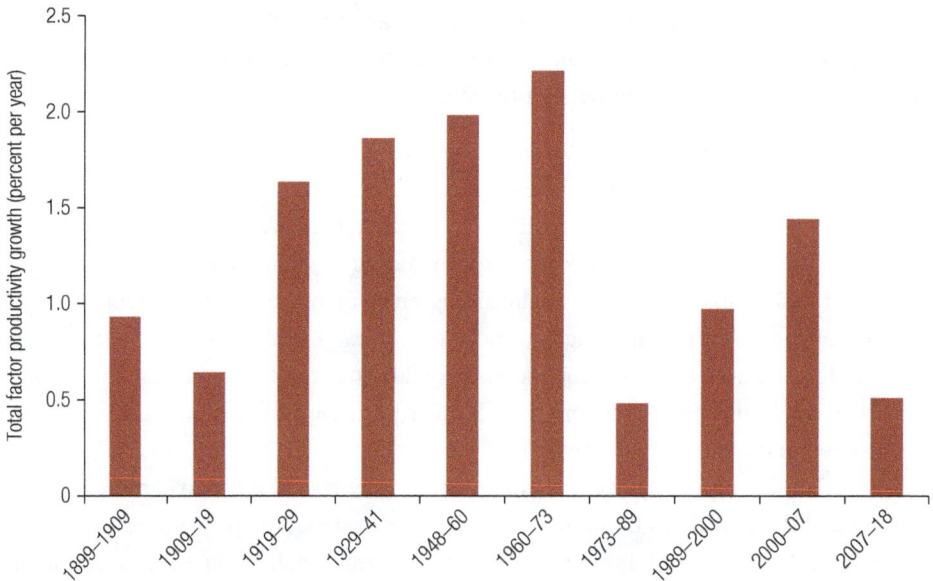

Source: Elaboration using Bakker, Crafts, and Woltjer, forthcoming, and Bureau of Labor Statistics.

Technological Progress and the Case of Missing Productivity

If both the long-term decline since the 1970s and that since 2007 are being driven by the increasing difficulty of generating new technological innovations, the problems are more profound than implementing reforms or working through the recession. The 2000s may represent a transient boomlet driven by ICT, but the overall trend from the 1960s might support Gordon's (2015) argument that the best fruits of the tree of knowledge have already been picked. The new harvests are shinier, but far less nourishing to growth. Bloom et al. (2017) show it takes progressively more researchers to generate a unit of TFP. The number of researchers has increased almost 25 times since 1950, suggesting that reaching fruit on the higher branches will become increasingly challenging. If true, then the future growth of the world economy will be permanently slowed, with attendant consequences for reducing global poverty and welfare.

However, the long-term deceleration in productivity growth has puzzled numerous observers in light of the arrival of what does appear to be an impressive array of new and powerful technologies and scientific tools. Mokyr (2013, 2014) argues these herald another boom: DNA sequencing machines and cell analysis through flow cytometry have revolutionized molecular microbiology; high-powered computers are helping research across vast domains of knowledge; new tools in astronomy, nano chemistry, and genetic engineering have led to radical changes in understanding in these fields. At the same time, the web and associated search systems permit the curating and searching of vast amounts and types of emerging knowledge.

Furthermore, as Aghion, Jones, and Jones (2017) argue, artificial intelligence (AI) may also change the production of new ideas themselves, solving complex problems in the near term, but also facilitating learning and imitation of technologies across firms, sectors, and activities, thus increasing the scope for knowledge externalities. AI could widen new product lines. For example, the recent boost in AI following the machine-learning revolution has spurred the invention of flying drones and advances toward self-driving cars. These tools of discovery multiply researcher's efforts and, when they lead to innovations brought to market, increase productivity.

Consistent with the idea that global growth was living off discoveries of the war years into the 1960s, it may be that, as box 1.1 discusses for the information technology (IT) industry, it takes time for new technologies to trickle through to the real economy. Brynjolffsson, Rock, and Syverson (2017) argue that the most impressive capabilities of AI, particularly those based on machine learning, have not been diffused widely yet. Furthermore, like other general-purpose technologies of the past, their full effects will not be realized until the necessary complementary innovations are developed and implemented.

Are the Current Productivity Lags Just the Calm before the Next Productivity Storm?

There is considerable evidence that information technologies (IT) were a key force behind productivity acceleration episodes in the late twentieth century (see, for example, Jorgenson, Ho, and Stiroh 2008), but these growth spurts appeared with a long lag, after a 20-year period (roughly 1974–94) of brisk investment in IT. The absence of an impact of IT on productivity during this period prompted Robert Solow to make his famous observation, "You can see the computer age everywhere but in the productivity statistics" (Solow 1987, 36). Recent works like Fernald 2014 and Byrne, Oliner, and Sichel 2013 have presented evidence that these IT-based gains have slowed over the past decade. But perhaps this represents a respite between periods of fast productivity growth. This view implies that while highly effective new technologies are being created, there are implementation and adjustment costs that must be paid before they can be effectively deployed to obtain noticeable improvements in productivity (see, for example, van Ark 2016).

History may offer some guidance on the issue of productivity gains from general-purpose technologies like IT. Syverson (2013) shows that the productivity growth from "portable power" technologies like electrification and the internal combustion engine arrived in two waves separated by a decade-long slowdown. While this prior diffusion hardly implies that a second IT wave is imminent, it does show that productivity accelerations from general-purpose technologies do not have to be one-off events. Just because their resultant productivity growth sped up in the late 1990s and early 2000s does not mean it cannot speed up again.

And while it may well be the case, as Bloom et al. (2017) note, that it takes more researchers per idea each year to advance the technological frontier, both the scope and the efficiency of that effort are increasing. On the one hand, more researchers are coming online globally who are capable of contributing new ideas that all economies can use: South Africa's early pioneering work in heart transplants, and Estonia's development of Skype, for example, are discoveries for all. The number of global researchers has doubled since 1995, with a disproportionate contribution from the developing world, which is rapidly converging to the level of the advanced economies (figure 1.4).

And these researchers can work progressively more efficiently than in the past. The internet allows greater search for ideas, but also permits real-time collaborations the likes of which Niels Bohr and far-flung colleagues exchanging ideas on the atom through snail mail could not imagine a century ago. Finally, as Branstetter, Li, and Veloso (2013) note in work supported by the World Bank, a new international division of innovation effort—effectively trade in research tasks—is emerging, analogous to standard international trade in goods. Figure 1.5 shows that while both India and China are making great advances in innovative capabilities and patenting, the bulk of patents registered with the United States Trademark and Patent Office are done under the auspices of foreign multinationals that are outsourcing the relatively routine and codified R&D segments of the knowledge production chain, while researchers in

FIGURE 1.4   **The Number of Global Researchers Has Doubled since 1995, with Most Growth in the Developing World**

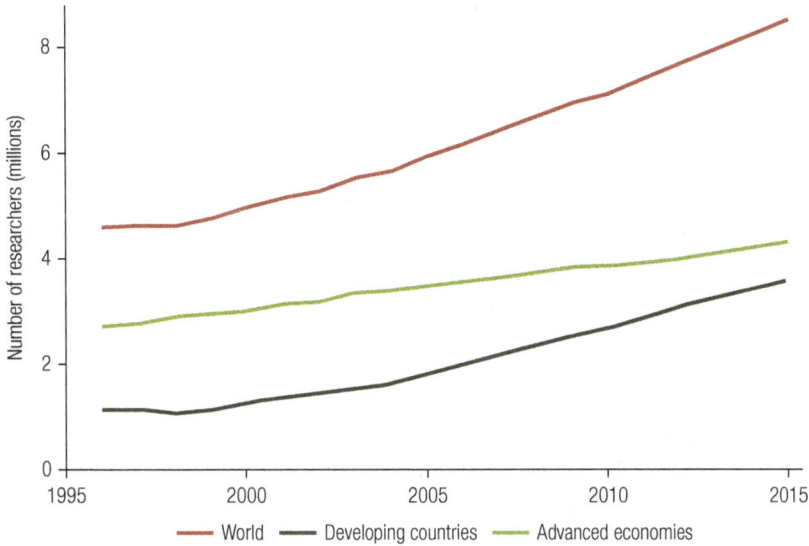

Source: Elaborations using UNESCO data.

FIGURE 1.5   **Most of the U.S. Patent and Trademark Office Patents in China and India Have Been Co-invented and Sponsored by Multinational Firms**

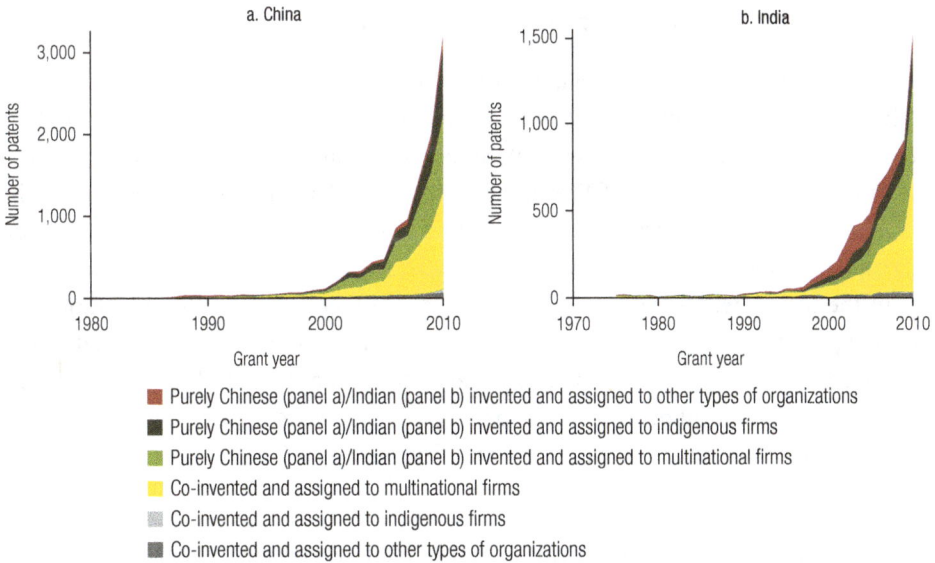

a. China

b. India

- ■ Purely Chinese (panel a)/Indian (panel b) invented and assigned to other types of organizations
- ■ Purely Chinese (panel a)/Indian (panel b) invented and assigned to indigenous firms
- ■ Purely Chinese (panel a)/Indian (panel b) invented and assigned to multinational firms
- ■ Co-invented and assigned to multinational firms
- ■ Co-invented and assigned to indigenous firms
- ■ Co-invented and assigned to other types of organizations

Source: Branstetter, Li, and Veloso 2013.

advanced economies may provide more sophisticated, creative, and high-level intellectual input. Hence, while new discoveries may be taking more and more research effort, the size and global productivity of that effort is increasing.

Are Measurement Issues Obscuring True Productivity Growth?

Some analysts have suggested that the deceleration in productivity is substantially illusory and represents a problem with measurement.[9] This "mismeasurement hypothesis" argues that products emerged in the mid-2000s, such as Google search, that are highly valued, but whose contributions to economic activity are difficult to capture in standard economic statistics because they are consumed at a zero price—or at least at a very low price relative to their social value. Hence the gains in true productivity are not reflected in the prevailing economic output statistics.

However, this hypothesis starts to falter when confronted by its implications for what can be measured in the data. Multiple recent systematic analyses using varied approaches and data have found that the slowdown is not primarily a mismeasurement phenomenon (see Cardarelli and Lusinyan 2015; Byrne, Fernald, and Reinsdorf 2016; Nakamura and Soloveichik 2015; and Syverson 2016). As one example, for the OECD, figure 1.6 plots the relationship between the size of a country's productivity slowdown (on the vertical axis) and two measures of the importance of IT products in that country's economy: on the demand side, the fraction of the country's households that have a broadband connection; and on the supply side, the share of value added accounted for by ICT-producing industries. Figure 1.6 reveals no obvious relationship to the eye, and a regression analysis confirms this.[10]

Brynjolfsson, Rock, and Syverson (2017) alternatively postulate that the delays in building the necessary intangible complements to innovations such as AI—including R&D, patents, trademarks and copyrights, or organizational or entrepreneurial capital—can distort the measurement of TFP because these complements are not well counted in the imperfect notion of gross domestic product (GDP). The early investments in labor and capital for these complements, which are not yet counted in GDP and whose output lies in the future, will appear as a decline in TFP. Brynjolfsson and his coauthors cite Brookings Institution research that investments in autonomous vehicles exceeded $80 billion from 2014 to 2017, with little consumer adoption of these technologies yet. This amounts to 0.44 percent of 2016 GDP (spread over three years). Adding in equally costly labor inputs would lower estimated labor productivity by 0.1 percent per year over the last three years.[11]

Another form of mismeasurement may arise from not taking important changes in industrial organization into account in the estimation of productivity. De Loecker and Eeckhout (2018) argue that the increase in industrial concentration of the U.S. economy (and in Europe as well) has increased markups and led to a corresponding fall in

FIGURE 1.6   There Is No Obvious Relationship between the Productivity Slowdown and the Prominence of Information Technology

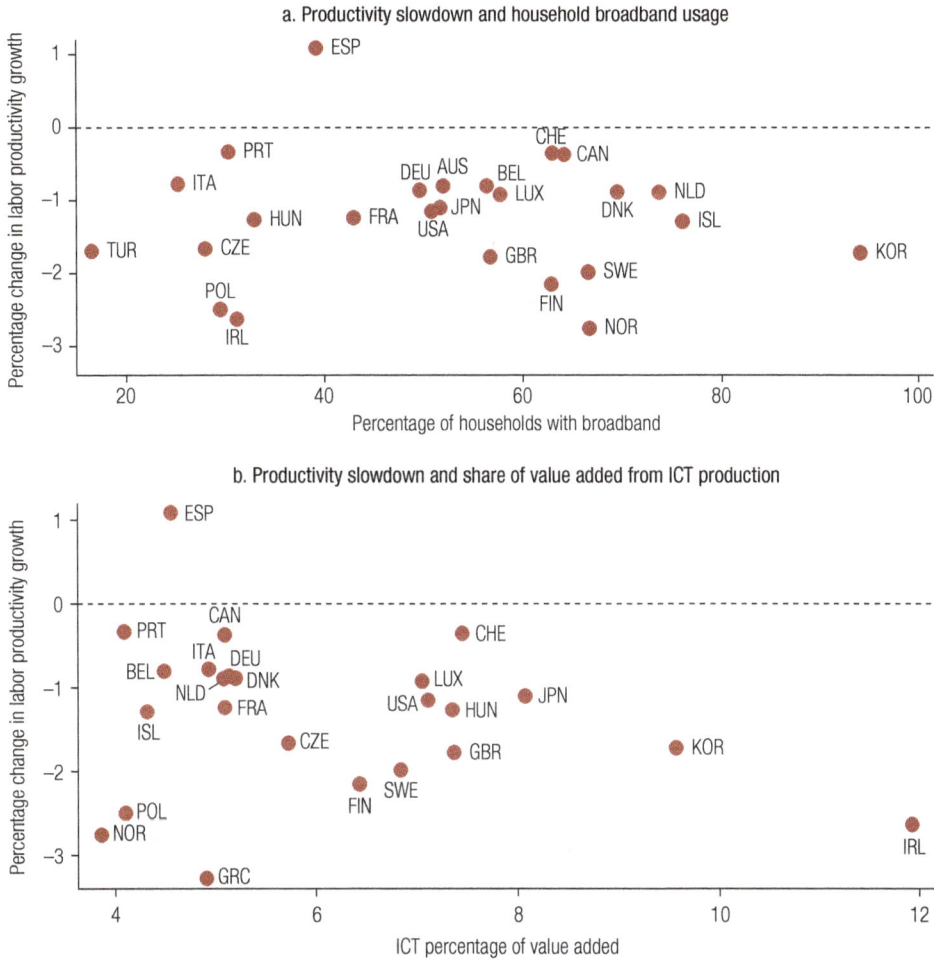

a. Productivity slowdown and household broadband usage

b. Productivity slowdown and share of value added from ICT production

Source: Syverson 2016.

Note: This figure plots the size of the measured productivity slowdown from 1995–2004 to 2005–14 in a country versus the share of the country's households with a broadband connection (panel a) or the value-added share of information and communication technologies (ICT) producers in the country (panel b). All data are from the Organisation for Economic Co-operation and Development. See chapter text and Syverson 2016 for details.

the share of income going to labor and capital. Taking these into effect, they find that productivity growth has *increased* since 1980 and has hovered around 3 percent–4 percent since the 2007 crisis. This, however, cannot explain why labor productivity, defined as output divided by number of workers, should also fall. Furthermore, De Loecker and Eeckhout (2018) show that Latin American markups have remained high, but have not increased over the last decades. Estimates from six representative countries do not suggest an increase in industrial concentration (figure 1.7) (see also Díez, Leigh, and Tambunlertchai 2018).

FIGURE 1.7 Industrial Concentration Has Not Increased in a Sample of Emerging Markets

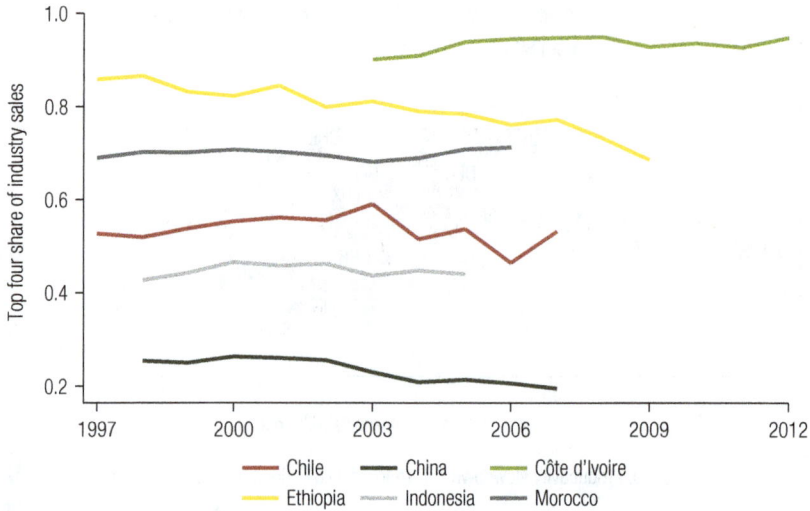

Source: Authors' elaboration using census data.

Note: The figure plots the average fraction of total manufacturing industry sales that is accounted for by the largest four firms within that industry in selected developing countries. Concentration ratios are calculated for each four-digit industry and then averaged across manufacturing using industry weights.

Hence, on balance, there are some reasons to think that production data are under-measuring at least the current and future impact of new technologies. In addition, there is something incongruous about the simultaneous concerns, on the one hand, that productivity growth is a thing of the past and on the other, that rapid progress in robotics and AI will displace masses of workers through productivity gains. Across the centuries, disruptive technologies have eliminated certain types of jobs (manual weavers being the iconic example) while creating entirely new professions (computer programmers, heart surgeons, automobile assemblers) that pay substantially better. The labor data do suggest that important employment effects of automation and technology-facilitated outsourcing are likely responsible for the polarization of advanced-economy labor markets.[12]

However, evidence of this effect for developing countries is still scattered and weak, perhaps partly because technology has not yet arrived in all these countries or because the intensity of use of these technologies has diverged (Comin and Mestieri 2018). Figure 1.8, using census data, confirms that for advanced economies, employment for workers engaged as machinery operators or in crafts has declined or stagnated compared with higher-end professional employment or lower-skilled clerks, service workers, or elementary occupations. Figure 1.9 suggests that, in fact, in advanced economies, more robots are associated with fewer jobs for manufacturing operators, although not necessarily more total jobs.

FIGURE 1.8 **Labor Markets Are Becoming More Polarized in Advanced Economies, but Not in Developing Countries**

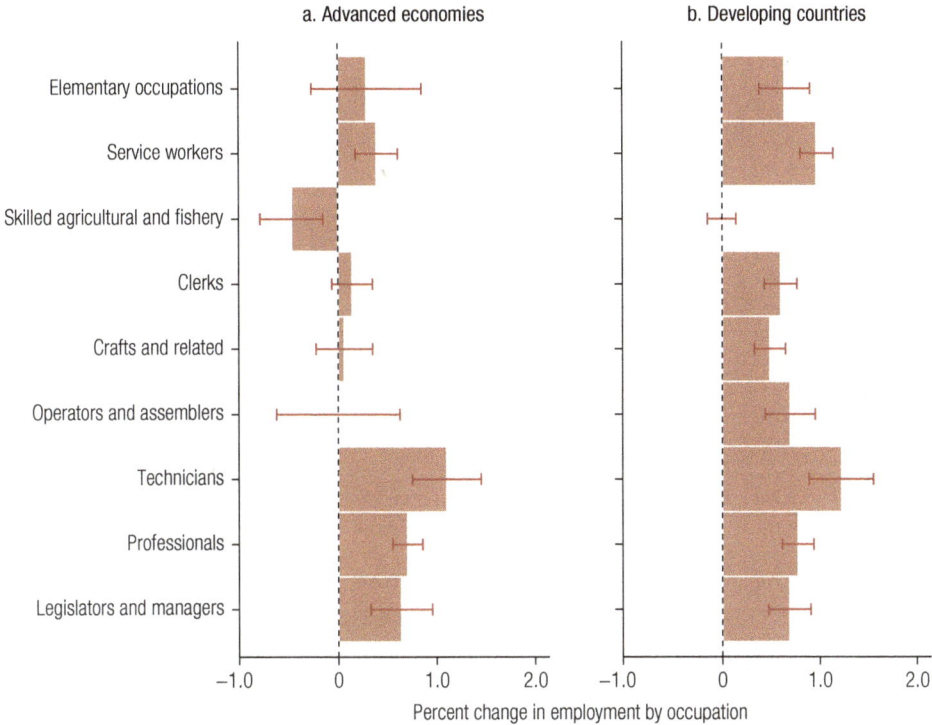

a. Advanced economies   b. Developing countries

Percent change in employment by occupation

Source: Maloney and Molina 2016. Calculations are based on IPUMS (Integrated Public Use Microdata Series) data.

Note: The figure plots the percent change in employment before and after 2000. Data span 1979–2012. Horizontal I-bars show confidence intervals.

The Weakness of Economic Convergence

The second area of preoccupation prompting new work on productivity is the continued failure of economic convergence over the long term. Even if advances were to come to a halt in the advanced economies, productivity in the follower nations would lag the frontier nations, offering the prospect of massive gains from technological catch-up.

The enduring question in development economics is why this catch-up has not been happening. The average GDP per capita of the richest 10 percent of countries in 2000 was 40 times higher than that of the poorest 10 percent of countries—meaning that the average person in an advanced economy produces in just over nine days what the average person in a follower country produces in an entire year, Restuccia (2013) finds (see also Caselli 2005). Numerous studies have documented that roughly half of this difference in income cannot be explained by differences in capital or other tangible factors of production and hence is attributed to differences in the efficiency with which they are combined—that is, to TFP (Klenow and Rodríguez Clare 1997;

FIGURE 1.9 Are Robots Displacing or Creating Manufacturing Jobs?

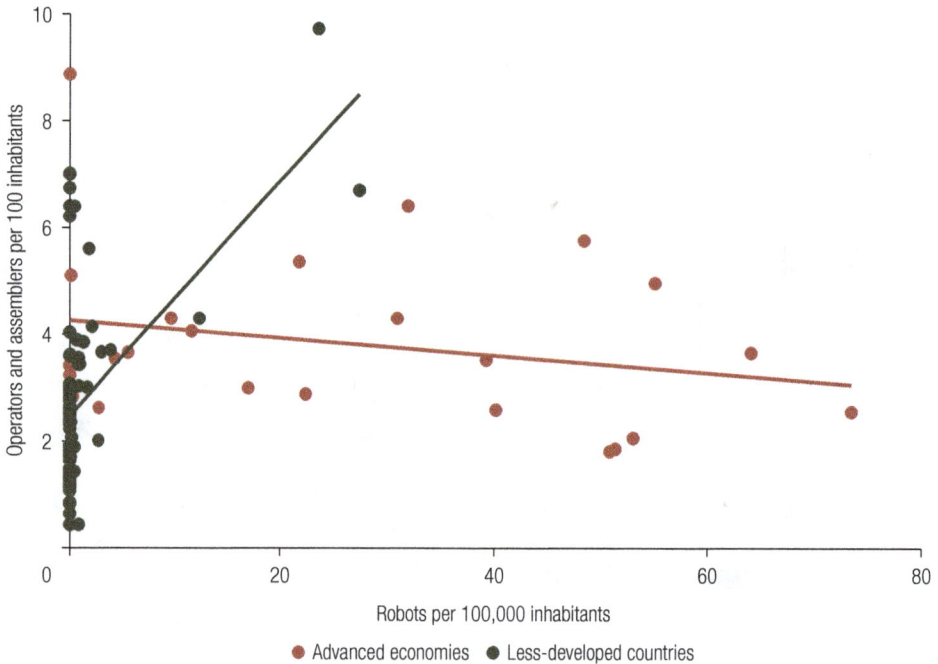

● Advanced economies ● Less-developed countries

Source: Maloney and Molina 2016. Calculations are based on IPUMS (Integrated Public Use Microdata Series) data.

Easterly and Levine 2001). The potential contribution to raising global productivity and reducing poverty of achieving convergence are immense.

Yet despite early arguments for a natural process of convergence among the now-frontier countries (Baumol 1986), it has subsequently proven statistically elusive (see, for example, De Long 1988). Furthermore, Pritchett (1997), among others, documents a "Great Divergence" of the last two centuries where, instead of follower countries catching up, advanced economies, with few exceptions, continue to pull ahead. The emergence of different "convergence clubs" (Quah 1996; Maasoumi, Racine, and Stengos 2007), in which follower countries converge to clumps of similar levels of income far from the frontier, has been documented to be largely a matter of differences in productivity growth. Convergence seems to be weakening even in the regions where it was assumed. A recent World Bank study, "Growing United" (Ridao-Cano and Bodewig 2018), shows that the productivity gap between southern and northern member states of the European Union has been widening since the early 2000s. Convergence is elusive at the subnational level as well.[13] What is clear is that reducing the between-country differences in productivity would contribute massively to global productivity growth. Yet convergence does not appear to be an inevitable natural force, like gravity.

This fact underlies what the previous volume in this series (Ciera and Maloney 2017) called the *innovation paradox,* focusing on the puzzle of why rates of technology adoption are low in developing countries, and how that inhibits convergence. The gains from adopting existing products, processes, and management techniques from abroad are thought to be large. Indeed, the radiation of ideas, products, and technologies to developing countries represents an externality of truly historic proportions. In fact, Comin and Hobijn (2004, 2010) and Comin and Ferrer (2013) argue that it is precisely the differences in the rate and intensity of adoption of new technologies that drives the magnitude of the Great Divergence.[14] Comin and Mestieri (2018) argue that a reduction in the average adoption lag by one year is associated with a 3.8 percent higher per capita income. Cutting the adoption lag faced by a country from 50 years longer than the United States to the U.S. level is associated with an increase in per capita income by a factor of seven![15] Recent estimates of the returns to one type of innovation investment, R&D, for the United States and Spain put them at a striking 40 percent to 60 percent annually.[16] Griffith, Redding, and Van Reenen (2004) and Goñi and Maloney (2017) show that returns rise much higher (potentially to the triple digits) with increased distance from the technological frontier for a while, reflecting the gains from Schumpeterian catch-up afforded to follower countries. Yet countries do not seem to exploit these potential gains.

Ironically, the lack of polarization observed in panel b of figure 1.8 for developing countries may be due partly to this low rate of technological adoption. The underlying data suggest perhaps incipient effects observed in more advanced economies like Mexico and Brazil, but the majority of countries in the sample show nothing. In fact, the exact reverse effect is observed in Vietnam and China, which may be because, as figure 1.9 suggests, in developing countries, robot density is associated with *higher* employment of operators and assemblers, in contrast to advanced economies. This may arise in cases where large-scale offshoring also involves the introduction of automation. As Maloney and Molina (2016) discuss, there are many reasons why automation and robots would be adopted more slowly in the majority of developing countries, ranging from the country's technological absorptive capacity to the skill of the workforce, its ability to mobilize resources for large capital investments, the capacity for maintenance, and attention to tolerances. As these problems are redressed, today's advanced-economy problems may, in fact, become those of the developing world tomorrow.

The Mechanisms of Productivity Growth: Second-Wave Analysis

In sum, there is no firm consensus on the first puzzle of the global productivity slowdown and, in fact, the causes may differ between advanced economies and developing countries. There appears not to be a pronounced fall in dynamism or increase in industrial concentration or shift toward lower-productivity services (see box 1.2) in developing countries that have been forwarded as explanations, for instance,

BOX 1.2

Structural Transformation Decompositions

Following in the spirit of economists from Kuznets to Chenery who have detailed the movement of labor from agriculture to manufacturing, McMillan and Rodrik (2011) and McMillan, Rodrik, and Verduzco-Gallo (2014) decompose labor productivity growth into two components: one that holds labor shares in different sectors constant but allows changes in average labor productivity, and another that holds sectoral productivity constant and allows for observed reallocation of labor. They find the latter component plays an important role in many high-growth countries.

Rogerson (2017), for this volume, examines data for Asia and broadly confirms their findings. Structural transformation—effectively the analog to the "between" dimension discussed earlier—does in some cases account for half of productivity growth (China, Thailand), although in many cases it accounts for less than 10 percent. Little structural transformation has occurred in high-growth Malaysia, and in both India and Indonesia structural transformation has been far less extensive than in China or Thailand (figure B1.2.1).

A second important takeaway is that the importance of reallocation diminishes with the level of income, accounting for very little in more advanced economies. In the United States, structural transformation never accounts for more than 0.1 percent of growth, while in Japan; Taiwan, China; and the Republic of Korea, the contribution is low or negative, despite having been important during their miracle periods. Baumol's cost disease, in which progressively more spending goes into sectors such as services where productivity is lower and slower, may partly explain these rates.

As the following chapters demonstrate, the interpretation of these patterns is not clear for policy. They are neither obviously capturing movements from high- to low-productivity sectors nor illustrating the underlying drivers of such movements.

FIGURE B1.2.1 **The Percentage of Productivity Growth Contributed by Structural Transformation Varies Widely by Country and over Time**

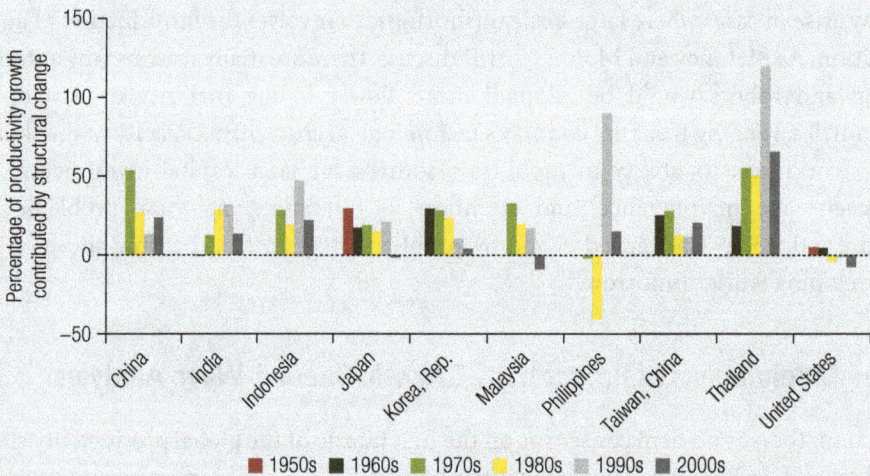

Source: Rogerson 2017.

in the United States. The second puzzle remains a long-standing analytical challenge that goes to the core of the World Bank's mandate.

This said, while the literature has not offered a definitive explanation for why the productivity engine has not regained its previous force or why followers are so slow in catching up to the leaders, it has, over the last 20 years, dramatically increased our understanding of the functioning of the underlying dynamics and mechanisms. More profoundly, it has revolutionized the conceptual and analytical tools for analyzing productivity and its determinants.

Productivity growth—both of the countries pushing the frontier and of those unevenly catching up—can be broken down mechanically into three components, as shown in figure 1.10.

Improved firm performance (within firm). At the center of productivity analysis is the firm. The within component is related to individual firms becoming more productive: that is, increasing the amount of output they produce with a constant amount of inputs (such as labor, capital, land, raw materials, and other intermediate inputs) because they have increased their internal capabilities, including managerial skills, workforce skills, innovation capacity, and technology-absorption capability.

Improved allocation of factors of production across firms (between-firm). Ideally, the most productive firms would attract the most resources, thereby ensuring the greatest possible output. However, myriad distortions—including poorly designed legislation or political patronage that prevents resources from moving from less efficient firms—can have large effects. The between-component is associated with the reallocation of factors of production and economic activity toward more efficient firms.

Improved entry and exit of firms (selection). Aggregate productivity growth can also be explained by the entrance of high-productivity firms (relative to the industry average) and the exit of low-productivity firms (again, relative to the industry average). Examining the factors that affect the entry of higher-quality firms moves into the study of entrepreneurship. Understanding the disincentives and barriers to exit involves issues of business climate and potentially social norms.

FIGURE 1.10   There Are Three Main Sources of Productivity Growth

The Productivity Margins That Matter Most: New Evidence for Developing Countries

The contribution of each of these margins to productivity growth is a subject of ongoing debate. Furthermore, as chapter 2 lays out, decompositions based on labor productivity or revenue-based TFP are misleading measures of efficiency. Backing out a reliable measure requires firm-level price information, which to date has been scarce. This volume has pulled together several unique databases from developing countries that collect firm-level prices.

Figure 1.11 offers the first decompositions for a sample of developing countries and emerging markets of one measure of efficiency, physical total factor productivity (TFPQ), into its distinct components. The within-component is relatively more important than the between-component in four of six cases, explaining roughly half or more of efficiency growth in these economies, especially in Ethiopia and China.[17] However, depending on the country, the other components also play important roles. In Chile and Colombia, the entry and exit of firms is the largest contributor. Reallocation is marginally the dominant contributor in India and comes a close second in Colombia.

As this volume discusses, going forward, the policy conclusions from these decompositions are not straightforward. One message is clear: productivity analytics and

FIGURE 1.11 **Which Dimension Contributes Most to Productivity Growth?**

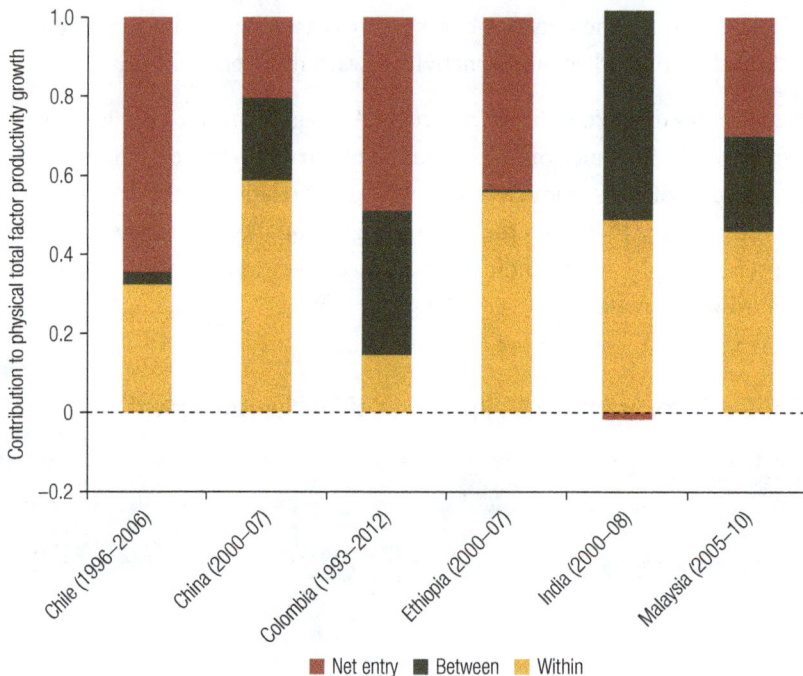

Net entry   Between   Within

Source: Physical total factor productivity decompositions using Melitz and Polanec's (2015) methodology.

policy need to encompass all three dimensions. Each of them entails different policy mixes. Productivity gains within firms may require a focus on firm management quality and technological learning and associated complements.[18] Improving the efficiency of entering firms may dictate focusing on factors particularly relevant to the incidence and quality of entering entrepreneurs and the entrepreneurial ecosystem. Facilitating reallocation requires structural reforms such as those associated with World Bank Doing Business indicators.

However, these decompositions are backward-looking and may reflect a particular stage in the reform or growth process. India's high contribution of reallocation might, for instance, reflect the effects of the far-reaching 1996 trade liberalization, while its very small share in Chile may reflect the fact that its major reforms were in the distant 1970s and 1980s. In fact, box 1.2, using the simpler and less reliable decompositions based on labor productivity characterizing the structural reform literature, suggests that the within-component becomes small and even negative in the most advanced economies. In addition, there are interactions among the three dimensions that dictate an integrated approach to productivity policy. Barriers to reallocation may be a drag on investments in new firms or firm upgrading; over the long term, further reallocation depends on the introduction of new processes, products, and startups that challenge existing firms for resources.

Plan of the Volume

Second-wave analysis has dramatically shifted how we analyze each of these margins. Across the next three chapters, this volume pulls together this recent thinking, extends it, and grounds it in the developing-country reality, using global trade and financial data and the handful of available developing-country data sets with characteristics that permit frontier estimation techniques. These span a representative cross-sample including Chile, China, Colombia, Ethiopia, India, Indonesia, Malaysia, and Mexico. The extensive empirical work and conceptual synthesis offers new guidance for productivity analysis and dictates a corresponding shift in how to approach policy.

Chapter 2 focuses on firm performance (the "within" component), explaining why conventional measures of productivity, like revenue-based total factor productivity (TFPR), are compromised measures of efficiency, and why analyses to date seeking to explain movements in productivity based on TFPR are correspondingly unreliable. Central to this approach is the need to treat productivity analysis and market power in an integrated way to disentangle them. The chapter also explores how the analysis of the determinants of firm performance needs to go beyond considerations of efficiency to incorporate broader aspects of product quality and demand.

Chapter 3 takes up the "between" margin, or reallocation component. It discusses how conceptually and empirically a popular measure of misallocation and distortion,

TFP dispersion, is not reliable. This measure conflates risk, adjustment rigidities, mark-ups, and quality, among other factors, and overstates the development effect of reallocation through reform. That said, the chapter argues that the effects of barriers to reallocation through the channels of investment in upgrading within firms and the entry of better firms are larger than previously thought.

Chapter 4 studies the "selection" margin and discusses four recent advances in thinking around the generation of high-quality entrants. First, it presents some of the earliest evidence on patterns of entry and exit in developing countries over time. Second, it provides a simple framework of entrepreneurship as experimentation that integrates both considerations of operational environment and a variety of types of human capital. Third, it explores the new literature on the role of personality and other characteristics of entrepreneurs that the emergence of detailed data sets has made possible. Finally, it approaches issues of culture, human capital, and environment, taking a longer view using historical examples.

Chapter 5 distills lessons from the previous chapters and maps the shifts in thinking around productivity policy that result. Chapter 6 concludes. A technical appendix lays out many of the critiques discussed in the text in mathematical form.

Notes

1. See Ivanic and Martin 2010, which argues that agricultural productivity growth benefits the poor most.
2. Four of the most cited papers in this area together account for about 9,400 Google Scholar cites. The earliest paper is from 1995.
3. This section draws heavily on Syverson 2016.
4. Projections are from The Conference Board, 2018 Total Economy Database.
5. These slowdowns are statistically significant. The U.S. figures are computed from quarterly data; equality of the two periods' productivity growth rates is rejected with a t-statistic of 2.7. The OECD values are from annual data across the 30 countries; the null hypothesis of equality is rejected with a t-statistic of 6.3. These slowdowns do not appear to reflect cyclical phenomena. Productivity decelerations are still observed in 25 of the 30 countries in the OECD data if growth rates from 2008–09, during the depths of the global financial crisis, are excluded from the totals. Furthermore, the average labor productivity growth across countries in the latter period (2005–14) remains a low 1.4 percent per year.
6. For example, if the production function is Cobb-Douglas with constant returns to scale $Y = AK^{\alpha}L^{1-\alpha}$, then $Y/L = A(K/L)^{\alpha}$, the relationship between labor productivity, TFP, and capital intensity is log-linear. More general production functions will imply a nonlinear relationship with (logged) capital intensity. This analysis remains agnostic about the form of the production function, other than imposing linear separability of (logged) TFP and inputs.
7. The 0.2 percentage point drop in labor productivity growth unexplained by TFP decline results from a reduction in the rate of ICT capital deepening. By contrast, non-ICT capital deepening plays little role in the change in labor productivity growth in the OECD sample. Interestingly, within countries at an annual level, non-ICT deepening is considerably *more* correlated with labor productivity growth (the correlation coefficient is 0.45) than ICT capital deepening (the correlation coefficient is 0.21). However, because there was essentially no change in the average

rate of non-ICT capital deepening between the two periods of the slowdown, accumulations of these other capital types had little effect on labor productivity (and what effect they did have was to slightly increase labor productivity growth between the periods).

8. This empirical work has focused on the United States. Analogous facts have not yet been established for other countries.

9. Proponents of this view include Brynjolfsson and McAfee (2011); Mokyr (2014); Byrne, Oliner, and Sichel (2013); Feldstein (2015); and Hatzius and Dawsey (2015).

10. The coefficient on broadband penetration is −0.001 (standard error = 0.008), which is not just a statistical zero but an economic zero as well, as the point estimate implies that a one standard deviation difference in broadband penetration is associated with a one-fiftieth of a standard deviation difference in the magnitude of the slowdown. The visual is not as obvious with the supply-side-based measure of ICT prominence in panel b of figure 1.6, but a regression again reveals a statistically insignificant relationship. The coefficient on ICT intensity is −0.111 (standard error = 0.095). Any economic relationship that might exist would be exclusively attributable to Ireland, which has an outlier ICT value-added share of 11.9 percent, double the sample average. Removing Ireland from the sample yields a regression coefficient of −0.030 (standard error = 0.123), which implies that a one standard deviation difference in ICT intensity corresponds to a one-sixteenth of a standard deviation change in the magnitude of the slowdown.

11. https://www.brookings.edu/research/gauging-investment-in-self-driving-cars/.

12. Autor, Katz, and Kearney (2006); Autor (2010); and Autor and Dorn (2013) document expanding job opportunities in both high-skill, high-wage occupations and low-skill, low-wage occupations, coupled with contracting opportunities in middle-wage, middle-skill white-collar and blue-collar jobs. In particular, job opportunities are declining in middle-skill white-collar clerical, administrative, and sales occupations and in middle-skill, blue-collar production, craft, and operative occupations. This especially hits the earnings and labor force participation rates of workers without college education, and particularly men. Goos, Manning, and Salomons (2014) document that this phenomenon has appeared in each of 16 European countries from 1993 to 2006: middle-wage occupations decline as a share of employment in all 16 countries with an unweighted average of 8 percentage points, while high-wage and low-wage occupations increased in the vast majority.

13. See, for example, Aroca, Bosch, and Maloney 2005 for Mexico and Massoumi and Wang 2008 for China, among others. A future volume in this series will also address this issue.

14. Likewise, Aghion, Howitt, and Mayer-Foulkes (2005) and Feyrer (2008) argue that Quah's (1996) finding that countries converge to "twin peaks" arises from diverging productivity as opposed to diverging physical capital or human capital accumulation, pointing again to knowledge-related barriers preventing catch-up. Numerous models (Aghion and Howitt 1990; Aghion, Howitt, and Mayer-Foulkes 2005) postulate situations in which countries enter a "stagnation equilibrium" far from the technological frontier because they are unable to incorporate new technologies.

15. Comin and Mestieri (2018) find that adoption lags between follower countries and advanced economies have recently converged; however, the intensity of use of adopted technologies of follower countries relative to advanced economies has diverged. The evolution of aggregate productivity implied by these trends in technology diffusion resembles the actual evolution of the world income distribution in the last two centuries. Cross-country differences in adoption lags account for a significant part of the cross-country income divergence in the nineteenth century. The divergence in intensity of use accounts for the divergence during the twentieth century.

16. This positive impact of innovation on productivity can be seen in both country-level and firm-level data. Hall, Mairesse, and Mohnen (2010), for example, review the substantial evidence over the last quarter century and find that R&D expenditures increase TFP and growth. Using firm-level data, Hall and Mohnen (2013) find that introduction of product or process innovation also increases productivity. Bloom, Schankerman, and Van Reenen (2013) and Bloom et al. (2017)

find social returns of 55.0–57.7 percent depending on the sample period, compared with a private return of 13.6–20.7 percent. Doraszelski and Jaumandreu (2013) find an average rate of return to R&D of 40 percent for Spain (1996–2000), roughly double that of, for instance, infrastructure.

17. Some researchers have argued that most productivity growth occurs within sectors and industries and *not* in the reallocation of factors among them (see Caselli 2005). From a very micro view, other evidence—for example, for Bangladesh, parts of Sub-Saharan Africa, and Vietnam—suggests that poverty transitions have been dominated not by changes in income sources from farm to nonfarm income, but by higher productivity within the same sector and often within firms (Christiaensen, Demrey, and Kuhl 2011). In China, increasing labor productivity in agriculture has been a key factor in reducing poverty in lagging Chinese provinces (Christiaensen, Pan, and Wang 2013).

18. These issues are discussed in the first volume in this series, *The Innovation Paradox* (Cirera and Maloney 2017).

References

Aghion, P., and P. Howitt. 1990. "A Model of Growth through Creative Destruction." NBER Working Paper 3223, National Bureau of Economic Research, Cambridge, MA.

Aghion, P., P. Howitt, and D. Mayer-Foulkes. 2005. "The Effect of Financial Development on Convergence: Theory and Evidence." *Quarterly Journal of Economics* 120 (1): 173–222.

Aghion, P., B. F. Jones, and C. I. Jones. 2017. "Artificial Intelligence and Economic Growth." NBER Working Paper 23928, National Bureau of Economic Research, Cambridge, MA.

Aroca, P., M. Bosch, and W. F. Maloney. 2005. "Spatial Dimensions of Trade Liberalization and Economic Convergence: Mexico 1985–2002." *World Bank Economic Review* 19 (3): 345–78.

Autor, D. H. 2010. "The Polarization of Job Opportunities in the US Labor Market: Implications for Employment and Earnings." Center for American Progress and The Hamilton Project, Washington, DC.

Autor, D. H., and D. Dorn. 2013. "The Growth of Low-Skill Service Jobs and the Polarization of the US Labor Market." *American Economic Review* 103 (5): 1553–97.

Autor, D. H., L. F. Katz, and M. S. Kearney. 2006. "The Polarization of the US Labor Market." *American Economic Review Papers and Proceedings* 96 (2): 189–94.

Bakker, G., N. Crafts, and P. Woltjer. Forthcoming. "The Sources of Growth in a Technologically Progressive Economy: the United States, 1899–1941." *Economic Journal*.

Baumol, W. J. 1986. "Productivity Growth, Convergence, and Welfare: What the Long-Run Data Show." *American Economic Review* 76 (5): 1072–85.

Baumol, W. J., and K. McLennan. 1985. *Productivity Growth and US Competitiveness*. New York: Oxford University Press for Committee for Economic Development.

Bloom, N. 2007. "Uncertainty and the Dynamics of R&D." *American Economic Review* 97 (2): 250–55.

Bloom, N., S. Bond, and J. Van Reenen. 2007. "Uncertainty and Investment Dynamics." *Review of Economic Studies* 74 (2): 391–415.

Bloom, N., C. I. Jones, J. Van Reenen, and M. Webb. 2017. "Are Ideas Getting Harder to Find?" NBER Working Paper 23782, National Bureau of Economic Research, Cambridge, MA.

Bloom, N., M. Schankerman, and J. Van Reenen. 2013. "Identifying Technology Spillovers and Product Market Rivalry." *Econometrica* 81 (4): 1347–93.

Branstetter, L. G., B. M. Glennon, and J. B. Jensen. 2018. "The IT Revolution and the Globalization of R&D." NBER Working Paper 24707, National Bureau of Economic Research, Cambridge, MA.

Branstetter, L. G., G. Li, and F. Veloso. 2013. *The Globalization of R&D: China, India, and the Rise of International Co-invention*. Draft Report. Washington, DC: World Bank.

Brynjolfsson, E., and A. McAfee. 2011. *Race against the Machine*. Lexington, MA: Digital Frontier.

Brynjolfsson, E., D. Rock, and C. Syverson. 2017. "Artificial Intelligence and the Modern Productivity Paradox: A Clash of Expectations and Statistics." In *Economics of Artificial Intelligence*. Chicago: University of Chicago Press.

Byrne, D. M., J. G. Fernald, and M. B. Reinsdorf. 2016. "Does the United States Have a Productivity Slowdown or a Measurement Problem?" *Brookings Papers on Economic Activity* 2016 (1): 109–82.

Byrne, D. M., S. D. Oliner, and D. E. Sichel. 2013. "Is the Information Technology Revolution Over?" *International Productivity Monitor* 25 (Spring): 20–36.

Cardarelli, M. R., and L. Lusinyan. 2015. "US Total Factor Productivity Slowdown: Evidence from the US States." Working Paper 15-116, International Monetary Fund, Washington, DC.

Caselli, F. 2005. "Accounting for Cross-Country Income Differences." In *Handbook of Economic Growth*, vol. 1A, edited by P. Aghion and S. Durlauf, 679–741. Amsterdam: Elsevier.

Cette, G., J. Fernald, and B. Mojon. 2016. "The Pre-Great Recession Slowdown in Productivity." *European Economic Review* 88: 3–20.

Christiaensen, L., L. Demery, and J. Kuhl. 2011. "The (Evolving) Role of Agriculture in Poverty Reduction—An Empirical Perspective." *Journal of Development Economics* 96 (2): 239–54.

Christiaensen, L., L. Pan, and S. Wang. 2013. "Pathways out of Poverty in Lagging Regions: Evidence from Rural Western China." *Agricultural Economics* 44 (1): 25–44.

Cirera, X., and W. F. Maloney. 2017. *The Innovation Paradox: Developing-Country Capabilities and the Unrealized Promise of Technological Catch-Up*. Washington, DC: World Bank.

Comin, D., and B. Hobijn. 2004. "Cross-Country Technology Adoption: Making the Theories Face the Facts." *Journal of Monetary Economics* 51 (1): 39–83.

———. 2010. "An Exploration of Technology Diffusion." *American Economic Review* 100 (5, December): 2031–59.

Comin, D., and M. Mestieri. 2018. "If Technology Has Arrived Everywhere, Why Has Income Diverged?" *American Economic Journal: Macroeconomics* 10 (3): 137–78.

Davis, S. J., and J. Haltiwanger. 2014. "Labor Market Fluidity and Economic Performance." NBER Working Paper 20479, National Bureau of Economic Research, Cambridge, MA.

Decker, R., J. Haltiwanger, R. S. Jarmin, and J. Miranda. 2015. "Where Has All the Skewness Gone? The Decline in High-Growth (Young) Firms in the US." NBER Working Paper 21776, National Bureau of Economic Research, Cambridge, MA.

De Loecker, J., and J. Eeckhout. 2018. "Global Market Power." Working Paper 24768, National Bureau of Economic Research, Cambridge, MA.

De Long, J. B. 1988. "Productivity Growth, Convergence, and Welfare: Comment." *American Economic Review* 78 (5): 1138–54.

Díez, F. J., D. Leigh, and S. Tambunlertchai. 2018. "Global Market Power and Its Macroeconomic Implications." IMF Working Paper 18/137, International Monetary Fund, Washington, DC.

Doms, M. E., R. S. Jarmin, and S. D. Klimek. 2004. "Information Technology Investment and Firm Performance in US Retail Trade." *Economics of Innovation and New Technology* 13 (7): 595–613.

Doraszelski, U., and J. Jaumandreu. 2013. "R&D and Productivity: Estimating Endogenous Productivity." *Review of Economic Studies* 80 (4): 1338–83.

Duval, R. A., G. H. Hong, and Y. Timmer. 2017. "Financial Frictions and the Great Productivity Slowdown." IMF Working Paper 17/129, International Monetary Fund, Washington, DC.

Easterly, W., and R. Levine. 2001. "What Have We Learned from a Decade of Empirical Research on Growth? It's Not Factor Accumulation: Stylized Facts and Growth Models." *World Bank Economic Review* 15 (2): 177–219.

Feldstein, M. 2015. "The U.S. Underestimates Growth." *Wall Street Journal*, May 18.

Fernald, J. 2014. "A Quarterly, Utilization-Adjusted Series on Total Factor Productivity." Federal Reserve Bank of San Francisco.

Feyrer, J. D. 2008. "Convergence by Parts." *BE Journal of Macroeconomics* 8 (1): 1–35.

Fischer, S. 1988. "Symposium on the Slowdown in Productivity Growth." *Journal of Economic Perspectives* 2 (4): 3–7.

Foster, L., J. C. Haltiwanger, and C. J. Krizan. 2001. "Aggregate Productivity Growth: Lessons from Microeconomic Evidence." In *New Developments in Productivity Analysis,* edited by Charles Hulten and Michael Parker, 303–72. Chicago: University of Chicago Press.

———. 2006. "Market Selection, Reallocation, and Restructuring in the US Retail Trade Sector in the 1990s." *Review of Economics and Statistics* 88 (4): 748–58.

Goñi, E., and W. F. Maloney. 2017. "Why Don't Poor Countries Do R&D? Varying Rates of Factor Returns across the Development Process." *European Economic Review* 94: 126–47.

Goos, M., A. Manning, and A. Salomons. 2014. "Explaining Job Polarization: Routine-Biased Technological Change and Offshoring." *American Economic Review* 104 (8): 2509–26.

Gordon, R. 2015. "Secular Stagnation: A Supply-Side View." *American Economic Review: Papers and Proceedings* 105 (5): 54–59.

Gorodnichenko, Y., and S. Ng. 2017. "Level and Volatility Factors in Macroeconomic Data." *Journal of Monetary Economics* 91: 52–68.

Griffith, R., S. Redding, and J. Van Reenen. 2004. "Mapping the Two Faces of R&D: Productivity Growth in a Panel of OECD industries." *Review of Economics and Statistics* 86 (4): 883–95.

Hall, B. H., J. Mairesse, and P. Mohnen. 2010. "Measuring the Returns to R&D." In *Handbook of the Economics of Innovation*, Vol. 2, 1033–82. North-Holland.

Hall, B. H., and P. Mohnen. 2013. "Innovation and Productivity: An Update." *Eurasian Business Review* 3 (1): 47–65.

Hatzius, J., and K. Dawsey. 2015. "Doing the Sums on Productivity Paradox v2. 0." *Goldman Sachs US Economics Analyst* 15 (30).

Ivanic, M., and W. Martin. 2010. "Poverty Impacts of Improved Agricultural Productivity: Opportunities for Genetically Modified Crops." *AgBioForum* 13 (4): Article 3.

Jorgenson, D. W., M. S. Ho, and K. J. Stiroh. 2008. "A Retrospective Look at the US Productivity Growth Resurgence." *Journal of Economic Perspectives* 22 (1): 3–24.

Khaldun, I. 1377. *The Muqaddimah: An Introduction to History*. Princeton, NJ: Princeton University Press. 2015 edition.

Klenow, P. J., and A. Rodríguez-Clare. 1997. "The Neoclassical Revival in Growth Economics: Has It Gone Too Far?" *NBER Macroeconomics Annual* 12: 73–103.

Krugman, Paul R. 1994. *The Age of Diminished Expectations*. Cambridge, MA: MIT Press.

Maasoumi, E., J. Racine, and T. Stengos. 2007. "Growth and Convergence: A Profile of Distribution Dynamics and Mobility." *Journal of Econometrics* 136 (2): 483–508.

Maasoumi, E., and L. Wang. 2008. "Economic Reform, Growth and Convergence in China." *Econometrics Journal* 11 (1): 128–54.

Maloney, W. F., and C. Molina. 2016. "Are Automation and Trade Polarizing Developing Country Labor Markets, Too?" Policy Research Working Paper 7922, World Bank, Washington, DC.

McMillan, M. S., and D. Rodrik. 2011. "Globalization, Structural Change and Productivity Growth." NBER Working Paper 17143, National Bureau of Economic Research, Cambridge, MA.

McMillan, M., D. Rodrik, and Í. Verduzco-Gallo. 2014. "Globalization, Structural Change, and Productivity Growth, with an Update on Africa." *World Development* 63: 11–32.

Melitz, M. J., and S. Polanec. 2015. "Dynamic Olley-Pakes Decomposition with Entry and Exit." *RAND Journal of Economics* 46 (2): 362–75.

Mokyr, J. 2013. "Is Technological Progress a Thing of the Past?" Vox EU, September 8.

———. 2014. "Secular Stagnation? Not in Your Life." Chapter 6 in *Secular Stagnation: Facts, Causes and Cures*, edited by C. Teulings and R. Baldwin. Vox EU e-book.

Nakamura, L., and R. Soloveichik. 2015. "Valuing 'Free' Media across Countries in GDP." Working Paper 15-25, Federal Reserve Bank of Philadelphia, July.

Phelps, E. 2013. *Mass Flourishing: How Grassroots Innovation Created Jobs, Challenge, and Change.* Princeton, NJ: Princeton University Press.

Pritchett, L. 1997. "Divergence, Big Time." *Journal of Economic Perspectives* 11 (3): 3–17.

Quah, D. T. 1996. "Twin Peaks: Growth and Convergence in Models of Distribution Dynamics." *Economic Journal* 106 (437): 1045–55.

Restuccia, D. 2013. "Factor Misallocation and Development." In *The New Palgrave Dictionary of Economics*, online edition, edited by S. N. Durlauf and L. E. Blume. Basingstoke, U.K.: Palgrave Macmillan.

Ridao-Cano, C., and C. Bodewig. 2018. *Growing United: Upgrading Europe's Convergence Machine.* Washington, DC: World Bank.

Rogerson, R. 2017. "Structural Transformation and Productivity Growth: Cause or Effect?" Background paper for *Productivity Revisited*, World Bank, Washington, DC.

Solow, R. M. 1987. "We'd Better Watch Out." *New York Times Book Review*, July 12, 36.

Syverson, C. 2013. "Will History Repeat Itself?" Comments on "Is the Information Technology Revolution Over?" *International Productivity Monitor* 25 (Spring): 37–40.

———. 2016. "Has a Worldwide Productivity Slowdown Started?" Background paper for *Productivity Revisited*, World Bank, Washington, DC.

van Ark, B. 2016. "The Productivity Paradox of the New Digital Economy." *International Productivity Monitor* 31 (Fall): 3–18.

Wolff, E. 1985. "The Magnitude and Causes of the Recent Productivity Slowdown in the U.S." In *Productivity Growth and U.S. Competitiveness*, edited by W. J. Baumol and K. McLennan, 29–57. New York: Oxford University Press for the Committee for Economic Development.

2. Enhancing Firm Performance

New Thinking about Within-Firm Productivity

The firm is the main creator of value added and productivity growth in the economy. As chapter 1 discusses, perhaps half of observed productivity growth is due to improvements within firms obtained by innovating, adopting new technologies, and implementing best managerial practices. The rapid and extensive gains of countries like Chile and China suggest that while removing distortions (such as imperfect financial markets, labor market regulations, or taxes) may yield large gains during initial reform periods, once the big distortions have been eliminated, productivity growth is more likely to come from the process of upgrading products and processes within existing firms and sectors, and from new firms.

How we conceive of and measure firm productivity has changed radically over the last 20 years for two reasons (De Loecker 2017). The first is the greater access to detailed individual firm–level data on output, intermediate inputs, workers, and capital—and, in some cases, on innovation investments, management quality, and, particularly, product prices. Second, the availability of this body of data has raised the bar in the academic literature on the estimation and identification of production functions. This has led to an expansion of the conception of firm performance beyond the standard efficiency concerns to a second set of considerations related to product prices. Just as importantly, it has led analysis to move away from the traditional simplification of assuming identical competitive firms to analysis in which firms sell differentiated products using differentiated inputs. In this way, it is bringing issues of market power and industrial organization more explicitly into productivity analysis.

Traditionally, productivity—captured by the measure of total factor productivity (TFP)—has been calculated as the part of firm-level revenue or sales that cannot be explained by the contribution of capital, labor, energy, or other factors. If all firms are assumed to be identical, then revenues can be deflated by industry-level price indexes to derive quantities produced. However, when prices vary across firms within an industry, industry-level deflation does not eliminate price influence. The literature now calls this traditional measure *revenue total factor productivity* (TFPR) to capture the fact that it is not free of price effects, and distinguishes it from *physical total factor productivity* (TFPQ), which is free of price effects—but can only be derived with individual firm prices. TFPR comprises TFPQ plus whatever is driving firm-level price variation (see appendix A).

This price variation, in turn, can be broken up into three components: differences in input prices, differences in market power, and differences in quality and other factors affecting demand for the product. These three components are captured in the first half of figure 2.1. The traditional TFP (TFPR) measure conflates both supply and demand factors. Breaking it apart into these components becomes critical to thinking more comprehensively about improved firm and industry performance over the long term. This new understanding suggests that many empirical conclusions based on traditional analysis of the drivers of productivity probably need to be reexamined. For instance, given that TFPR conflates market concentration with efficiency, simple structural transformation calculations, or inferences to date about the impact of trade liberalization or procompetitive policies, appear to be unreliable.

The great benefit of this new understanding is that it forces policy makers to think more broadly about what policy to improve firm performance should be. Growth is driven not only by narrow efficiency considerations but also by other dimensions of firm performance on the demand side. Higher prices may arise from increased market power and increase profitability for a while—although, as discussed later, the long-term implications are ambiguous. Or, a firm's value may rise because, with the same inputs, it produces a higher quality product that commands a higher price or sells greater volume. Policy makers may therefore proceed beyond a narrow focus on improving efficiency to taking into account demand-side investments such as upgrading quality, connecting to digital platforms, or marketing.

This chapter presents some of the latest thinking on these and other issues, some of which radically call into question how we think about policy. It also presents World Bank work on several countries that illustrates what can be learned from this new approach. That said, this is the beginning of a new analytical agenda, not the culmination. Hence the

FIGURE 2.1 Decomposing Firm Performance

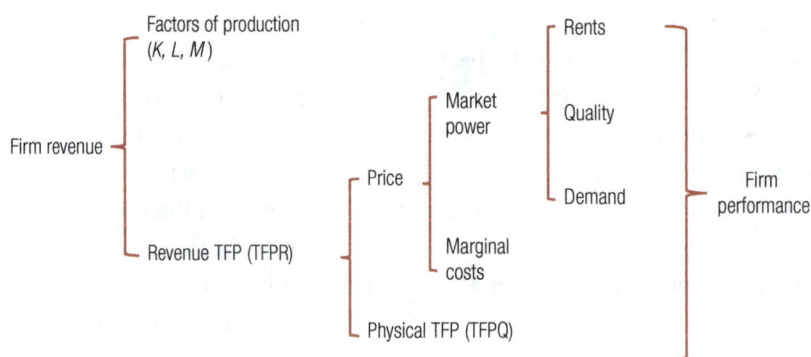

Note: K = capital; L = labor; M = materials; TFP = total factor productivity.

results must be seen as grist for renewed policy debate, rather than the definitive word on where policy should go.

Firm Performance: Beyond Efficiency

A firm's performance on balance sheets is measured as revenues over costs. Figure 2.1 breaks this into constituent parts in finer detail than in the preceding discussion. Beginning from the left, firm performance can increase through higher prices, higher efficiency, or both. Prices are, in turn, a function of costs of production on the one hand, and markups on the other. Markups, in turn, may both reflect product market competition in the traditional sense and require investments like upgrading quality, advertising, and marketing as well.

The Good and the Bad of Markups and Market Power

In the narrowest sense, higher markups, in which prices exceed marginal costs, may be good for GDP. Exporters of scarce natural resources around the world receive prices high above extraction costs, and these rents show up as higher GDP. Similarly, inventors who hold a patent on their new ideas receive the temporary rents (quasi-rents) from their innovations—again, with prices above costs. Schumpeter argued that higher rents (higher markups) offer firms a greater incentive to innovate.

On the other hand, markups often signal market power arising from anticompetitive behavior or barriers to entry that a long literature documents are likely to be a disincentive to increasing productivity in existing firms[1] or allow unproductive firms to continue (see discussion in chapter 4). The radical restructurings of the economies of Chile, India, and many Eastern European countries when opened to foreign competition illustrate how important this effect can be. Market power increases firm profits in the short term, but may have detrimental long-term dynamic effects on investment by destroying the incentives to invest in productivity-enhancing activities.

However, the impact of more competition and lower markups may be ambiguous. Aghion et al. (2005) argue that the effect of competition on innovation has an inverted U-shape: firms competing "neck and neck" with frontier firms will innovate seeking room to "escape competition." On the other hand, firms too far from the frontier may find profits so low that they will not or cannot upgrade, and thus Schumpeter's effect dominates.

The analysis of markups and efficiency has regained increased attention in recent years for several reasons. Evidence on global market power shows that markups have risen most in North America and Europe, and least in emerging markets in Latin America and Asia, partly because in the latter markups were originally high and thus there was limited scope for further increments (De Loecker and Eeckhout 2018). Recent findings for India (De Loecker et al. 2016) and World Bank evidence for Chile (Cusolito, García-Marin, and Maloney 2017), Malaysia (Zaourak 2018), and Mexico (Cusolito, Iacovone, and Sanchez 2018) show that firms that are highly efficient charge higher markups. While the higher price-costs margins could be a result of supply and demand complementarities, meaning that more efficient firms have an advantage to vertically differentiate their products, they can also reflect imperfect pass-through.

Moreover, empirically, the presence of market power can lead to faulty empirical inferences (and thus faulty policy prescriptions) because measures of TFPR conflate efficiency with markups. This issue was highlighted by Katayama, Lu, and Tybout in 2003. The authors show that the resultant revenue-based productivity indexes have little to do with technical efficiency, product quality, or contributions to social welfare. Nonetheless, they are likely to be correlated with policy shocks and managerial decisions in misleading ways. Two examples from recent work sponsored by the World Bank suggest why breaking these apart is essential for evidence-based policy inference (Cusolito, García Marín, and Maloney 2017; Cusolito, Iacovone, and Sanchez 2018).

A Better Allocation of Resources or Increased Market Concentration?

Reallocation of resources from low-TFP to high-TFP firms may imply transferring resources not to more efficient firms, but rather to firms with more market power. In this case, a common measure used to suggest a healthy allocation of resources—a higher covariance between TFPR and employment—may actually reflect the reverse. A similar problem arises from the structural transformation exercises discussed in chapter 1. Large differences in labor productivity among sectors can suggest that efficiency can be gained by transferring workers to more productive sectors. To the degree that labor productivity is capturing rents due to barriers to entry, this approach amounts to arguing for transferring workers to the more distorted and inefficient parts of the economy. This may well be the explanation for the finding of McMillan and Rodrik (2011) that the effect of structural transformation in Latin America was negative. Chile, before liberalization, had tariffs on automobiles totaling hundreds of percent and had as many assembly plants as the United States. In Argentina in 1980, virtually every car on the street was an early 1960s model Ford Falcon built with 1960s technology, protected by high tariffs and generating clear monopoly rents. Liberalization cut heavily into these sectors and led to workers being transferred to what, on paper, looked like less productive sectors—but which, in reality, were a better growth bet over the long term.

Documenting the Benefits of Trade Liberalization

Similarly, regressions of TFPR on measures of competition or liberalization can be misleading because an increase in upstream and downstream competition may have two countervailing effects: lowering prices and markups, while increasing efficiency. For instance, recent studies finding that tariff liberalization, increased imports from China, and liberalized flows of foreign direct investment increase TFPR (see Ahn et al. 2016; Ahn and Duval 2017) may actually understate the effect on efficiency, and seem to support the usual "escape from competition" effect. However, breaking apart the different components of TFPR offers a much richer perspective and insight into the mechanisms through which trade reforms work. For instance, De Loecker et al. (2016) show that after India's trade reform in 1991, markups increased, inflating TFPR and overstating apparent efficiency gains. Factory-gate prices indeed fell with declines in output tariffs, but marginal costs fell by more in response to input tariff liberalization, leading to big gains for producers and smaller gains for consumers than trade theory would predict. One of the central messages of De Loecker et al. (2016) is that understanding the drivers that underlie this imperfect pass-through on the product side is clearly necessary to complement the productivity analysis.

These findings further raise the question of where, precisely, the efficiency-enhancing effects of trade liberalization come from. World Bank work by Cusolito, García Marín, and Maloney (2017) argues that it may rather work through the Schumpeterian effect already discussed. These authors find a strong positive relationship between markups and within-plant TFPQ, on average, with half of the effect being due to investments in innovation. This is broadly consistent with more of Chile's firms being on the laggard side of the inverted U-shaped curve described by Aghion et al. (2005).

Finally, the Chilean case also suggests that the Schumpeterian effect of higher rents on innovation for firms that are relatively far from the frontier may be conflated with being able to substitute for missing markets from higher earnings. The positive effects of markups on innovation are stronger in industries that are more dependent on external sources of financing, suggesting that as much as raising the returns to innovation, higher markups raise cash flow that relieves credit market constraints, thus allowing firms to cover the fixed costs of innovating, including upgrading their managerial and technical capabilities.[2]

These capabilities, in turn, appear important to how firms react to increased competition. Chilean firms with higher preliberalization TFPQ, part of which reflects greater innovation ability, showed increased productivity in response to increased competition compared with low-TFPQ firms, which showed a decrease. This is consistent with Hombert and Matray (2018), who show that while rising imports from China led to slower sales growth and lower profitability for U.S. manufacturing firms, these effects are significantly smaller for firms with a larger stock of research and development (R&D), reflecting their ability to differentiate their products. Bloom, Draca, and Van Reenen (2016) similarly find that in sectors more exposed to Chinese imports, job and survival rates fell in firms with low patenting intensity, but firms with high patenting intensity were relatively sheltered. In all cases, raising innovative capability broadly construed appears to be an important complement to competition.

The above complications clearly do not negate the positive competitive effects of trade liberalization; domestic tradable prices do fall as a result of competing imports. But the channels through which the distribution of firm performance changes appear more complex than previously thought. Furthermore, the examples confirm the importance of empirically separating efficiency effects from markup effects, and more importantly, the need to conceptually treat productivity and market structure in an integrated way.

Quality

While the focus on firm performance has tended to be on efficiency, raising the quality of a product also has the potential to boost firm profits and advance growth. Prices within very narrowly defined product categories differ vastly and to an important degree reflect quality. For instance, a bottle of "red wine, 750 ml" may sell for $2 (by Charles Shaw, known as Two Buck Chuck) or $40,000 (Domaine de la Romanée-Conti Grand Cru). Within the category of "leather women's shoes," Manolo Blahnik's shoes can sell for $1,500—easily 100 times more expensive than basic Payless pumps. In Japan, snips of Ruby Roman grapes can sell for $5,000; Densuke watermelons sell for more than $2,000 each; and musk melons have sold for more than $10,000 apiece. Part of this reflects the care in the growing process, and thus higher production costs. Sekai ichi apples ($20 apiece) are individually pollinated. But part also reflects that fruit has been elevated from mere nourishment to the status of a luxury product, and features heavily in Japan's gift-giving culture, along with other gourmet foodstuffs including frozen steaks, whisky, and black tea.[3] More generally, using data on exports to the United States from the rest of the world, Schott (2008) shows that prices (proxied by export unit values) of identically defined goods from different countries vary enormously.[4]

In many cases, different qualities of products can be thought of as reflecting insufficient disaggregation in the prevailing systems of industrial classifications: a better-quality product could be considered a different product and both quality levels could be sold in different competitive markets. Steel comes in many different qualities that are not registered at the 10-digit (HS-10) level of disaggregation in the Harmonized System of industrial classification. On the other hand, many high-end products benefit from investments in advertising and branding that create market power—and hence positive markups. For such products, however, the markups are arising from investments in R&D, as Sutton (1998) terms them, and resulting product differentiation rather than artificial barriers to entry, and thus contribute to growth. Chile aspires to the day when its fine wines have the cachet of French Bordeaux, which would allow them to earn higher profits per bottle, increasing firm performance and growth.

Quantifying quality also poses challenges. Some fraction of observed price differences may represent differences in the cost of production or inefficiency, rather than quality (Khandelwal 2010). But a large fraction is due to desirable characteristics for which consumers are willing to pay. To take one narrowly defined product—wine—Combris, Lecocq, and Visser (1997) find that the information listed on the bottle of

Bordeaux—including Cru, Grand Cru, or the vineyard—accounted for 66 percent of differences in price. World Bank work by Cusolito, García, and Juvenal (2018) pursues this further with Chilean wines to permit closer examination of the relationship between TFPR, quality, price, and efficiency. Using quality rankings collected from the *Wine Spectator* and *Descorchados* magazines,[5] figure 2.2 shows that wine prices are correlated with high prices of materials in panel a and c. These higher prices of inputs could reflect less efficient sourcing, but may reflect better quality inputs and better skilled labor that permit producers to make higher-quality products—as found in previous studies for Colombia (Kugler and Verhoogen 2011), China (Manova and Zhang 2012), and Portugal (Bastos, Silva, and Verhoogen 2018). Furthermore, prices are also very clearly related to the quality ratings in panels b and d. The diverging unit values

FIGURE 2.2 **The Price of Wines Is Clearly Related to the Price of Materials and the Quality Rating They Receive**
(Wine experts' scores and wine prices)

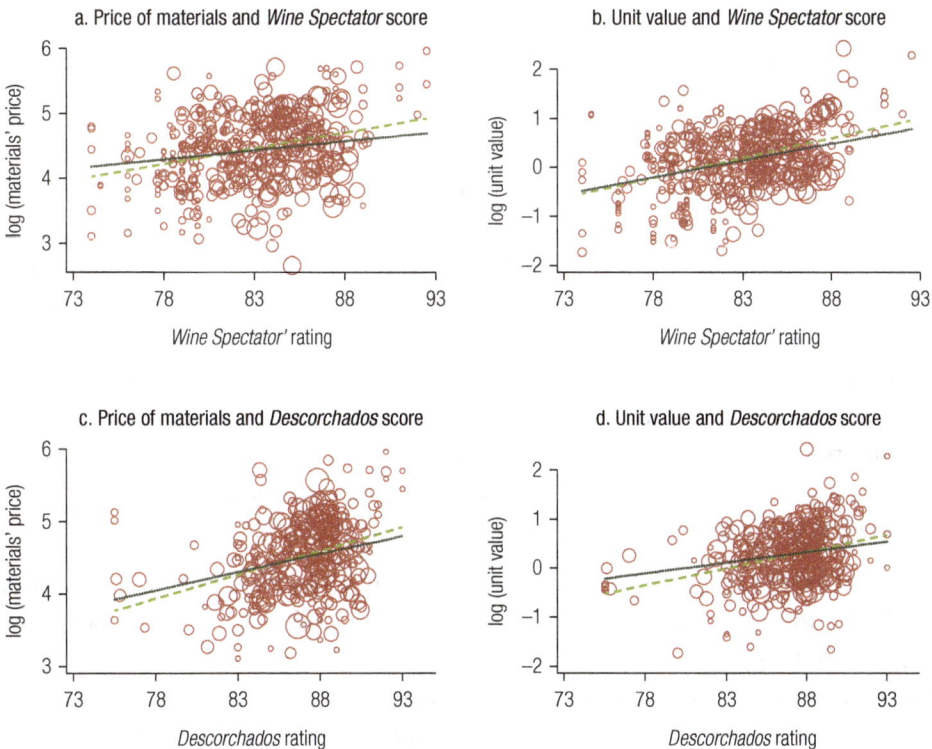

a. Price of materials and *Wine Spectator* score

b. Unit value and *Wine Spectator* score

c. Price of materials and *Descorchados* score

d. Unit value and *Descorchados* score

Source: Cusolito, García, and Juvenal 2018.

Note: The figure displays the relation between the average rating by *Wine Spectator* (panels a and b) and *Descorchados* (panels c and d) for each winery-year observation and different plant-level outcomes. The size of each circle reflects the number of *Wine Spectator* reviews available for the winery in the respective year. All panels include regression lines. The dashed-red regression line corresponds to unweighted regression, while the dotted-green regression line weights observations by the number of reviews in *Wine Spectator*.

FIGURE 2.3 **TFPQ Estimations Exhibit a Downward Bias When Quality Is Not Controlled For**
(Wine experts' scores and TFPQ)

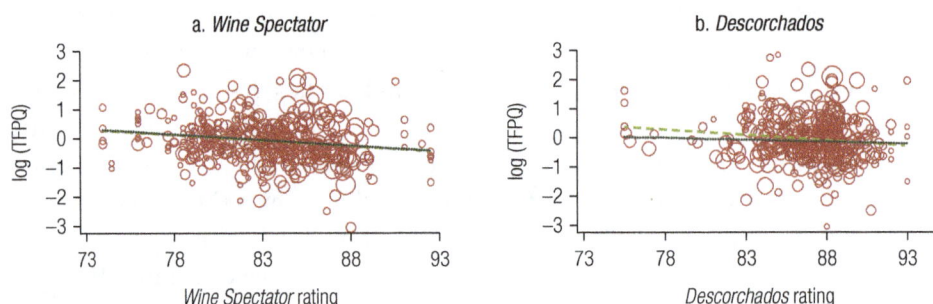

Source: Cusolito, García, and Juvenal 2018.

Note: The figure displays the relation between *Descorchados'* average rating for each winery-year observation and different plant-level outcomes. The size of each circle reflects the number of *Wine Spectator* reviews available for the winery in the respective year. The dashed-red regression line corresponds to unweighted regression, while the dotted-green regression line weights observations by the number of reviews in *Wine Spectator*. TFPQ = physical total factor productivity.

reflect not only differences in the ability to produce a vertically superior product, but also all that the superior characteristic implies with it—from design capacity, to different sets of inputs, to marketing and advertising (Sutton 1998).[6]

Figure 2.3 suggests that higher quality may come with an apparent cost in terms of efficiency when efficiency measures do not take into consideration the quality of each bottle; the number of bottles produced per worker declines with quality in this case. However, better quality may allow product differentiation that permits higher overall firm profitability and revenue productivity per worker. Again, simply looking at efficiency may hide important gains in firm performance and value added, and furthermore, estimating TFPQ without controlling explicitly for quality can make high-quality producers look unproductive (see annex 2A). And to the degree that quality upgrading requires a higher level of skills in workers, captured in higher input and factor prices, a better quality of jobs is generated.

This is not to say that the overall structure of the wine market may not make it as profitable to produce a lower-quality good given a large mass market (Two Buck Chuck), and high-performing firms may decide to produce goods at multiple price points. However, Krishna, Levchenko, and Maloney (2018) for this report show that there is a correlation between the level of a country's development and price, suggesting that the ability to generate higher quality increases with the stage of development (figure 2.4).

In this sense, the broad co-evolution of average quality and underlying national productivity offers another window on firm performance: despite the evidence from

FIGURE 2.4   Average Product Quality Increases with the Level of Development

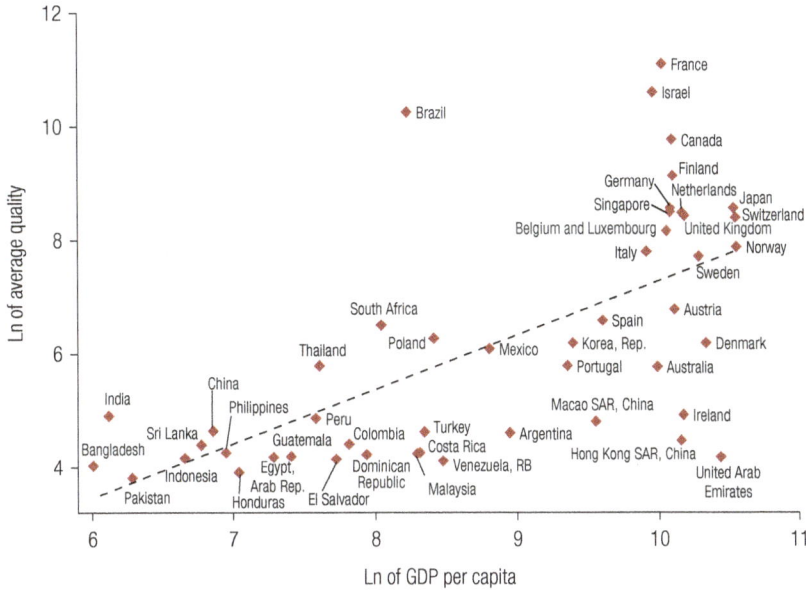

Source: Krishna, Levchenko, and Maloney 2018.

Note: The figure plots average cross-good unit values standardized by the 90th value of HS-10 against log GDP per capita for countries with more than 50 products. Ln of average quality versus ln of gross domestic product per capita. Slope = 0.956 (*t*-statistic = 5.73). HS-10 = 10-digit level of disaggregation in the Harmonized System of industrial classification.

the wine industry presented earlier, in the aggregate better managed, more sophisticated firms could be expected to be better at quality and physical productivity.

In sum, though discussions of productivity tend to focus on efficiency, quality is an integral part of firm performance and improving it is a core component of an overall growth strategy.

Demand

Whether higher quality leads to higher prices depends on customers' willingness to pay. Thus, the preceding discussion sheds light on recently initiated debate about which is more important for firm performance and growth: increasing demand for firms' products or increasing efficiency. Focusing on one very homogeneous product, concrete, with similar quality and production costs across firms, Foster, Haltiwanger, and Syverson (2016) show that the growth of U.S. concrete firms is mostly due to the slow process of building up demand through different types of "soft" investments, like advertising, marketing, and development of a network of clients. Furthermore, they show that new firms without a strong demand base enter with a lower price but higher productivity. Here again, the conflation of the two in TFPR leads to the mistaken conclusion that entrants have lower efficiency.

FIGURE 2.5 Demand Is More Important than TFPQ at Mature Stages: Colombia

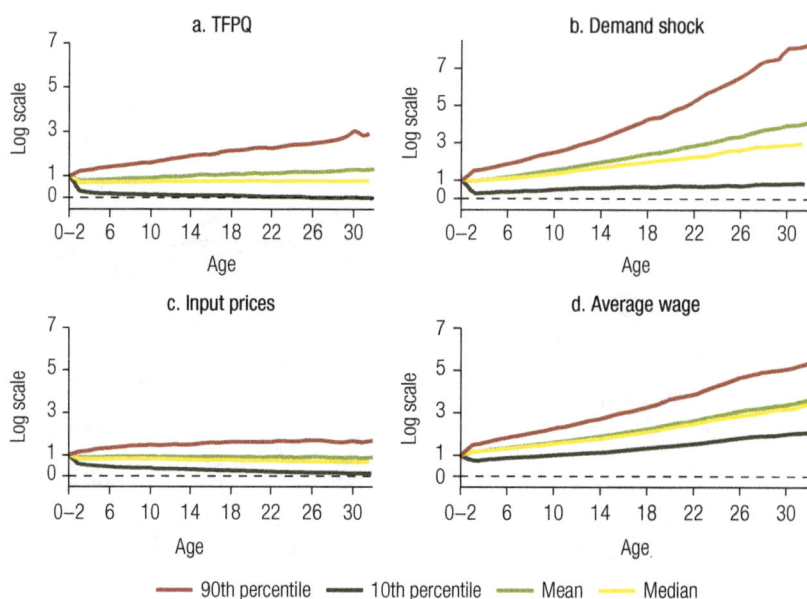

Source: Eslava and Haltiwanger 2017.
Note: The data include year and sector fixed effects. TFPQ = physical total factor productivity.

World Bank evidence on the contributions to firm growth of demand versus efficiency and quality over the life cycle for the manufacturing sector in Chile, Colombia, Malaysia, and Mexico finds similar results. For Colombia, Eslava and Haltiwanger (2017) study the relative importance of TFPQ and demand shocks, input and output prices, and distortions as determinants of firm growth over a firm's life cycle, since 1982.[7] As with the case of concrete, panel a of figure 2.5 suggests that demand considerations appear more important at mature stages than the evolution of physical productivity. Furthermore, the increase in input prices and wages suggests quality upgrading as a partial explanation for the evolution of the demand. However, since the expansion of the demand component is much larger than the observed increase of input prices, the evidence suggests that other factors beyond pure upgrading of product quality, like the establishment of a brand name, have affected consumers' willingness to pay a higher price for the goods they buy.

Figure 2.6 for Malaysia shows very similar patterns across the four panels. Both demand shocks and TFPQ grow, but demand grows on average by a factor of almost 3 by the time firms have reached the age of 27, relative to a factor of 1.7 in the case of TFPQ. The findings again confirm a story of quality upgrading over the life cycle. The latter is inferred from the rise in material prices and wages, which all increase with age. Furthermore, figure 2.7 establishes that what underlies the increasing wages is a rise in the ratio of skilled to unskilled workers. Higher efficiency gets passed along

FIGURE 2.6 Demand Is More Important than TFPQ at Mature Stages: Malaysia

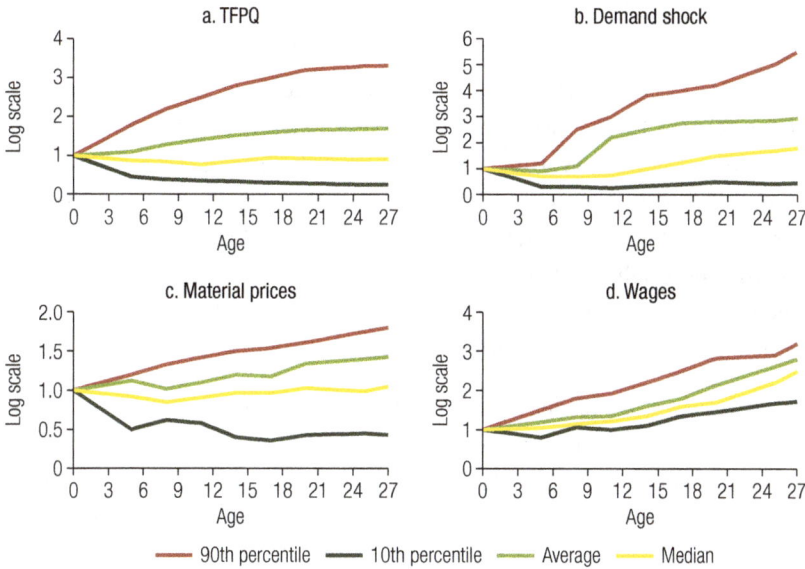

a. TFPQ

b. Demand shock

c. Material prices

d. Wages

— 90th percentile — 10th percentile — Average — Median

Source: Zaourak 2018.

Note: Controlled by year and sector fixed effects. Outliers below the 3rd percentile and above the 97th percentile are trimmed. TFPQ = physical total factor productivity.

FIGURE 2.7 Firms Hire More Skilled Labor and Use Higher-Quality Inputs as They Raise Quality during Their Life Cycle

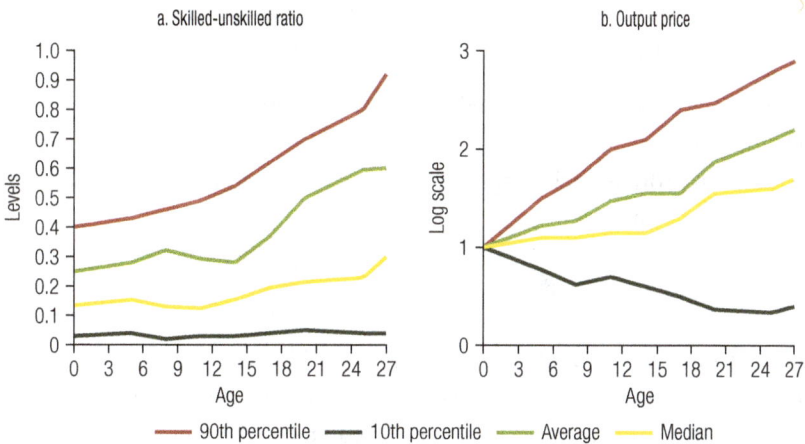

a. Skilled-unskilled ratio

b. Output price

— 90th percentile — 10th percentile — Average — Median

Source: Zaourak 2018.

Note: Controlled by year and sector fixed effects. Outliers below the 3rd percentile and above the 97th percentile are trimmed.

to workers in the form of higher earnings, but quality upgrading increases demand for more skilled workers.

These results are confirmed for Mexico, where Cusolito, Iacovone, and Sanchez (2018) find that TFPQ increases modestly over the life cycle, with markups explaining most of the gains in firm performance at mature stages. A comparison between single and multiproduct firms reveals that markups and changes in markups are higher for multiproduct firms than for single-product ones. Thus, the evidence suggests a higher scope for product differentiation for firms that sell more than one good and operate in sectors with long quality ladders. Last, Canales and García Marín (2018) show that across the life cycle of high-growth firms in Chile, roughly 20 percent of firm growth is due to efficiency gains and about 80 percent is due to increased demand.

In fact, the evolution of demand and efficiency cannot be treated as independent. Firms able to access foreign markets learn by exporting (De Loecker 2013; Atkin, Khandelwal, and Osman 2017). Mayer, Melitz, and Ottaviano (2014) document how demand shocks in export markets led French multiproduct exporters to shift their product mix toward those with greater productivity. Cusolito, Fernandes, and Maemir (2018) for this report find similar evidence for Romania. Broadly following Mayer, Melitz, and Ottaviano (2016), they show that three different types of demand shocks, at the country, industry, and firm levels, increase average exports per product and the number of exported products. This increase causes multiproduct exporters to change their export product mix toward their best-performing products, which, in turn, increases both labor productivity and TFPR (figure 2.8). Although changes in TFPR can reflect positive price variations due to the demand shock, the authors find little evidence in this direction (figure 2.8), suggesting that improvements in TFPR are mainly related to efficiency gains after the demand shock.

Suggesting another channel, Lederman et al. (2018), using linked employer-employee data for Brazil, find that for large firms, higher export intensity increases the margins of firm growth, including TFPQ, product appeal, markups, and production scale, through the demand for more skilled workers.

Firm Size and Development

The preceding discussion offers some keys to unlocking the puzzle of the large differences in mature firm sizes viewed across countries and the development process. Hsieh and Klenow (2014) document that in the United States, the average 40-year-old plant employs more than seven times as many workers as the typical plant that is 5 years old or younger. In contrast, over the same age range, plants in India and Mexico only double in size. Furthermore, the growth trajectories are closely matched by the evolution of TFP. Figure 2.9, drawing on the World Bank Enterprise Surveys, show that this is a broader phenomenon, with firm size clearly increasing with the level of development. This is consistent with findings discussed earlier that efficiency and quality tend to be

FIGURE 2.8 **Increased Demand from Trade Causes Firms to Concentrate on Their Best-Performing Products but Has Little Impact on Product Price**

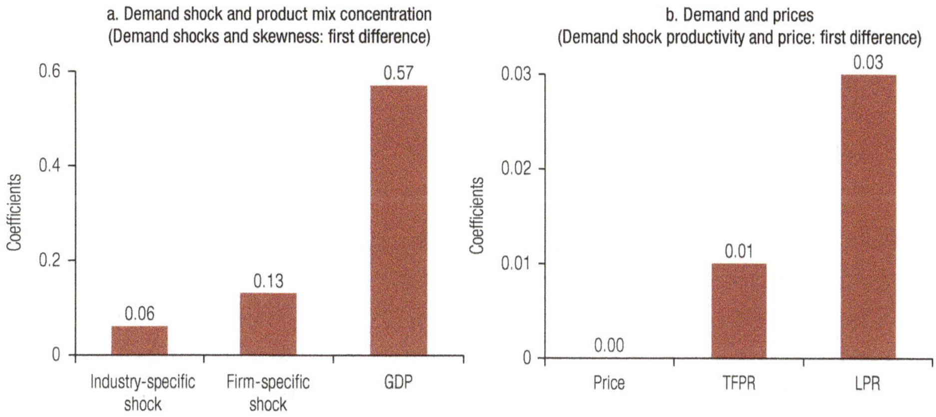

a. Demand shock and product mix concentration
(Demand shocks and skewness: first difference)

b. Demand and prices
(Demand shock productivity and price: first difference)

Source: Cusolito, Fernandes, and Maemir 2017.

Note: Panel a displays the coefficients of the regression of the Theil index on three types of demand shocks: country, industry, and firm. Panel b shows the coefficients of the regression of labor productivity (LPR), revenue total factor productivity (TFPR), and price on the firm-level demand shock.

FIGURE 2.9 **Firm Size Increases with the Level of Development**

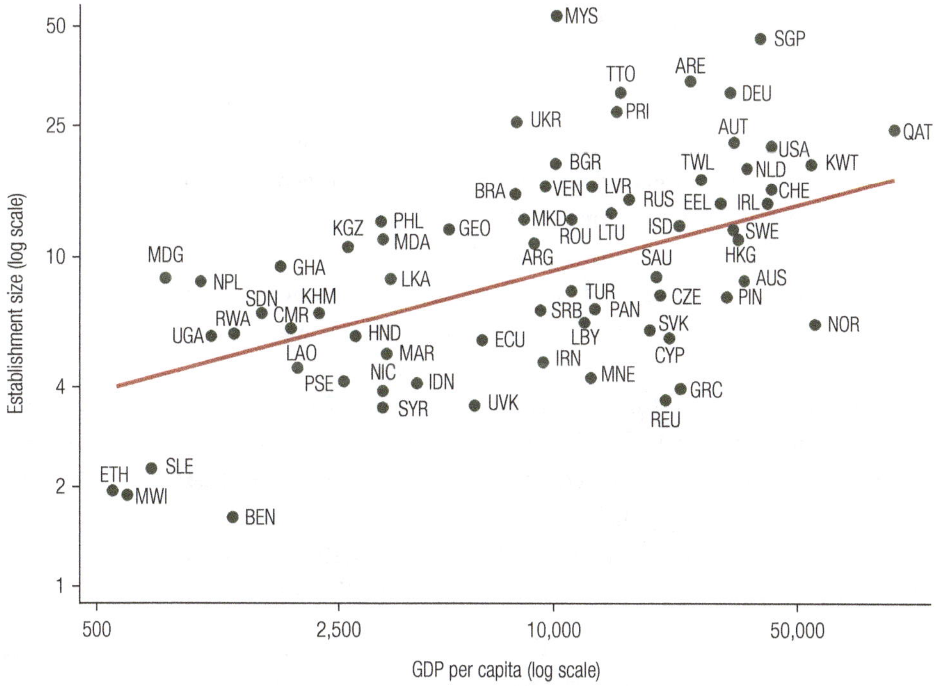

Source: Bento and Restuccia 2017.

lower in developing countries, as may well be the ability to amass a large client base. All three can be restrained by problems in the operating environment and deficient human capital and firm capabilities.

Concluding Remarks

This chapter documents the major shifts in measurement and conceptualization of firm productivity. It has two important implications for policy.

First, it challenges much of the empirical literature to date that has worked with standard measures of TFPR and asks for a reexamination of a long list of revenue-based productivity studies linking productivity (efficiency) changes to policy changes such as trade liberalization or market deregulation. As shown here, important identification problems can lead to misleading conclusions and policy prescriptions. Of great importance is the need to approach the analysis of productivity and market structure in an integrated fashion, to understand both how policy initiatives work their way through the market structure and how firms subsequently respond.

Thus, this chapter seeks to initiate an ambitious new empirical agenda for developing countries that requires a commitment to collect systematic data on prices, specifically at the firm-product level. This report has identified and worked with industrial data sets from Brazil, Chile, China, India, Colombia, Ethiopia, Malaysia, and Mexico that have such data, but most countries do not.

Second, the chapter argues that policies to improve firm performance and growth need to move beyond a narrow focus on efficiency to explore the upgrading of product quality and the cultivation of demand. All require improvements both on the human capital side and in the operating environment. Both efficiency and quality require strengthening the ability of firms to identify, adapt, and implement new productive technologies and processes (that is, technology transfer). Both require investments in "innovation," broadly construed, ranging from improving managerial practices to licensing of technologies, and R&D, supported by the kinds of policies discussed at length in *The Innovation Paradox* (Cirera and Maloney 2017), as well as specific initiatives in quality infrastructure and marketing. In terms of cultivating demand, the findings in this chapter suggest the need to rebalance business support services toward this end, as well as exploring policies to reduce search, matching, and informational frictions, strengthen links to multinational firms and facilitate access to global value chains, develop networks, and facilitate investments in marketing and advertising.

The next chapter discusses how the distortions or market failures in the operating environment can lead to the misallocation of factors across firms and hence inhibit productivity growth along the first margin. Moreover, it also explores in depth how they may also affect both the within-firm upgrading discussed in this chapter and the entry of more efficient and higher-quality firms as well.

Annex 2A. Quality and Physical Total Factor Productivity Estimation

As discussed, quality differences across firms could have implications for the estimation of productivity (TFPQ). Indeed, even if output and input price data at the firm level are available, which allows the production function to be estimated in physical units, not controlling explicitly for quality generates biased production elasticities and productivity measures. Why? Because high-quality production processes typically use higher quantities of inputs to produce the same product. For instance, high-quality wine production uses only the best vines, leading to more waste of grapes per unit of wine produced. Thus, not controlling for quality differences could lead to the mistaken conclusion that a plant producing high-quality products is relatively more inefficient, even if data on inputs and outputs are available in terms of physical units. This explanation sounds reasonable, but the challenge is to empirically prove it, given that product quality is often an unobservable variable.

To bridge that gap, Cusolito, García, and Juvenal (2018) focus on the wine industry in Chile and create a new and unusually rich database at the firm level that merges several sources of information, including the manufacturing census, export transaction data, and observable measures of quality coming from publicly available experts' wine rankings.

The authors first confirm that ignoring quality biases TFPQ downward, making high-quality firms look unproductive. That finding also challenges the standard approach of inferring the quality content embedded in a product by estimating the residual of a demand function and instrumenting prices with TFPQ (when firm-level prices are observed). If the production elasticities are biased and contaminated for the parameter meant to capture the relative importance of quality on output, then TFPQ still contains quality determinants, and it is not orthogonal to the demand residual—thus invalidating the condition needed for a valid instrument. Furthermore, the finding shows that one cannot, as Schott (2008) does, simply treat output prices as measures of quality. Hence, the task of separating efficiency from quality—which requires controlling for quality—becomes challenging, even when firm-level prices are available.

Notes

1. Schmitz (2005), for example, analyzing the U.S. and Canadian iron ore industries when faced with increased competition from Brazil, documents a doubling of labor productivity arising from investment in management practices (raising worker competencies and reorganizing work schedules, leading to better capital utilization) and a loosening of restrictive work practices, including overstaffing. Dunne, Klimek, and Schmitz (2008) also note that TFP in the U.S. cement industry had been falling for decades until the entry of firms from Australia, Japan, Mexico, and Spain, among others, in the 1980s. In the following decade, TFP increased by 35 percent among U.S. cement makers, with 75 percent of that increase arising from within plants. Again, the increased ability to adjust the workforce and the relaxation of some workplace regulations were central factors in generating these improvements. Both studies argue that the previous rents made possible work rules that

prohibited plants from firing workers to make way for the adoption of new technologies or machinery, and hence had impeded innovation. De Loecker (2011) shows that productivity rose in Belgian textiles when important tariffs were reduced. See also Holmes and Schmitz (2010).

2. Duval, Hong, and Timmer (2017) show that credit constraints impeded firms' emergence from the financial crisis.

3. "Why Is Fruit So Expensive in Japan?" *The Independent*, July 16, 2014, https://www.independent .co.uk/life-style/food-and-drink/features/why-is-fruit-so-expensive-in-japan-9605105.html.

4. The goods were identified as identical as classified by the Harmonized System of industrial classification at the 10-digit (HS-10) level of disaggregation.

5. The *Wine Spectator* is perhaps the most comprehensive guide to wines around the globe. Each year, it provides scores for about 300–400 Chilean wines. The ratings are given on a scale of 50 to 100 points—where a higher score indicates higher quality—for a sample of wines within firms. Varieties are uniquely identified according to the name of the producer, the commercial name of the wine, the wine grape, and vintage year. *Descorchados* is a Chilean wine publication that provides scores for an average of 1,000 wines each year, as well as information on prices per bottle. Wine tasters working for *Descorchados* make a first selection of the top wines within a vineyard, called recommended, and provide a quality ranking per vineyard, based on blind tasting, and information about the ratio of tasted wines to recommended wines, which can also be used to construct categorical quality variables at the vineyard level.

6. Sutton (1998), in fact, lumps investments in these dimensions together as R&D.

7. To control for quality differences, the study relies on a nested constant elasticity of substitution structure for preferences for goods produced by multiproduct firms (Hottman, Redding, and Weinstein 2016).

References

Aghion, P., N. Bloom, R. Blundell, R. Griffith, and P. Howitt. 2005. "Competition and Innovation: An Inverted-U Relationship." *Quarterly Journal of Economics* 120 (2): 701–28.

Ahn, J. B., E. Dabla-Norris, R. A. Duval, B. Hu, and L. Njie. 2016. "Reassessing the Productivity Gains from Trade Liberalization." Working Paper 16/77, International Monetary Fund, Washington, DC.

Ahn, J. B., and R. A. Duval. 2017. "Trading with China: Productivity Gains, Job Losses." IMF Working Paper 17/122, International Monetary Fund, Washington, DC.

Atkin, D., A. K. Khandelwal, and A. Osman. 2017. "Exporting and Firm Performance: Evidence from a Randomized Experiment." *Quarterly Journal of Economics* 132 (2): 551–615.

Bastos, P., J. Silva, and E. Verhoogen. 2018. "Export Destinations and Input Prices." *American Economic Review* 108 (2): 353–92.

Bento, P., and D. Restuccia. 2017. "Misallocation, Establishment Size, and Productivity." *American Economic Journal: Macroeconomics* 9 (3): 267–303.

Bloom, N., M. Draca, and J. Van Reenen. 2016. "Trade-Induced Technical Change? The Impact of Chinese Imports on Innovation, IT and Productivity." *Review of Economic Studies* 83 (1): 87–117.

Canales, M., and A. García Marín. 2018. "Productividad, tamaño y empresas súper-estrella: Evidencia microenonómica para Chile." Working paper, University of Chile.

Cirera, X., and W. F. Maloney. 2017. *The Innovation Paradox: Developing-Country Capabilities and the Unrealized Promise of Technological Catch-Up*. Washington, DC: World Bank.

Combris, P., S. Lecocq, and M. Visser. 1997. "Estimation of a Hedonic Price Equation for Bordeaux Wine: Does Quality Matter?" *Economic Journal* 107 (441): 390–402.

Cusolito, A. P., A. M. Fernandes, and H. Maemir. 2018. "Cross-Country Evidence on the Effects of Demand Shocks on the Product Mix." Background paper for *Productivity Revisited,* World Bank, Washington, DC.

Cusolito, A. P., M. García, and L. Juvenal. 2018. "Quality and Efficiency in the Wine Industry." Background paper for *Productivity Revisited,* World Bank, Washington, DC.

Cusolito, A. P., A. García Marín, and W. F. Maloney. 2017. "Competition, Innovation and Within-Plant Productivity: Evidence from Chilean Plants." Background paper for *Productivity Revisited,* World Bank, Washington, DC.

Cusolito, A. P., L. Iacovone, and L. Sanchez. 2018. "The Effects of Chinese Competition on All the Margins of Firm Growth." Background paper for *Productivity Revisited,* World Bank, Washington, DC.

De Loecker, J. 2011. "Product Differentiation, Multiproduct Firms, and Estimating the Impact of Trade Liberalization on Productivity." *Econometrica* 79 (5): 1407–51.

———. 2013. "Detecting Learning by Exporting." *American Economic Journal: Microeconomics* 5 (3, August): 1–21.

———. 2017. "Productivity Analysis Using Micro Data. Where Do We Stand?" Background paper for *Productivity Revisited,* World Bank, Washington, DC.

De Loecker, J., and J. Eeckhout. 2018. "Global Market Power." Working Paper, Katholieke Universiteit Leuven.

De Loecker, J., P. K. Goldberg, A. K. Khandelwal, and N. Pavcnik. 2016. "Prices, Markups, and Trade Reform." *Econometrica* 84 (2): 445–510.

Dunne, T., S. Klimek, and J. Schmitz. 2008. "Does Foreign Competition Spur Productivity? Evidence from Post-WWII US Cement Manufacturing." Working Paper, Federal Reserve Bank of Minneapolis.

Duval, R. A., G. H. Hong, and Y. Timmer. 2017. "Financial Frictions and the Great Productivity Slowdown." IMF Working Paper 17/129, International Monetary Fund, Washington, DC.

Eslava, M., and J. Haltiwanger. 2017. "The Drivers of Life-Cycle Growth of Manufacturing Plants." Background paper for *Productivity Revisited,* World Bank, Washington, DC.

Foster, L., J. Haltiwanger, and C. Syverson. 2016. "The Slow Growth of New Plants: Learning about Demand?" *Economica* 83 (329): 91–129.

Holmes, T. J., and J. A. Schmitz Jr. 2010. "Competition and Productivity: A Review of Evidence." *Annual Review of Economics* 2 (1): 619–42.

Hombert, J., and A. Matray. 2018. "Can Innovation Help US Manufacturing Firms Escape Import Competition from China?" *Journal of Finance,* June 5, https://doi.org/10.1111/jofi.12691.

Hottman, C., S. Redding, and D. E. Weinstein. 2016. "Quantifying the Sources of Firm Heterogeneity." *Quarterly Journal of Economics* 131 (3): 1291–364.

Hsieh, C. T., and P. J. Klenow. 2014. "The Life Cycle of Plants in India and Mexico." *Quarterly Journal of Economics* 129 (3): 1035–84.

Katayama, H., S. Lu, and J. Tybout. 2003. "Why Plant-Level Productivity Studies Are Often Misleading, and an Alternative Approach to Interference." NBER Working Paper 9617, National Bureau of Economic Research, Cambridge, MA.

Khandelwal, A. 2010. "The Long and Short (of) Quality Ladders." *Review of Economic Studies* 77 (4): 1450–76.

Krishna, P., A. Levchenko, and W. Maloney. 2018. "Growth and Risk: The View from International Trade." Unpublished, World Bank, Washington, DC.

Kugler, M., and E. Verhoogen. 2011. "Prices, Plant Size, and Product Quality." *Review of Economic Studies* 79 (1): 307–39.

Lederman, D., G. Miion, R. Prado-Provenca, and J. Silva. 2018. "Trade, Skills, and Productivity." Working Paper, World Bank, Washington, DC.

Manova, K., and Z. Zhang. 2012. "Multi-product Firms and Product Quality." NBER Working Paper 18637, National Bureau of Economic Research, Cambridge, MA.

Mayer, T., M. J. Melitz, and G. I. Ottaviano. 2014. "Market Size, Competition, and the Product Mix of Exporters." *American Economic Review* 104 (2): 495–536.

———. 2016. "Product Mix and Firm Productivity Responses to Trade Competition." NBER Working Paper 22433, National Bureau of Economic Research, Cambridge, MA.

McMillan, M. S., and D. Rodrik. 2011. "Globalization, Structural Change and Productivity Growth." NBER Working Paper 17143, National Bureau of Economic Research, Cambridge, MA.

Schmitz Jr., J. A. 2005. "What Determines Productivity? Lessons from the Dramatic Recovery of the US and Canadian Iron Ore Industries Following their Early 1980s Crisis." *Journal of Political Economy* 113 (3): 582–625.

Schott, P. K. 2008. "The Relative Sophistication of Chinese Exports." *Economic Policy* 23 (53): 6–49.

Sutton, J. 1998. *Technology and Market Structure.* Cambridge, MA: MIT Press.

Zaourak, G. 2018. "Quality-Upgrading over the Life Cycle. Evidence for Malaysia." Background paper for *Productivity Revisited,* World Bank, Washington, DC.

3. Misallocation, Dispersion, and Risk

Chapter 2 focuses not only on efficiency but also on new ways of conceiving of firm performance and approaches to improving it through the accumulation of physical, human, and knowledge capital. Ideally, a well-functioning economy would ensure that these factors flowed to those firms that can use them most productively, grow most rapidly, and create the most jobs. Conceptually, the returns to, for instance, an additional unit of physical investment should be equated across all firms: no productivity gains can be reaped by taking resources from one firm and giving it to another. In reality, however, distortions and market failures—such as missing financial markets, labor market regulations, and taxes—exist in all economies to a greater or lesser degree. Hence, dispersion occurs in marginal products, potentially indicating misallocation. Hence, in explaining differences in levels of development, it is not only the level of accumulation of physical, human, and knowledge capital that matters, but how they are allocated across heterogeneous firms.

Olley and Pakes (1996) offer a way of capturing the contribution of reallocation to growth that underlies the Melitz-Polanec decompositions in chapter 1. The key contribution of Hsieh and Klenow (2009) was to offer a quantification of just how large the cost to societies of such misallocation may be—in a sense, demonstrating how microeconomic distortions plausibly have large macroeconomic consequences. By interpreting the dispersion in revenue total factor productivity (TFPR) as a direct measure of distortions, they argue that if capital and labor in China and India are hypothetically reallocated to reduce dispersion to the extent observed in the United States, their benchmark country, the "static" or one-off gains in manufacturing total factor productivity (TFPR) are 30 percent to 50 percent in China and 40 percent to 60 percent in India.

Part of the attraction of the Hsieh-Klenow framework was its tractability and apparent ease of replicability. Figure 3.1 presents comparable statistics for how much could be gained if all dispersion were eliminated for 10 developing countries plus the United States. TFPR would have ranged from 40 percent higher even in the United States to 160 percent higher in Kenya. The impressive magnitude of these potential gains has led to focusing policy on removing the driving distortions, for instance, by improving the popular Doing Business rankings.

FIGURE 3.1 More Misallocation (Higher TFP Dispersion) May Partly Explain Lower GDP
(Gains from reallocation versus GDP)

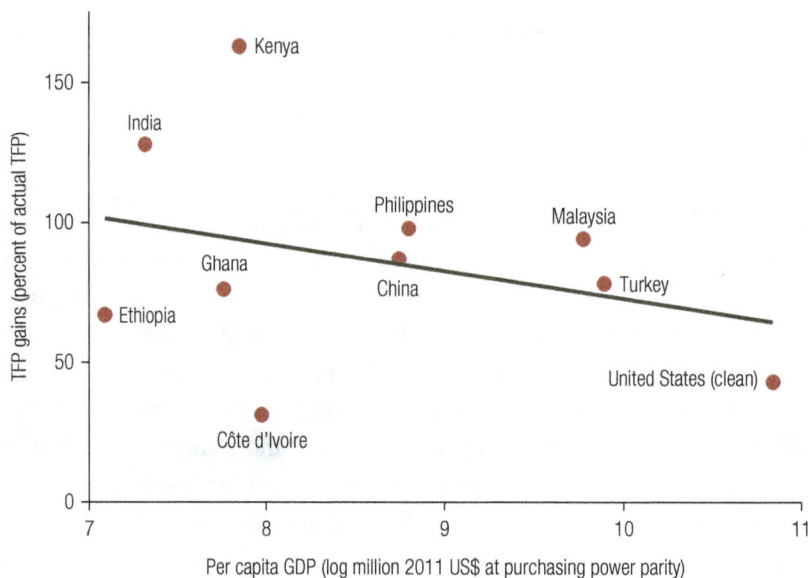

Source: Elaborations using the Hsieh-Klenow (2009) framework.

Note: Data are for the following years: China (2005), Ethiopia (2011), Ghana (2003), India (1994), Kenya (2010), Malaysia (2010), Philippines (2014), Turkey (2014), United States (1997: Hsieh-Klenow base year). "Clean" means data were cleaned using U.S. Census Bureau methodology. TFP = total factor productivity.

However, over the last 10 years, there has been a reconsideration of this focus or at least of its dominance in the policy dialogue and whether it has come too much at the expense of the within-firm and entry-exit margins. For starters, the accumulated empirical results are not obviously supportive. Figure 3.1 shows, for instance, that the calculated gains from reallocation seem very tentatively correlated with productivity as measured by GDP per capita. Yes, Kenya and the United States mark extremes that broadly correspond to income levels, but Ethiopia and Ghana appear with fewer potential gains than Malaysia or Turkey, substantially higher-income countries.[1] As Nishida et al. (2017) note, a substantial literature seems to find a very small or even negative impact of dispersion on income and growth. For instance, despite India's dramatic reforms of the 1990s and an increase in annual aggregate productivity growth of close to 5 percent, studies and new World Bank evidence suggest that reallocation plays a relatively unimportant role relative to within-plant gains in explaining gains in technical efficiency (Sividasan 2009; Bollard, Klenow, and Sharma 2013).

Second, the conceptual underpinnings underlying the Hsieh-Klenow interpretation of TFPR dispersion as uniquely capturing distortions have been challenged as unrealistic. It is important to remember that the approach was meant as a proof of concept more than a workhorse diagnostic. However, these challenges do leave policy makers uncertain as to what dispersion really captures and, more fundamentally, what the optimal level of dispersion should be. As shown later in this chapter, dispersion may reflect differences in technology, quality, markups, adjustment costs to capital coupled with volatility in sales, or even different levels of experimentation—and potentially say nothing at all about distortions. Finally, measurement and data cleaning issues have called into question comparative exercises such as those in figure 3.1 or, indeed, the original Hsieh-Klenow findings.

This said, the second half of the chapter contributes to an important emerging literature exploring previously unexamined dynamic effects of distortions through both the innovation and entrepreneurship channels. In the end, while this chapter calls into question the usefulness of popular comparative measures of misallocation in developing and advanced economies in prioritizing policies, the heuristic framework remains a useful arrow in the productivity analytics quiver.

Reconsidering the Hsieh-Klenow Model

A recent body of academic literature has revisited the Hsieh-Klenow approach on four broad fronts: (1) the assumptions embedded in the Hsieh-Klenow framework, (2) possible drivers of dispersion not related to misallocation, (3) the assertion that dispersion of TFPR has a negative effect on aggregate productivity, and (4) how errors in measurement and data processing may undermine the comparisons of relative distortion across countries. While technical, each of these points highlights themes important in devising and implementing policies to address distortions. The discussion that follows explores these issues. Figure 3.2 presents a heuristic that guides the discussion.

How Restrictive Are the Hsieh-Klenow Assumptions? What Are Their Policy Implications?

Dispersion in marginal products of labor and capital can, conceptually, be generated by a variety of differences across firms, including technology, managerial practices,

FIGURE 3.2 What Does Total Factor Productivity Dispersion Really Tell Us?

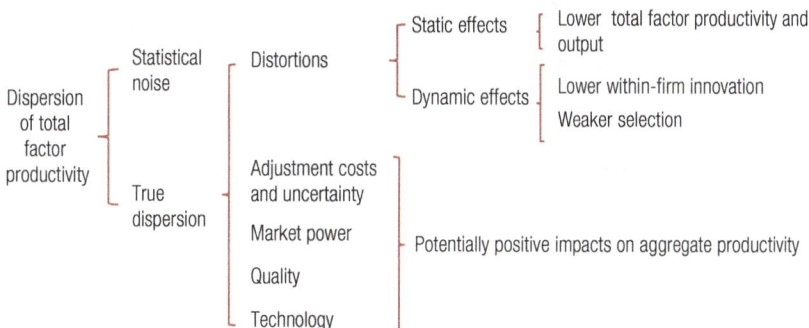

market power, quality, demand, and decision making. To be able to infer distortions in a compact way, the Hsieh-Klenow framework requires imposing theoretical assumptions that recent analysis suggests are not realistic (Haltiwanger, Kulick, and Syverson 2018).

To begin, the methodology interprets any difference across firms in TFPR as reflecting distortions, despite allowing underlying productivities—that is, physical total factor productivity (TFPQ)—to vary. For this to be the case, the methodology needs to assume that any increase in productivity is fully offset by a fall in prices (that is, that the elasticity of prices to technological improvements = −1). Empirical work with census data about U.S. firms suggests that industry-level elasticities are generally substantially less than 1, and overall, closer to 0.5 or 0.6, consistent with the common finding of a positive correlation between TFPQ and TFPR. That is, only about half of a rise in efficiency would be offset by a fall in prices, and that rise would therefore increase measured TFPR (Haltiwanger, Kulick, and Syverson 2018).

Recent empirical work from follower countries is not supportive either. For example, studies for Argentina (Chen and Juvenal 2016), Chile (Cusolito, García Marín, and Maloney 2017), Colombia (Eslava and Haltiwanger 2017), India (De Loecker et al. 2016), and Slovenia (De Loecker and Warzynski 2012) show incomplete pass-through of productivity to prices. Cusolito, García Marín, and Maloney (2017), Cusolito, Iacovone, and Sanchez (2018), and Zaourak (2018b) for this volume find that firms with high TFPQ in Chile, Mexico, and Malaysia charge higher markups. As an example, figure 3.3, for Malaysia, suggests that firms with lower marginal costs, as expected, produce more output, but also have higher markups, suggesting that pass-through is not complete.[2]

This underlying pass-through relationship could break down at two steps. First, any increase in productivity needs to be translated proportionately into a decrease in marginal costs. Second, the decrease in marginal costs needs to be translated proportionately into lower prices. The first condition requires constant-returns-to-scale production technology, which ensures that increases in demand will not change prices or TFPR. This is probably empirically questionable. Haltiwanger, Kulick, and Syverson (2018) find that TFPR is positively correlated with firm-specific demand shocks, consistent with chapter 2.

For the second condition, most common demand functions (such as linear ones) generate less than proportional pass-through of marginal costs into prices. Together, these suggest that rather than TFPR and TFPQ being independent, the two are positively related: dispersion of TFPR can reflect the dispersion of underlying productivity and demand. Also, unlike the Hsieh-Klenow assumptions, it allows markups to differ across firms.

More prosaically, it is not just that different underlying values of the elasticities across countries will make comparisons of Hsieh-Klenow distortion measures

FIGURE 3.3 **Pass-Through Is Imperfect in Malaysia**

a. Markups and marginal costs

b. Marginal costs and quantity

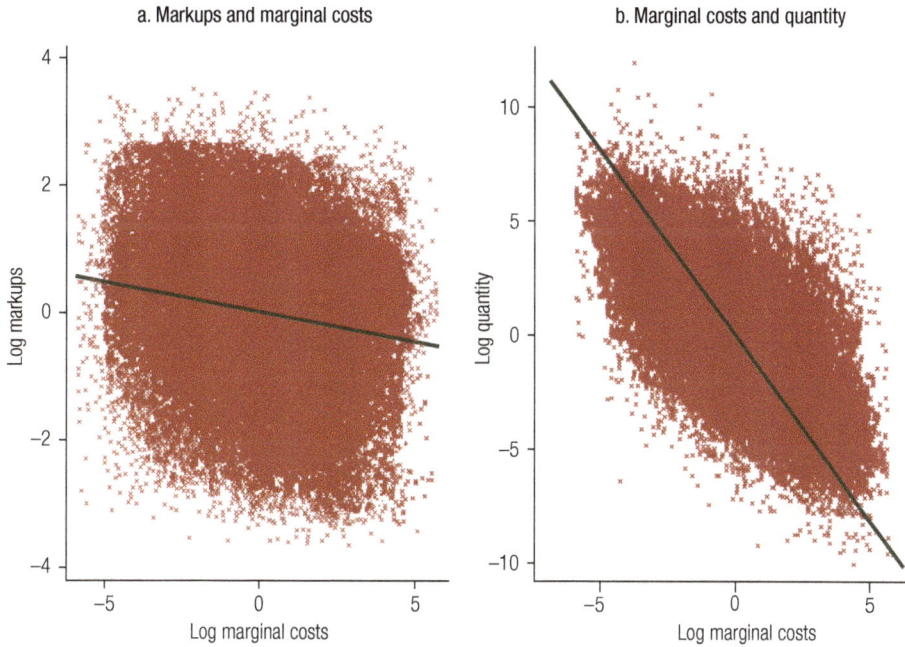

Source: Zaourak 2018b, using the Manufacturing Census from the Department of Statistics, Malaysia.

Note: The panels plot the log of estimated firm markups and quantity against marginal costs. Variables are de-meaned by product-year fixed effects. Markups, costs, and quantity outliers are trimmed below and above the 3rd and 97th percentiles.

difficult, but they will vary within the manufacturing sector, making even within-country diagnostics difficult. In addition, as Kasahara, Nishida, and Suzuki (2017) document, the assumption that all firms have the same underlying production processes (technology) is probably too strong. Looking at the Japanese knitted garment industry, they find that heterogeneity in technology accounted for perhaps 20 percent of measured increases in dispersion in the five years after the bubble burst in Japan.

In work for this volume, David et al. (2018) use Orbis data for a larger number of countries and find that heterogeneity in firm-level technologies potentially explains between one-quarter and one-half of the dispersion in the marginal product of capital (figure 3.4).[3] This is an important result, as it suggests that a nonnegligible portion of observed dispersion may not entail "misallocation" at all, while markup dispersion is generally modest. Taken together, these latter two factors—technology heterogeneity and markups—can explain as much as 50 percent of the observed dispersion.

Ideally, as Haltiwanger, Kulick, and Syverson (2018) suggest, policy makers might rather look for more direct measures of distortions, at least to see if there is any correlation with the measures derived from the Hsieh-Klenow framework. This is taken up in

FIGURE 3.4 **Between One-Quarter and One-Half of the Dispersion in the Average Revenue Product of Capital Can Potentially Be Explained by Heterogeneity in Firm-Level Technologies**

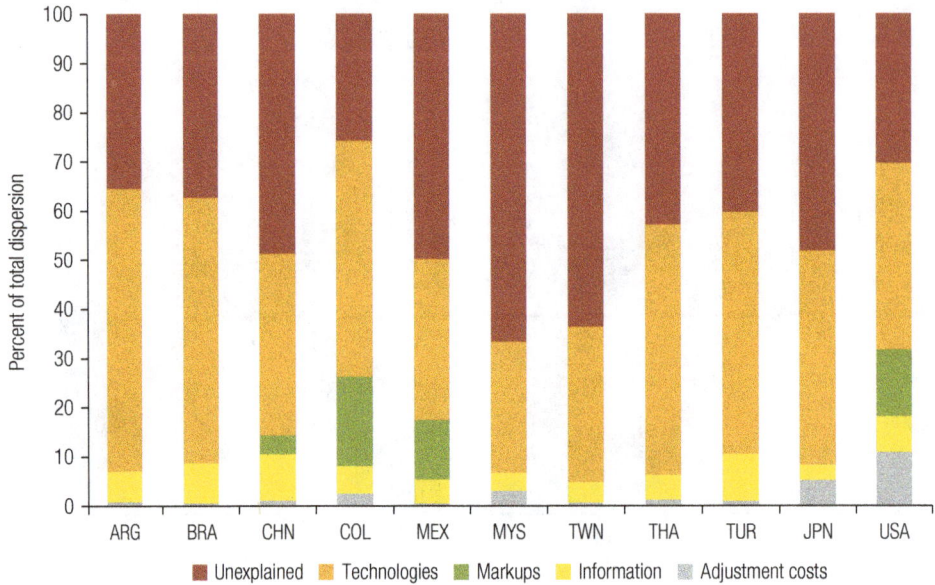

Source: David et al. 2018.

Note: The figure presents a decomposition of the contribution of different determinants of the dispersion of the average revenue product of capital using the methodology of David and Venkateswaran (2017).

the discussion that follows. Fundamentally, however, the central conclusion is that dispersion is likely driven by many factors, including shifts in productivity or demand, and therefore cannot be uncritically taken as a measure of distortion. The next section explores some of these factors.

What Else Could Be Driving Dispersion?

Adjustment Costs

The Hsieh-Klenow framework implicitly also assumes that all firms are in their long-run steady state: they hold the capital and labor that they ideally want, given costs and demand. This assumption simplifies too much. For instance, increased demand for a particular firm's product may increase its price and hence the returns to factors and TFPR, relative to unaffected firms. Eventually, the firm will need to expand its capital or other investments to respond to this demand and returns will fall again to the market level.

However, as Asker, Collard-Wexler, and De Loecker (2014) argue, if there are adjustment costs that prevent this wedge from being quickly arbitraged away, the

FIGURE 3.5 **Sixty Percent to Ninety Percent of Dispersion May Reflect Adjustments to Shocks**

(Variance in the marginal revenue product of capital against volatility of demand shocks)

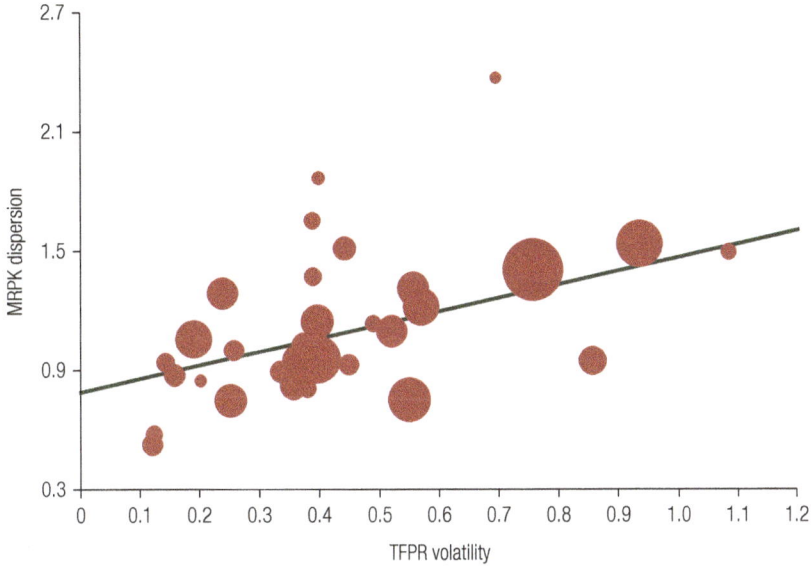

Source: Asker, Collard-Wexler, and De Loecker 2014.

Note: The figure draws on the World Bank Enterprise Survey (WBES) and eight high-quality census panel data sets. For each of the 33 countries in the WBES database, the standard deviation of the marginal revenue production of capital (MRPK) is plotted against the standard deviation in the change in revenue total factor productivity (TFPR).

calculated dispersion in the Hsieh-Klenow framework will rise. That is, dispersion may simply reflect the interaction of sales volatility and adjustment costs rather than distortions. There is abundant evidence for both dynamics, especially in developing countries. Figure 3.5 draws on eight high-quality census panel data sets and the World Bank Enterprise Survey micro data set covering about 33 countries. It shows a strong correlation between demand volatility and the returns to capital that holds across countries, across country-industries, and across industries within a country. Calibrations suggest that 60 percent to 90 percent of dispersion can be accounted for by this effect.

Despite this high potential explanatory power, these findings do not necessarily mean that distortions do not matter. They do suggest that policy makers need to focus more on reducing volatility, however it is driven. Volatility could be a function of pure dynamism of the economy—entrepreneurs placing many bets and winning some and losing some. In this case, more dispersion is better. However, if dispersion is driven by other sources of uncertainty—such as fickle government policy (Bloom et al. 2013)—then clearly the discussion returns to distortions, albeit through a different lens. Furthermore, policy makers may still ask why adjustment is not instantaneous and whether distortions may not explain why adjustments are faster in some countries than others. It could be for reasons of uncertainty, limited access to capital, or barriers to purchasing necessary capital goods.

In addition, David and Venkateswaran (2017) argue that theoretically just looking at dispersion is not enough to separate out all relevant effects and may overstate the possible contribution of adjustment effects to explaining dispersion.[4] They offer an integrated framework that combines ingredients of the two previous approaches, and uses not only dispersion, but several other statistical moments of the data to identify the respective importance of the individual effects.[5] In the case of manufacturing firms in China, they find only a modest role for uncertainty and adjustment costs, and a larger role for other factors. They find the reverse for large U.S. firms, though permanent firm-specific factors remain important. So again, it may be that removing distortions is more important for countries at lower levels of development, while for advanced economies, the more pressing issue is adjustment costs.

Quality

As discussed in chapter 2, better quality is often manifested through higher prices and may lead to markups resulting from product differentiation. Conceptually, additional price variance that is not driven by marginal costs will show up as dispersion. In addition, quality dispersion may increase with the level of quality. Krishna, Levchenko, and Maloney (2018) explore the patterns of quality upgrading in disaggregated bilateral exports to the United States, at the 10-digit (HS-10) level of disaggregation in the Harmonized System (HS) of industrial classification. Export unit values serve as a proxy for product quality. Figure 3.6 shows that as the average standardized quality rises, so does the dispersion and TFP. This may make sense: firms or countries capable of producing higher-quality products may still find it profitable to produce at the lower end for a different market.

Risk

Pulling together the last sections also raises the question of the role of risk and uncertainty in driving dispersion. Economic development is, by nature, a continuous process of placing wagers, making uncertain investments in new products, new firms, new management techniques, new production processes, and the like. The outcome in terms of higher productivity or quality of a firm or sector is uncertain and leads to dispersion in TFPR over the medium term.

As empirical support for this effect, Doraszelski and Jaumandreu (2013) show that engaging in risky innovation, such as research and development (R&D) activities, roughly doubles the degree of uncertainty in the evolution of a producer's productivity level. As it is well documented that investments in R&D as a share of GDP rise with the

FIGURE 3.6 **Higher Country Product Quality Is Associated with Higher Dispersion of Quality**

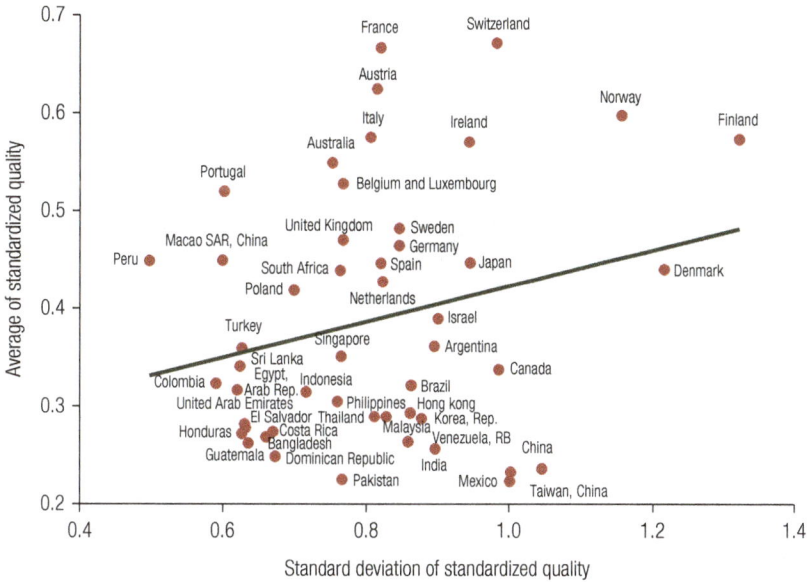

Source: Krishna, Levchenko, and Maloney 2018.

Note: For countries with more than 50 products, the figure plots the country average of standardized export (HS-10) unit values against their variance. HS-10 = 10-digit level of disaggregation in the Harmonized System (HS) of industrial classification.

level of development, greater dispersion should be expected in productivity in more advanced economies. Confirming evidence appears for quality as well. Consistent with their framework of risky quality-upgrading by firms, Krishna, Levchenko and Maloney (2018) show that the mean of the rate of quality growth and the cross-sectional variance of quality growth move together (figure 3.7). That is, as in financial investments, more risk appears associated with higher returns. But this also implies that faster quality growth will be accompanied by more variance and hence greater dispersion. More dispersion may therefore be found in more risk-taking economies and be positively correlated with growth.

To sum up, the assumptions that the Hsieh-Klenow model requires to guarantee that dispersion only captures distortions and hence lower income or growth are probably not reasonable in both the United States and in developing countries. Furthermore, dispersion will reflect firms that are in the process of adjustment, even if in that steady state there might not be any dispersion. Finally, increases in productivity and quality—and the risk surrounding investments in them—will also appear. Hence, again, increased risk, and increased dispersion, would seem to be good for growth in aggregate outcomes, in contrast to what the Hsieh-Klenow framework shows under certain conditions.

FIGURE 3.7   Faster Quality Growth Is Riskier Quality Growth

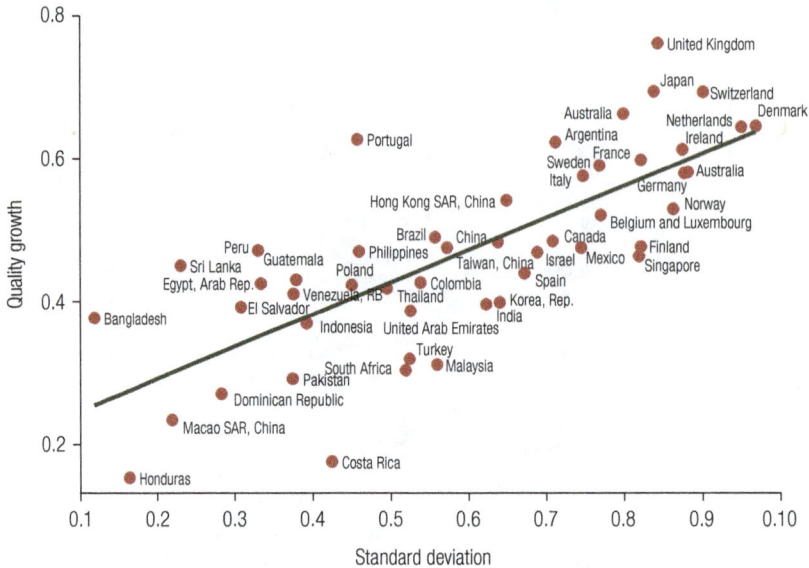

Source: Krishna, Levchenko, and Maloney 2018.

Note: For countries with more than 50 products, the figure plots the country average of standardized export (HS-10) unit values growth rates against the variance of those growth rates. Slope = 0.67 (*t*-statistic = 7.83). HS-10 = 10-digit level of disaggregation in the Harmonized System (HS) of industrial classification.

Product-Related Externalities

As a final note, the allocation of resources across firms and industries will be inefficient if there are positive externalities—benefits to society, such as knowledge spillovers, that are not captured by prices per se—pertaining to a good or sector. The vigorous discussion in the development community around the wisdom of supporting individual sectors presumes this to be the case and the attendant policy recommendation is, by definition, to "distort" the market allocation of resources and, as a by-product, create dispersion. As chapter 5 discusses, the measurement of such externalities is extremely difficult.

Is It All Measurement Noise, Anyway?

All the previous conceptual discussions presume comparability in data collection and processing across the different data sources. Recent findings suggest that is probably not the case.

First, different methodological approaches and variables used can generate radically different results. Nishida et al. (2017) argue that the finding of no impact of reallocation in the Indian example discussed previously is a function of using value added productivity measures instead of revenue-based ones. When they revisit the analysis with revenue-based measures, they find substantially greater impact. This result simply highlights the important role that different variables play in the quantifications generated.

How data are treated across countries also winds up being critical. For starters, authorities often impute missing data to fill gaps in surveys or censuses caused by non-responses. White, Reiter, and Petrin (2018) show that for 2002, imputation rates for the U.S. Census of Manufactures ranged between 20 percent and 40 percent for key production variables, and how this is done affects measured dispersion. Using a methodology different from that used by the U.S. Census Bureau (classification and regression trees),[6] they find in their comparison that in 2007, 51 percent of industries had ratios of TFPR in the top 75 percent to the bottom 25 percent that are at least 10 percentage points higher than in the Census database. This suggests that TFPR dispersion is higher than currently thought. They also find that TFPQ dispersion is 27 percent higher and price dispersion is 58 percent higher.

Eliminating extreme values or outliers also has important effects. For the United States, Rotemberg and White (2017) show that using raw untreated Census data leads to predicted gains from reallocation of an extraordinary 4,293 percent, which falls to 165 percent when fully cleaned Census data are used. If 1 percent of the extreme values are trimmed, which is more or less standard in this literature, gains in the Census-cleaned data fall to 62 percent, or one-third of the untrimmed result. This suggests that country measures of misallocation depend tremendously on the data processing by national authorities. This is vital to knowing what table 3.1 really tells us. With uncleaned data, the United States would have the highest value in figure 3.1 and the original Hsieh-Klenow result would be reversed. Analysts might be attributing the pattern to more aggressive risk-taking by U.S. entrepreneurs rather than to distortions.

In general, this kind of processing of the U.S. data is not possible with many developing country data sets. As an alternative, Rotemberg and White (2017) undertake a careful comparison with Indian data (table 3.2). Overall, they cannot reject the finding that India and the United States have similar levels of dispersion.

TABLE 3.1   How Data Are Cleaned Dramatically Affects the Measure of Misallocation
(Percentage of measured misallocation in the 2007 U.S. Census of Manufactures)

	Trimming		
	0%	**1%**	**2%**
Census-cleaned	165	62	43
Raw	4,293	371	263

Source: Rotemberg and White 2017.

Note: Values in the table follow Hsieh and Klenow 2009. Each cell represents a different starting point: either the Census-cleaned or raw data and trimming the 0, 1, or 2 percent extremes for physical total factor productivity, the capital wedge, and the output wedge.

TABLE 3.2 **India and the United States Have Similar Levels of Dispersion after Data Are Similarly Cleaned**
(Percent)

Country	Raw data trimming			Clean data trimming		
	0%	1%	2%	0%	1%	2%
United States	4,293	371	264	65	48	40
India	147	91	76	63	58	53

Source: Rotemberg and White 2017.

FIGURE 3.8 **Is Dispersion Correlated with Higher GDP? Without Common Data Cleaning Methods, It Is Impossible to Know**

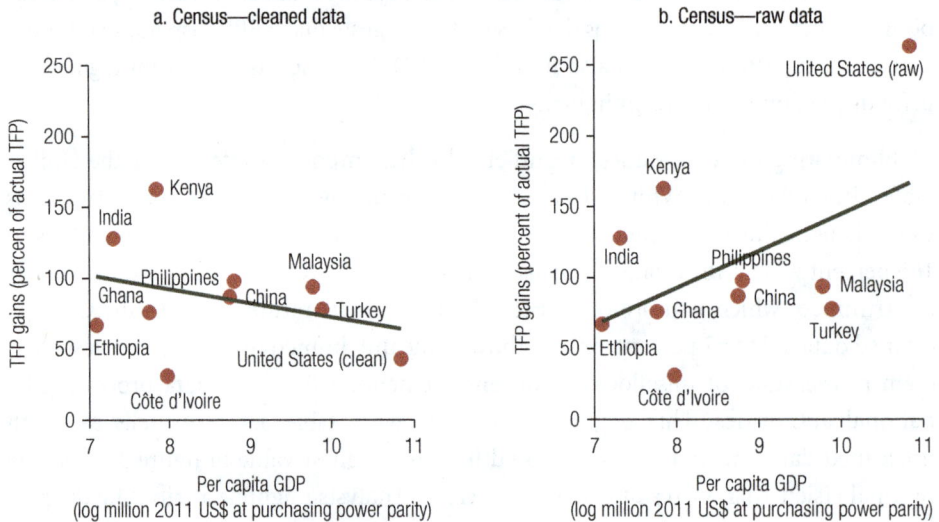

Source: Elaboration based on World Bank studies and Rotemberg and White (2017) results.

Note: The figure plots the relationship between the level of per capita GDP and TFP gains from equalizing TFPR within industries for selected countries. In panel a, the bullet for the United States is based on Census-cleaned data. In panel b, it is based on raw data. TFP = total factor productivity; TFPR = revenue total factor productivity.

Furthermore, just using the raw U.S. data to calculate dispersion instead of the Census-cleaned data reverses the relationship between the calculated "gains from reallocation" and GDP in figure 3.1. Figure 3.8 now shows that the most advanced economies have the most to gain from reallocation. The U.S. value here is likely extreme, but the exercise shows that without confidence that cleaning methods are comparable across countries, it is difficult to infer *any* relationship and reject, for example, a hypothesis that the entrepreneurial dynamism of the United States drives greater dispersion.

In a similar spirit, Bils, Klenow, and Ruane (2017) revise Hsieh and Klenow's (2009) findings when accounting for measurement errors in India and the United States and find that for Indian manufacturing plants from 1985 to 2011, the true marginal products are only half as dispersed as measured average products, and the potential gains from reallocation are reduced by two-fifths.

The bottom line is that it is impossible to draw a straight line between TFPR dispersion and the degree of distortion in the economy. More dispersion may reflect a more dynamic economy in which entrepreneurs are placing more risky bets, both losing but also winning more, and hence growing more. It may therefore be more productive to identify what policies or distortions appear to be influencing dispersion (see Restuccia and Rogerson 2017).

A strand of research tries to do this, exploring the role of adjustment costs in labor and capital (Hopenhayn and Rogerson 1993), taxes (Guner, Ventura, and Xu 2008), informality (Busso, Madrigal, and Pagés 2013); government regulations (Hsieh and Moretti 2015; Fajgelbaum et al. 2015; Brandt, Tombe, and Zhu 2013), property rights (Besley and Ghatak 2010; Banerjee 1999; Deininger and Feder 2001), trade protection (Pavcnik 2002; Trefler 2004), and financial frictions (Buera, Kaboski, and Shin 2015). Ideally, analysis would treat these all simultaneously to better isolate the relative contribution of each driver so as to potentially help order policy priorities. Correa, Cusolito, and Pena (2017) use the World Bank Enterprise Survey database and apply the De Loecker (2013) methodology and explore the contribution of a large set of determinants that includes policy variables related to the business environment.

Figure 3.9 presents the explanatory contribution to TFPR dispersion of four variables of interest for low-income and high-income countries according to the World Bank country classification. In all cases, the direction of the impact is the same at both

FIGURE 3.9 Potential Drivers of TFPR Dispersion

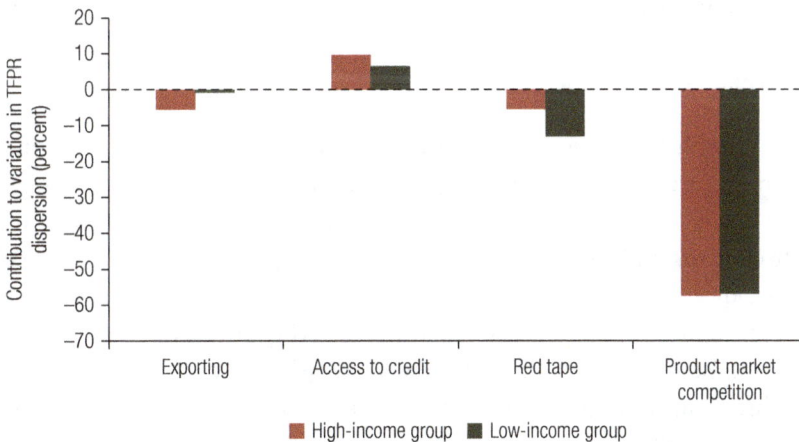

Source: Correa, Cusolito, and Pena 2017, using World Bank Enterprise Survey data.

Note: The figure presents the contribution of the main determinants of the dispersion of estimated revenue total factor productivity (TFPR).

income levels. The number of reported competitor firms and an increase in the number of exporting firms reduce TFPR dispersion. Product market competition has the greatest impact of all variables—arguably because it forces the exit of unproductive firms, thereby trimming the left tail of the TFPR distribution and reducing dispersion. This is in line with the Hsieh-Klenow interpretation of distortions driving dispersion. However, the effect of better access to credit and a decrease in distortionary red tape is to *increase* dispersion, probably because both help finance experimentation.

Though product competition enters with the largest explanatory power (50–60 percent), the combined access to credit and red tape variables account for a non-negligible 15–20 percent. While only a first step toward a more complete mapping of drivers of dispersion, the analysis again highlights the difficulty of inference from dispersion.

Dynamic Effects of Distortions

The previous discussion focuses on methodological and measurement issues that cast doubt on TFPR dispersion as a reliable guide to the likely importance of reallocation to explaining aggregate income differentials. The finding from chapter 1 that most productivity growth has, in fact, been driven by within-firm improvements for a sample of important developing countries would also seem to point to deemphasizing the distortion-reallocation agenda. However, recent research suggests that even if the gains envisaged by Hsieh-Klenow are smaller and certainly less clear, there are other unexplored channels that may magnify the impacts of distortions and barriers to reallocation. In particular, there may be important dynamic effects through the decisions that firms make about investments, firm upgrading, and entry and exit. Hence, while most productivity gains may be through within-firm improvement, these may be importantly affected by the distortions generally associated with the reallocation margin.

Effects through Intermediate Inputs

Distortions may have additional effects working through the interactions among firms and sectors. In particular, in research prepared for this volume, Krishna and Tang (2018) show that efficiency gains from removing distortions may be larger because of additional effects across industries. For example, policy distortions, such as taxes on output and inputs, lower firms' output and raise their prices for upstream firms. This, in turn, will raise the input prices of downstream firms, lowering production below the socially optimal level. Removing such distortions will have efficiency gains that are magnified through this channel. Guided by an extended version of the Hsieh-Klenow framework, Krishna and Tang (2018) find that the average value of the input-output multiplier for China—the size of the magnification of a distortion in inputs—for the manufacturing sector is 3.57, while the multiplier for India is about 2.21. Despite these substantial magnitudes, Krishna and Tang (2018) find that aggregate TFP losses from resource misallocation are similar and sometimes even smaller than those computed using the core Hsieh-Klenow (2009) approach and subsequent studies. The surprising results are due to the fact that the dispersion in the marginal revenue product of materials across firms is substantially smaller than those of labor and capital.

Political Economy Effects

Taxes and financial frictions are frequently cited distortions. In a recent paper, Zaourak (2018a) presents a political economy framework and explores the role of lobbying for capital tax benefits in amplifying the effects of misallocation due to financial frictions. Matching data on lobbying activities in the United States to Compustat firm-level data, Zaourak finds that lobbying for capital tax benefits together with financial frictions increases the dispersion in the marginal product of capital and amplifies the negative effect of the credit shock on output by one-third. The framework is able to explain 80 percent of the decline in output and almost the entire drop in total factor productivity observed for the nonfinancial corporate sector during the financial crisis of 2008–09.

Disproportionate Impact of Distortions on More Productive Firms

In reality, distortions probably penalize the more productive firms more heavily. Thus, the measures available to date probably understate the impact of aggregate measures of distortion (Restuccia and Rogerson 2008; Hsieh and Klenow 2009, 2014). In India, for example, rigid labor laws become binding for firms that have hired 10 workers, thereby making it harder for the more productive (larger) firms to adjust their workforces. In Mexico, the penalties for reducing the workforce to adopt new technologies were higher than for simply downsizing the workforce, penalizing firms that were more open to technological advance (Maloney 2009). To show that these effects may be larger in developing countries, Bloom et al. (2013) and Iacovone, Maloney, and Tsivanidis (2018) argue that weak contracting laws and institutions prohibit firms from hiring skilled managers. Clearly, weak financial intermediation, and thus lack of credit, will penalize firms whose underlying productivity would dictate that they grow to a larger size, or diversify the risk implied in upgrading in productivity or quality. Hence, these *correlated distortions* may have larger impacts than envisaged originally by Hsieh and Klenow.

Arguing that disturbances are more correlated in developing countries, Bento and Restuccia (2017), using the World Bank Enterprise Surveys, estimate the productivity elasticity of distortions: to what extent the Hsieh-Klenow measures of distortion actually lead to declines in measured productivity. Figure 3.10 shows that the elasticities are larger for developing countries.

These differential effects may help explain why countries with similar measured distortion can have such different levels of development.

FIGURE 3.10 Distortions Have Larger Impacts in Developing Countries
(GDP per capita and productivity elasticity of distortions)

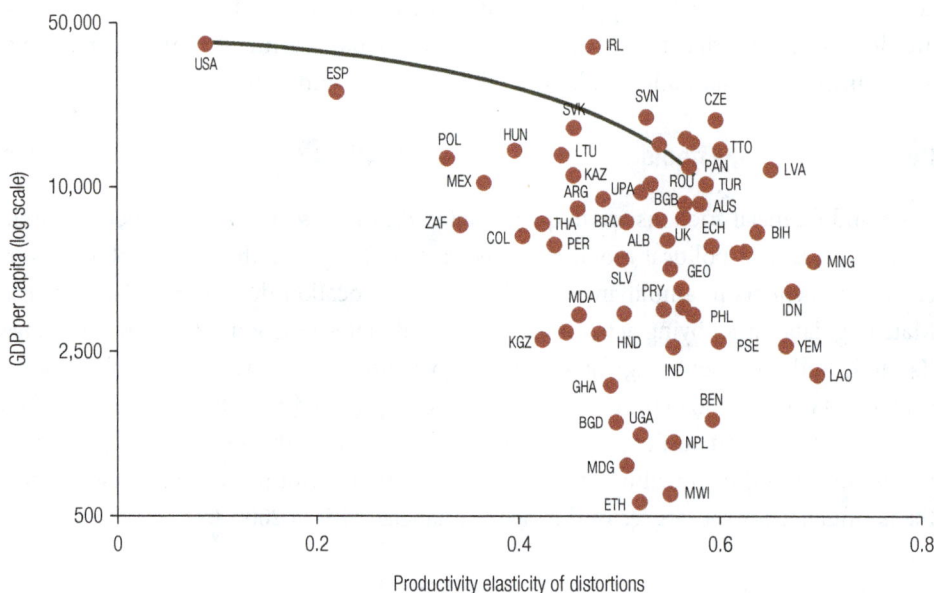

Source: Bento and Restuccia 2017.

Dynamic Effects

Several recent lines of work have focused on how distortions can affect firm dynamics—firms' decisions about investment and entry and exit.

Hsieh and Klenow (2014) acknowledge that the estimates of the impact of misallocation in their 2009 paper, even if taken as correct, could explain only one-third of the gaps in aggregate manufacturing TFP between the United States and China or India. This means that, consistent with the Melitz-Polanec decompositions in the first chapter, most of the productivity gap is due to differences in plant productivity.

The relevant question is why plant productivity is so low in developing countries. Hsieh and Klenow (2014) argue that correlated disturbance disproportionately harms large establishments, inhibiting them from investing in new technologies, developing new markets, or diversifying into more and higher-quality products. These dynamic effects can explain why a 40-year-old U.S. plant is, on average, four times as large as a comparable Mexican plant and six times larger than a comparable Indian plant. These sizes correspond to gaps between high-productivity and low-productivity firms that are five to six times larger than in the United States. To the degree that this is due to a differential impact on large firms of distortions, as opposed to, for instance, management quality, as discussed in chapter 2, this is potentially a potent long-term channel affecting growth.

In particular, Hsieh and Klenow see this channel working first, by retarding investment in intangible capital[7] in existing firms; second, by increasing the entry of firms because of reduced competition by incumbents and thereby lowering average firm size; and third, by increasing the presence of marginal entrants that are less productive than firms that otherwise would have entered. By focusing on these life-cycle effects, their calibrations can account for one-third of the differential between the United States and India, but explain substantially more of the difference between the United States and Mexico.

Incorporating the productivity elasticities of distortions discussed into a model of life-cycle growth yields different but important investment effects. Bento and Restuccia (2017) simulate the impact if the productivity elasticity of distortions increases from 0.09 in the United States to 0.5 in India and find that aggregate output and average establishment size fall by 53 percent and 86 percent, respectively, compared with 37 percent and 0 percent in the standard factor misallocation model. This pattern is presented in figure 3.11. As the productivity elasticity of distortions increases, the return to investing in productivity decreases and existing firms invest less in upgrading. This leaves more room for entrants, but for similar reasons, they also choose a lower level of investment and productivity. The life-cycle investments of firms have little amplifying power because of the offsetting impact of increased entry. Bento and Restuccia's data suggest that, broadly consistent with Hsieh and Klenow, firm size rises with a country's level of development (see figure 3.11, panels e and f). The results suggest that accounting for entry and endogenous productivity roughly doubles the implied impact of correlated distortions, relative to a model with only factor misallocation.

Buera and Fattal Jaef (2018) use those mechanisms to explore the patterns of development dynamics resulting from mitigating distortions. Their emphasis has been on understanding how allocative distortions interact with the incentives of the firms to invest in innovation and other forms of intangible capital in shaping both the magnitude of long-term losses in productivity and the speed of transitional dynamics following reforms aimed at alleviating these distortions.

They consider separately two types of convergence episodes: sustained growth accelerations in the postwar period, and transitions to a more market-oriented economy by two former communist countries (Hungary, Romania) and one current communist country (China). Figure 3.13 shows the average behavior of TFP and investment rates for Hungary, Romania, and China, and four acceleration episodes (Singapore, Japan, Chile, and the Republic of Korea). The former group of countries is plotted in panel a, and the latter group is plotted in panel b. Despite the initial slump in the case of Hungary, Romania, and China, both TFP and the investment rate increase over time. This pattern of behavior has been noted before in the literature as a challenge for the standard neoclassical growth model, the workhorse model for studying transitions, because it suggests that TFP should decrease as the country

FIGURE 3.11 **Higher Productivity Elasticity of Distortions Is Correlated with Lower GDP Per Capita and Smaller Firm Size**

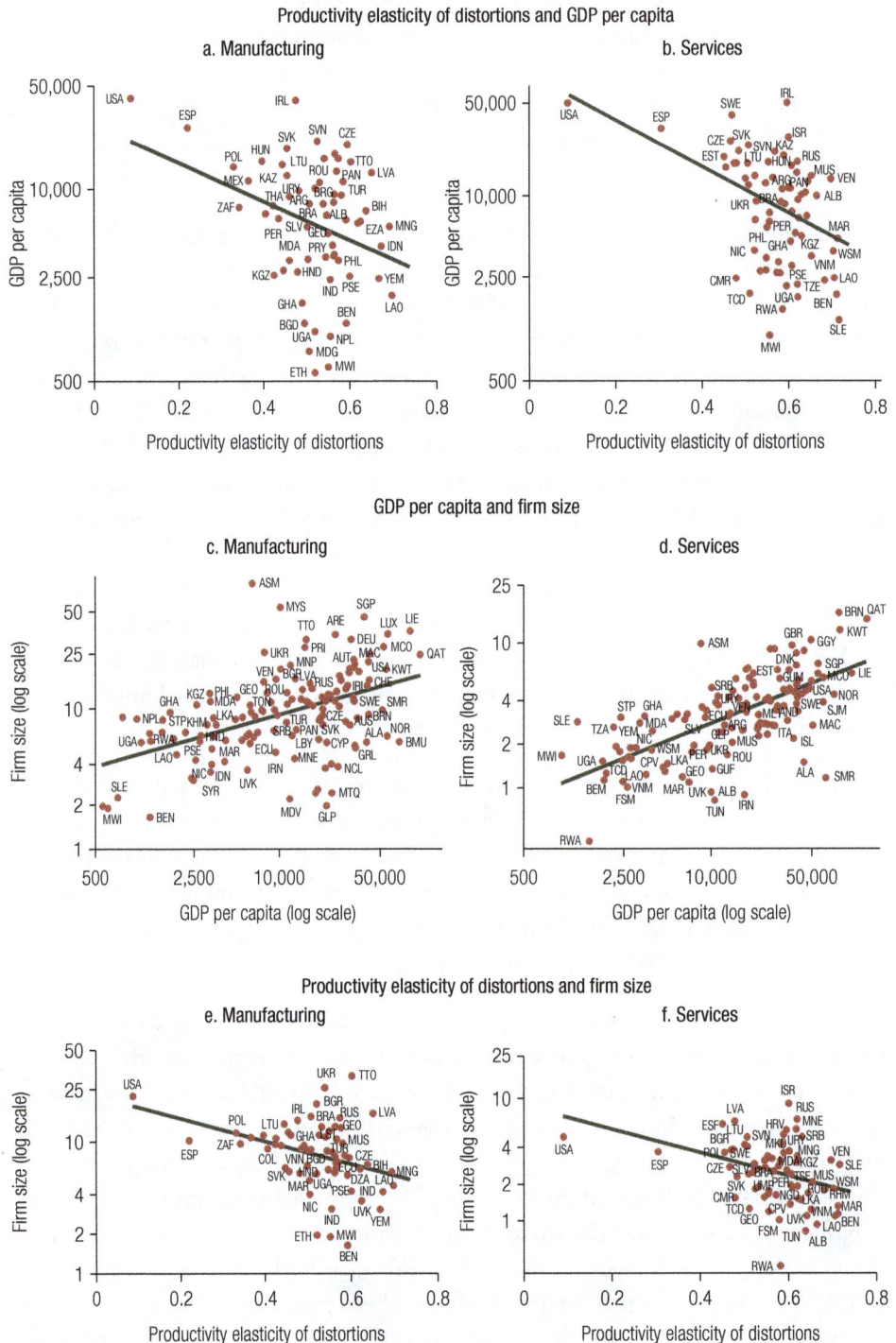

Productivity elasticity of distortions and GDP per capita

a. Manufacturing

b. Services

GDP per capita and firm size

c. Manufacturing

d. Services

Productivity elasticity of distortions and firm size

e. Manufacturing

f. Services

Source: Bento and Restuccia 2016.

FIGURE 3.12   TFP and Investment-Output Ratio during Acceleration Episodes and Postliberalization Transitions

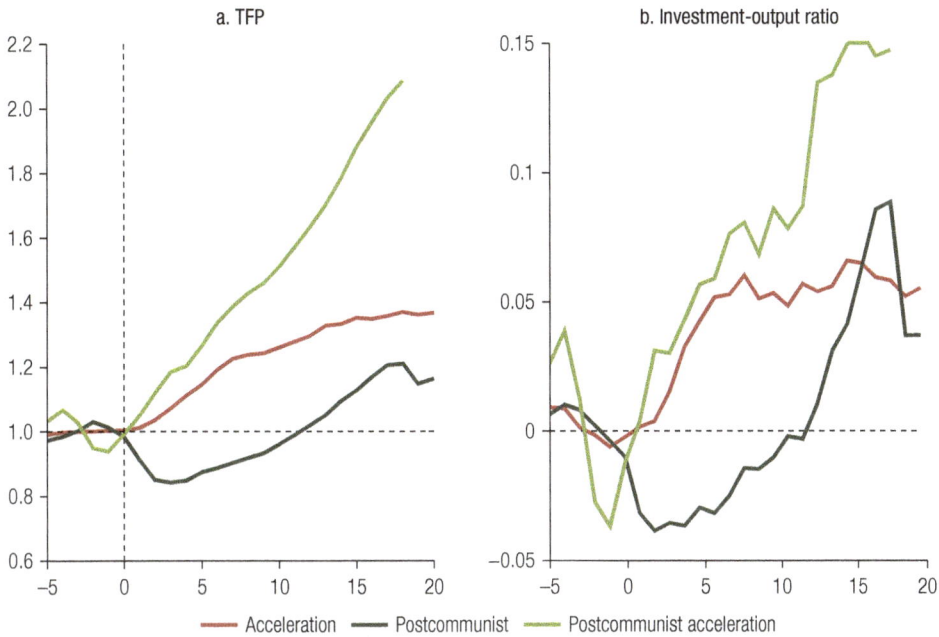

Source: Buera and Fattal Jaef 2018.

Note: The figure uses the "postcommunist" terminology of Buera and Fattal Jaef (2018). Panel a plots total factor productivity (TFP) dynamics for the simple average of postcommunist transitions and acceleration episodes. Panel b illustrates the average of investment rates. The horizontal axis measures years with respect to the beginning of each episode, which is labeled period 0. For postcommunist transitions, period 0 is dated 1990. For growth accelerations, period 0 is the start of the growth take-off. TFP dynamics are measured relative to the TFP level in period 0, while the investment rates are expressed as absolute deviations from the period 0 levels.

approaches its new equilibrium with a higher capital stock. Here, consistent with the two exercises above, releasing distortions increases investment in intangible capital.

Although they exhibit similar characteristics in the aggregate, acceleration episodes and "postcommunist" transitions differ notably in the adjustments taking place at the micro level, particularly regarding the size distribution of firms. To see this, figure 3.13 reproduces the dynamics of the average size of a manufacturing firm in terms of employment. Figure 3.13 shows a divergence in the behavior of average firm size across episodes. While the average size increases by a factor of 2 some 20 years into an acceleration path, the typical firm shrinks by almost 70 percent in the case of Hungary, Romania, and China. Allocative distortions in Chile generate a 19 percent decline in TFP and a 24 percent decline in output relative to the levels in the undistorted stationary equilibrium. The average firm size conditional on 10 or more workers is only 44 percent of the size in the United States. In China, the combination of misallocation and profit taxes drag aggregate productivity down by 50 percent and output by 60 percent. The average size in this case becomes three times as high as in the United States.

FIGURE 3.13 Variations in Size Dynamics during Acceleration Episodes and Postliberalization Transitions

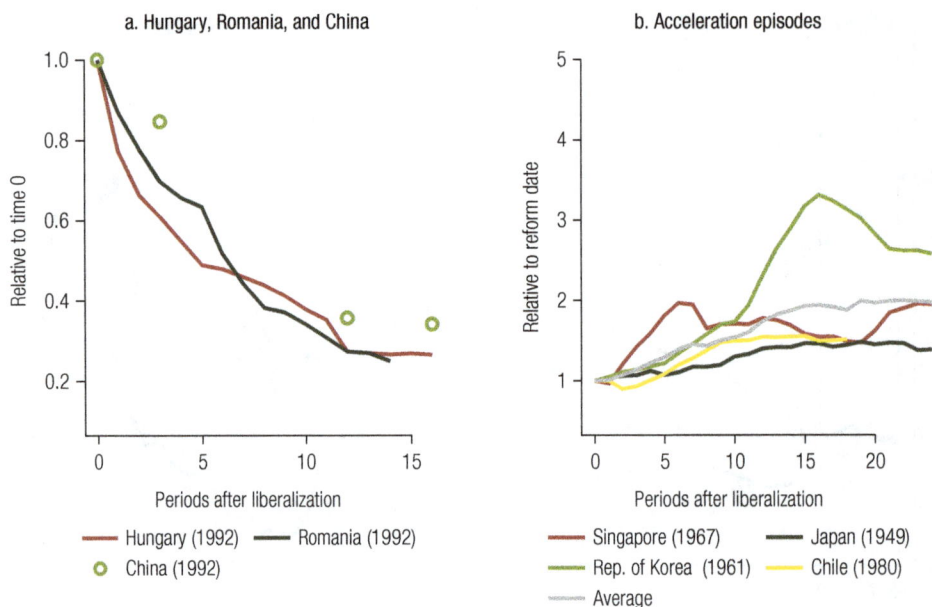

Source: Buera and Fattal Jaef 2018.

Note: The figure uses the "postcommunist" terminology of Buera and Fattal Jaef (2018). Panel a illustrates average size dynamics for "postcommunist" countries. Panel b plots acceleration episodes for comparators. Horizontal axes measure years after period 0, which corresponds to the year of reforms, in the case of accelerations, and the first available year with firm-level data, in the case of "post-communist" transitions. Given the substantial difference in average size dynamics across growth accelerations, the figure also plots the behavior of the simple average of average size dynamics across these episodes. In all cases, the vertical axes measure the average size relative to period 0.

Accounting for the effect of distortions on firms' incentives to innovate and accumulate intangible capital is thus essential for capturing the protractedness that Buera and Fattal Jaef (2018) note in the growth episodes. Otherwise, convergence would have been much faster, with TFP jumping to the new steady-state level upon liberalization as soon as the misallocation had been reversed, and with decreasing dynamics of investment rates, typical of neoclassical growth models and counterfactual with the data.

The results suggest that convergence dynamics will depend importantly on the intensity of the innovation efforts of the firms. The dynamic component of TFP (the innovation decisions) accounts for the bulk of the total gains coming from the removal of distortions, in both Chile's and China's benchmark experiments, with the majority of the productivity increases occurring during the 15–20 years after the reform. In Chile, after resolving misallocation, TFP is still 11 percent below the undistorted value, while in China aggregate productivity is still 50 percent below the efficient level.

Hence, the impact of distortions on firm investment and entry decisions are potentially quite large. Firm productivity issues cannot be separated from distortions.

Concluding Remarks

Allocating factors of production to the most productive firms is a critical function of a well-functioning economy. The growth literature over the last decades has moved barriers to reallocation to center stage as an explanation for cross-country income differences, largely on the basis of vast differences in levels of economic distortions and dispersion of TFPR.

However, the decompositions in chapter 1 suggest that reallocation of factors of production has been an important driver of productivity growth, although not the dominant one, in the past for several developing countries, accounting for perhaps 25 percent of efficiency growth. Furthermore, as this chapter shows, the Hsieh-Klenow framework relies on very strong assumptions that, once rendered more realistic, make it difficult to disentangle distortions, on the one hand, from adjustment lags and risk or differences in technology, quality, markups, or even levels of experimentation on the other. Empirically, conducting comparisons across countries has proved much more perilous than generally assumed; in one exercise, the United States shows more dispersion than most developing countries, and in general, the derived potential impacts from reallocation vary greatly across sets of assumptions.

Conceptually, however, the framework has proven to be an influential starting point for thinking about how distortions affect the economy and remains salient. The work here argues that even if the static "one-off" gains from reallocation are not as great as thought, distortions in the operating environment also have "dynamic" impacts on investments in managerial and technical capabilities, or the R&D required to raise efficiency and product quality. Likewise, they contribute to the decisions of potentially high-productivity firms to enter, and low-productivity firms to exit. This margin and the interactions between human capital factors and operating environment are the subject of the next chapter.

Notes

1. Baily, Hulten, and Campbell (1992) document that about half of overall productivity growth in U.S. manufacturing in the 1980s can be attributed to factor reallocation from low-productivity to high-productivity establishments.

2. Alternatively, it is possible that highly efficient firms may also invest more in quality or product differentiation that generates rents.

3. Orbis is Bureau van Dijk's global database containing production and financial data based on balance sheets of companies across the world.

4. Indeed, the authors show that the use of a single statistical moment like dispersion is not enough to disentangle the importance of a specific factor in explaining (mis)allocation. Their strategy uses readily observable moments in firm-level data, such as capital and revenues, to measure the contributions of technological and informational frictions, as well as a rich class of (potentially distortionary) firm-specific factors.

5. These effects are the variance of investment, the autocorrelation of investment, the correlation of investment with past fundamentals, and the covariance of the marginal (revenue) product of capital with fundamentals.

6. Classification and regression trees are machine-learning methods for imputing data or predicting models. The data space is partitioned recursively and each partition is used to make a prediction (Burgette and Reiter 2010).

7. Intangible assets lack physical substance and include patents, copyrights, franchises, goodwill, trademarks, and trade names, and can, under some definitions include software and other intangible computer-based assets.

References

Asker, J., A. Collard-Wexler, and J. De Loecker. 2014. "Dynamic Inputs and Resource (Mis)Allocation." *Journal of Political Economy* 122 (5): 1013–63.

Baily, M. N., C. Hulten, and D. Campbell. 1992. "The Distribution of Productivity in Manufacturing Plants." *Brookings Papers: Microeconomics 1992*, 187–267.

Banerjee, A. 1999. "Land Reforms: Prospects and Strategies." Conference Paper, Annual World Bank Conference on Development Economics, Washington DC; and MIT Department of Economics Working Paper No. 99-24.

Bento, P., and D. Restuccia. 2016. "Misallocation and Technology: Amplification Effects of Policy Distortions." Background paper for *Productivity Revisited*, World Bank, Washington, DC.

———. 2017. "Misallocation, Establishment Size, and Productivity." *American Economic Journal: Macroeconomics* 9 (3): 267–303.

Besley, T., and M. Ghatak. 2010. "Property Rights and Economic Development." In *Handbook of Development Economics*, edited by D. Rodrik and M. Rosenzwieg, Vol. 5, 4525–95. New York: Elsevier.

Bils, M., P. J. Klenow, and C. Ruane. 2017. "Misallocation or Mismeasurement?" In *2017 Meeting Papers* (No. 715), Society for Economic Dynamics.

Bloom, N., B. Eifert, A. Mahajan, D. McKenzie, and J. Roberts. 2013. "Does Management Matter? Evidence from India." *Quarterly Journal of Economics* 128 (1): 1–51.

Bollard, A., P. J. Klenow, and G. Sharma. 2013. "India's Mysterious Manufacturing Miracle." *Review of Economic Dynamics* 16 (1): 59–85.

Brandt, L., T. Tombe, and X. Zhu. 2013. "Factor Market Distortions across Time, Space and Sectors in China." *Review of Economic Dynamics* 16 (1): 39–58.

Buera, F. J., and R. N. Fattal Jaef. 2018. "The Dynamics of Development: Innovation and Reallocation." Policy Research Working Paper 8585, World Bank, Washington, DC.

Buera, F. J., J. Kaboski, and Y. Shin. 2015. "Entrepreneurship and Financial Frictions: A Macro-development Perspective." *Annual Review of Economics* 7 (August): 409–36.

Burgette, L. F., and J. P. Reiter. 2010. "Multiple Imputation for Missing Data via Sequential Regression Trees." *American Journal of Epidemiology* 172 (9): 1070–76.

Busso, M., L. Madrigal, and C. Pagés. 2013. "Productivity and Resource Misallocation in Latin America." *B. E. Journal of Macroeconomics* 13 (1): 903–32.

Chen, L., and N. Juvenal. 2016. "Quality, Trade, and Exchange Rate Pass-Through." *Journal of International Economics* 100 (May): 61–80.

Correa, P. G., A. P. Cusolito, and J. Pena. 2017. "Identifying and Quantifying the Effects of Private Sector Policies on Productivity Dispersion." Background paper for *Productivity Revisited*, World Bank, Washington, DC.

Cusolito, A. P., A. García Marín, and W. F. Maloney. 2017. "Competition, Innovation and Within-Plant Productivity: Evidence from Chilean Plants." Background paper for *Productivity Revisited*, World Bank, Washington, DC.

Cusolito, A. P., L. Iacovone, and L. Sanchez. 2018. "The Effects of Chinese Competition on All the Margins of Firm Growth." Background paper for *Productivity Revisited*, World Bank, Washington, DC.

David, J., and V. Venkateswaran. 2017. "The Sources of Capital Misallocation." NBER Working Paper 23139, National Bureau of Economic Research, Cambridge, MA.

David, J. M., V. Venkateswaran, A. P. Cusolito, and T. Didier. 2018. "Capital Allocation in Developing Countries." Background paper for *Productivity Revisited*, World Bank, Washington, DC.

Deininger, K., and G. Feder. 2001. "Land Institutions and Land Markets." *Handbook of Agricultural Economics*, edition 1, volume 1A, *Agricultural Production*, edited by B. L. Gardner and G. C. Rausser, chapter 6, 287–331. New York: Elsevier.

De Loecker, J. 2013. "Detecting Learning by Exporting." *American Economic Journal: Microeconomics* 5 (3): 1–21.

De Loecker, J., P. Goldberg, A. Khandelwal, and N. Pavcnik. 2016. "Prices, Markups, and Trade Reform." *Econometrica* 84 (2, March): 445–510.

De Loecker, J., and F. Warzynski. 2012. "Markups and Firm-Level Export Status." *American Economic Review* 102 (6, October): 2437–71.

Doraszelski, U., and J. Jaumandreu. 2013. "R&D and Productivity: Estimating Endogenous Productivity." *Review of Economic Studies* 80 (4): 1338–83.

Eslava, M., and J. Haltiwanger. 2017. "The Drivers of Life-Cycle Business Growth." Background paper for *Productivity Revisited*, World Bank, Washington, DC.

Fajgelbaum, P. D., E. Morales, J. C. S. Serrato, and O. M. Zidar. 2015. "State Taxes and Spatial Misallocation." NBER Working Paper 21760, National Bureau of Economic Research, Cambridge, MA.

Guner, N., G. Ventura, and Y. Xu. 2008. "Macroeconomic Implications of Size-Dependent Policies." *Review of Economic Dynamics* 11 (4): 721–44.

Haltiwanger, J., R. Kulick, and C. Syverson. 2018. "Misallocation Measures: The Distortion That Ate the Residual." NBER Working Paper 24199, National Bureau of Economic Research, Cambridge, MA.

Hopenhayn, H., and R. Rogerson. 1993. "Job Turnover and Policy Evaluation: A General Equilibrium Analysis." *Journal of Political Economy* 101 (5): 915–38.

Hsieh, C. T., and P. J. Klenow. 2009. "Misallocation and Manufacturing TFP in China and India." *Quarterly Journal of Economics* 124 (4): 1403–48.

———. 2014. "The Life Cycle of Plants in India and Mexico." *Quarterly Journal of Economics* 129 (3): 1035–84.

Hsieh, C. T., and E. Moretti. 2015. "Housing Constraints and Spatial Misallocation." NBER Working Paper 21154, National Bureau of Economic Research, Cambridge, MA.

Iacovone, L., W. Maloney, and N. Tsivanidis. 2018. "Family Firms and Contractual Institutions." Unpublished working paper.

Kasahara, H., M. Nishida, and M. Suzuki. 2017. "Decomposition of Aggregate Productivity Growth with Unobserved Heterogeneity." Discussion Paper 17083, Research Institute of Economy, Trade and Industry (RIETI), Tokyo.

Krishna, P., A. Levchenko, and W. Maloney. 2018. "Growth and Risk: The View from International Trade." Background paper for *Productivity Revisited*, World Bank, Washington, DC.

Krishna, P., and H. Tang. 2018. "Production Networks, Trade and Misallocation." Background paper for *Productivity Revisited,* World Bank, Washington, DC.

Maloney, W. F. 2009. "Mexican Labor Markets: Protection, Productivity, and Power." In *No Growth without Equity? Inequality, Interests, and Competition in Mexico,* edited by S. Levy and M. Walton. Washington, DC: World Bank and Palgrave Macmillan.

Nishida, M., A. Petrin, M. Rotemberg, and T. White. 2017. "Are We Undercounting Reallocation's Contribution to Growth?" Center for Economic Studies Paper No. CES-WP-13-55, U.S. Census Bureau, Washington, DC.

Olley, G. S., and A. Pakes. 1996. "The Dynamics of Productivity in the Telecommunications Equipment Industry." *Econometrica* 64: 1263–97.

Pavcnik, N. 2002. "Trade Liberalization, Exit, and Productivity Improvements: Evidence from Chilean Plants." *Review of Economic Studies* 69 (1): 245–76.

Restuccia, D., and R. Rogerson. 2008. "Policy Distortions and Aggregate Productivity with Heterogeneous Establishments." *Review of Economic Dynamics* 11 (4): 707–20.

———. 2017. "The Causes and Costs of Misallocation." *Journal of Economic Perspectives* 31 (3): 151–74.

Rotemberg, M., and T. Kirk White. 2017. "Measuring Cross-Country Differences in Misallocation." Working Paper, New York University and U.S. Census Bureau.

Sivadasan, J. 2009. "Barriers to Competition and Productivity: Evidence from India." *B.E. Journal of Economic Analysis and Policy* 9 (1): 1–66.

Trefler, D. 2004. "The Long and Short of the Canada-US Free Trade Agreement." *American Economic Review* 94 (4): 870–95.

White, T. Kirk, J. P. Reiter, and A. Petrin. 2018. "Imputation in U.S. Manufacturing Data and Its Implications for Productivity Dispersion." *Review of Economics and Statistics* 100 (3): 502–9.

Zaourak, G. 2018a. "Lobbying for Capital Tax Benefits and Misallocation of Resources during a Credit Crunch." Working Paper 8384, World Bank, Washington, DC.

———. 2018b. "Quality-Upgrading over the Life Cycle. Evidence for Malaysia." Background paper for *Productivity Revisited,* World Bank, Washington, DC.

4. Entry and Exit: Creating Experimental Societies

Entry of more productive firms and exit of less productive firms account for roughly one-quarter of productivity growth, as the decompositions in chapter 1 show. However, that contribution varies greatly by country. While plant entry and exit account for 25 percent of U.S. productivity growth, Foster, Haltiwanger, and Krizan (2001) find, it accounts for 72 percent in China, according to Brandt, Van Biesebroeck, and Zhang (2012).[1] In the long run, when static gains from reallocation through the elimination of distortions are exhausted, entry and exit must account for a significantly larger share because technological advance and firm upgrading will be the only drivers of reallocation—and firm entry and exit are a key vector of that advance. Finding ways to promote the entry of productive firms and exit of unproductive ones is central to the productivity reform agenda.

Here, too, there is fresh thinking on the determinants of entrepreneurship. While the traditional concerns of market failures and barriers to entry and exit remain critical, the field over the last decade has seen an expansion of investigation focusing on the following three topics: thinking of entrepreneurship as a process of experimentation, the personal characteristics and human capital necessary to facilitate the process, and long historical processes underlying growth.

Treating entrepreneurship as an experimental process requires a greater focus on how individuals process information and perceive, tolerate, and manage risk, as well as on the framework institutions that support this process. Though these issues have been discussed in the context of scientific discovery (Moscarini and Smith 2001) and venture capital (Kerr, Nanda, and Rhodes-Kropf 2014), their application to productivity growth in developing countries is newer. Often a particular product, process, or technology has never been tried in the local context and the firm contemplating doing so is facing great uncertainty. An entrepreneurial sector as a whole needs to learn how to identify projects, evaluate risk, and judge when to continue and when to exit. Countries go through a process of discovery of what products and industries will work in their context (see Hausmann and Rodrik 2003, for example).

As to the personal characteristics and human capital that drive productivity growth, studies of entrepreneurial personality have enjoyed a resurgence, partly as a result of radical increases in data, and partly due to a twenty-first century fascination with start-up culture, as Kerr, Kerr, and Xu (2017) argue. This resurgence has occurred jointly with the focus on behavioral economics (Astebro et al. 2014), psychology, and advances in the study of management quality (Bloom, Bond, and Van Reenen 2007).

The focus on both experimentation and personality or human capital dovetails with a focus on national learning dominant in Schumpeterian or evolutionary economics approaches to explaining the Asian miracles. As discussions of changing institutions, culture, and personality necessarily involve centuries-long processes, the economics literature has also seen a renewed interest in historical approaches to explaining different growth experiences. This chapter follows this trend, as well.

Paralleling chapter 1, this chapter treats entrepreneurship as a response to technological opportunity. It presents measures of entrepreneurial activity and reveals a puzzle in the low number of capable entrepreneurs in developing countries, given the available technological opportunities. It then offers a simple framework for thinking about why this might be so, comprising both operational environment factors and those relating to the quality of entrepreneurs. In the process, the chapter discusses factors impeding exit, as well.

Drivers of Entry and Exit

Entrepreneurs can be seen as agents who identify and take advantage of the opportunities accompanying the disequilibria brought on by technological advance (see Schultz 1980; Schmitz 1989; and Holmes and Schmitz 1990). On the one hand, the appearance of new technologies offers new possibilities for profit in the advanced economies. On the other, the possibilities of bringing frontier technologies to developing countries offers huge business opportunities. Reframing the two puzzles from chapter 1, why have entrepreneurs in advanced economies become less dynamic, and where are the missing entrepreneurs in developing countries who would propel their countries to the frontier?

The Global Slowdown in Productivity and Its Relationship to Entry

Part of the answer to the first puzzle, as Haltiwanger et al. (2017) and Decker et al. (2018) note, is that the decline in productivity growth in advanced economies is matched by a decline in entry (or exit) and the reallocation it triggers. Although the entry and churning of firms has no social value per se, it potentially plays an important role in boosting productivity and job quality if newcomers are more productive than incumbents and they draw away labor and capital. New small firms are often very good at identifying new market opportunities (Lerner 2000), where new technologies can be applied to meet specific customers' needs. Start-ups are quick to introduce new products that allow them to reap the benefits of unexploited market niches. Small young firms hire more workers via poaching from other firms than they lose to other firms (Haltiwanger et al. 2017); that is, compared with large mature firms, small young firms exhibit positive net flows of jobs through poaching. To the degree that the decline in productivity in the advanced economies represents a cyclical downturn, the entry rate of firms tends to be more cyclical than the exit rate (Lee and Mukoyama 2015).

Figure 4.1 shows that the employment shares for young firms (those less than five years old) across many sectors have declined steadily since the early 1980s and can be shown with some care in sectoral analyses to broadly track the decline in productivity. This suggests either that new firms are not entering or that old firms are not exiting, with the exception of the information sector, which experienced a huge spike in employment in the mid-1990s to early 2000s.

Evidence for developing countries is limited because of constraints to data access for firm-level censuses. However, World Bank analysis for this volume, using data from regionally representative countries, suggests, if anything, a reverse trend (figure 4.2). Other measures for these countries similarly suggest different patterns. With the exception of perhaps Morocco and a very volatile China, entry is broadly stable or increasing, and exit—again with the exception of China—is broadly increasing. Two other barometers of dynamism, the dispersion in growth rate of sales and employment,

FIGURE 4.1   **Employment Shares for Young U.S. Firms Have Declined Steadily since the Early 1980s in Most Sectors**

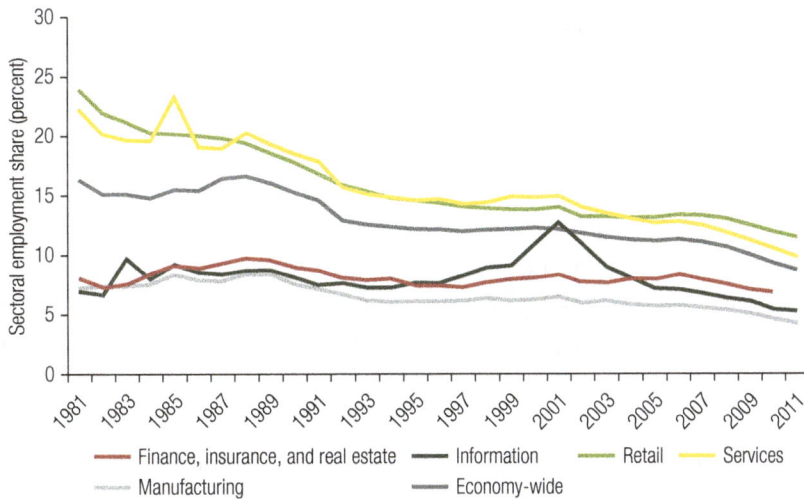

Source: Haltiwanger 2016.

Note: Young firms are defined as those less than five years old. Industries are defined on a consistent North American Industry Classification Scheme (NAICS) basis. Data include all firms (new entrants, exiters, and continuers).

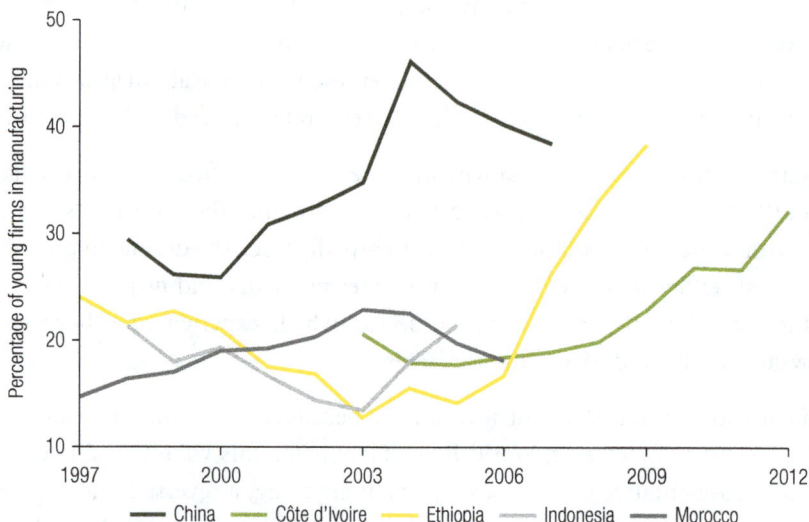

Source: Elaborations using firm-level census data.

Note: This figure plots the aggregate proportion of young firms in the manufacturing sector of selected developing countries. Young firms are defined as those less than five years old.

similarly show no strong pattern across the period—again, perhaps with a decline in China (figure 4.3). In sum, the data are imperfect; coverage varies by country and measures of dynamism are very sensitive to data noise. However, it is hard to tell a story for developing countries of a steady decline in business dynamism over the period such as the one above for the United States.

What Drives Entry and Exit Rates?

The decline in entry, like the slowdown in reallocation discussed in chapter 3, can be broken down into two components.

First, there may be a decline in opportunities for entrepreneurs. A decline in entry could then be driven by a decline in technological advance. Variation in start-up rates may endogenously reflect changes in the pace of innovation in an industry for the reasons hypothesized by Gort and Klepper (1982): a period of rapid innovation leads to a surge in entry, reallocation, and subsequent productivity growth from the innovation. That an important part of reduced entry in the United States might be due to reduced opportunities is suggested precisely by the rise in the share of young firms in the information industry in the late 1990s. Entrepreneurs reacted to the new profit opportunities presented by the arrival of information and communication technologies. The overall decline might be consistent with the

FIGURE 4.3 **Measures of Entrepreneurial Dynamism in Developing Countries Show No Clear Pattern of Reduced Entrepreneurial Dynamism, 1997–2012**

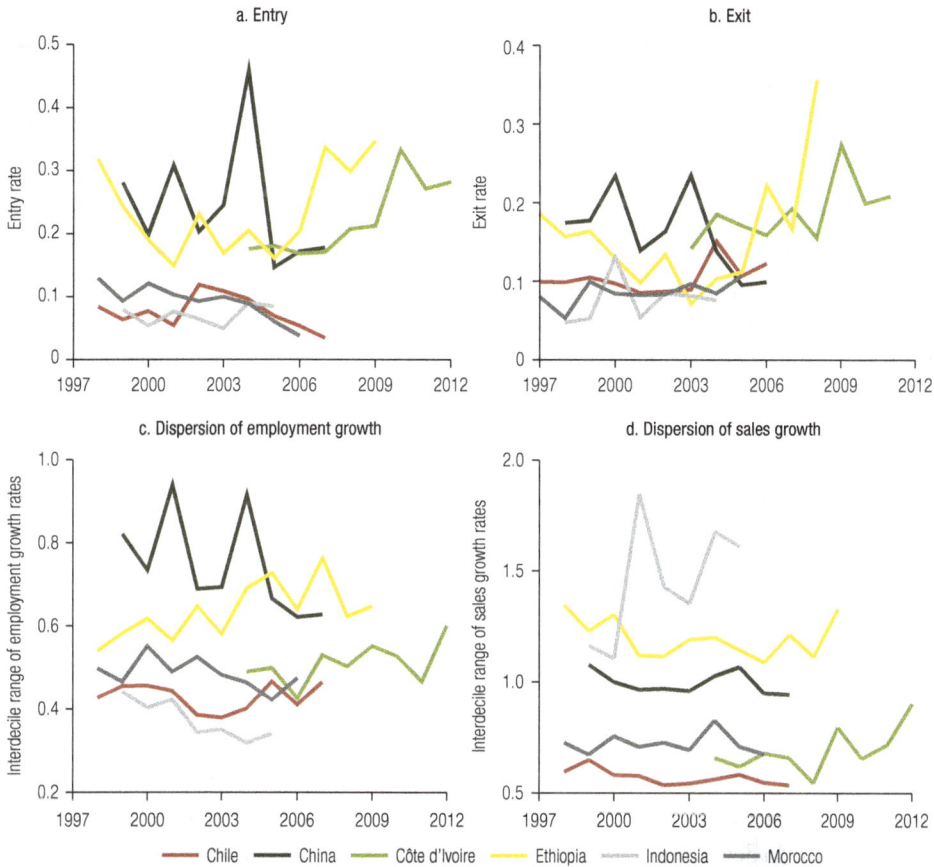

a. Entry

b. Exit

c. Dispersion of employment growth

d. Dispersion of sales growth

Chile ▬▬ China ▬▬ Côte d'Ivoire ▬▬ Ethiopia ▬▬ Indonesia ▬▬ Morocco

Source: Elaborations using firm-level census data.

Note: Panel a (panel b) plots the aggregate rate of entry (exit) in the manufacturing sector of selected developing countries. The rate of entry (exit) is defined as the number of new firms in the market (number of firms leaving the market) divided by the total number of firms. Panel c (panel d) plots the dispersion of firm-level employment (sales) growth in the manufacturing sector of selected developing countries. Dispersion is defined as the interdecile range of the unweighted distribution of employment (sales) growth rates; growth rates are computed such that the denominator is the average employment (sales) level between $t-1$ and t.

technological pessimism discussed in chapter 1, as argued by Gordon (2015), who states that the big technological advances have been reaped in the past, or Bloom et al. (2017), who show that it is taking progressively more and more engineers to produce an additional unit of total factor productivity.

However, turnover might also be due to a decline in the responsiveness to those opportunities. Haltiwanger et al. (2014) and Decker et al. (2018) undertake a decomposition of the two components and argue that the shocks have been more or less constant across time in the United States, but the responsiveness to shocks, particularly on the exit and reallocation side, has weakened. The rise of productivity responsiveness in the high-tech sector before 2000 and the fall after 2000 coincide with the rise and fall of aggregate productivity growth in the United States, which was concentrated in information and communication technology–related industries (Fernald 2014). This fall in responsiveness occurred in all industries and within every age group of firms. Older low-productivity firms were more likely to survive (not exit). Some 18 percent of the decline in the information sector in the period after 2000 was accounted for by activity of new firms, so selection is clearly an important aspect, if not the whole story.

As mentioned in chapter 1, the factors undermining the responsiveness to opportunities could be increased uncertainty, increased frictions (barriers to entry and exit), or a reduction in population (reducing the pool of entrepreneurs) (Pugsley and Sahin 2015). World Bank work for this volume by García (2018) undertakes the same decompositions for Chile and documents similar findings across Chile's period of stagnating productivity growth: shocks to the economy have been more or less constant, but the responsiveness has fallen. In the case of Chile, an increase in policy uncertainty, a tightening of labor regulations, or a reduction of financing across the financial crisis could all be relevant. An increase in the average age of firms is clear, as well.

Weak Technological Convergence by Developing Countries

The importance of technological opportunity just discussed has its cross-country analog in the gaps in the technological level between the advanced economies and follower countries and the opportunities those gaps offer for rapid catch-up. By the same logic that a shift in the technological frontier should induce entrepreneurs to exploit new opportunities—as appears to be the case in the high-tech sectors—we should expect a tremendous number of entrepreneurs in developing countries to exploit the possibilities of catch-up, given the huge expected returns documented in chapter 2. In fact, as Comin shows in various papers (Comin and Mestieri 2018; Comin and Hobijn 2010, 2011) the average rate of technological adoption grows more *slowly* with distance from the frontier. More specifically, it is more the intensity of adoption that slows. The question is then, Where are the entrepreneurs who should be taking advantage of the vast potential technological arbitrage?

Panel a of figure 4.4 shows the share of the workforces around the world that are self-employed. At first glance, the pattern would suggest that, in fact, as predicted, the share of self-employed or employers increases with distance from the technological frontier. However, panel b reveals the reverse pattern, focusing only on those firms that have at least one employee (call them entrepreneurs), as a measure of the firm having some minimal dynamism or potential to grow into a sophisticated firm. It is the member countries of the Organisation for Economic Co-operation and Development (OECD) that have the highest rate of dynamic entrepreneurship.

Panel c further shows that the labor market share of self-employment by individuals who are likely to be able to recognize serious technological opportunities and act upon

FIGURE 4.4 **Despite Higher Opportunities from Technological Adoption, Productive Entrepreneurship Is Not Higher in Developing Countries**

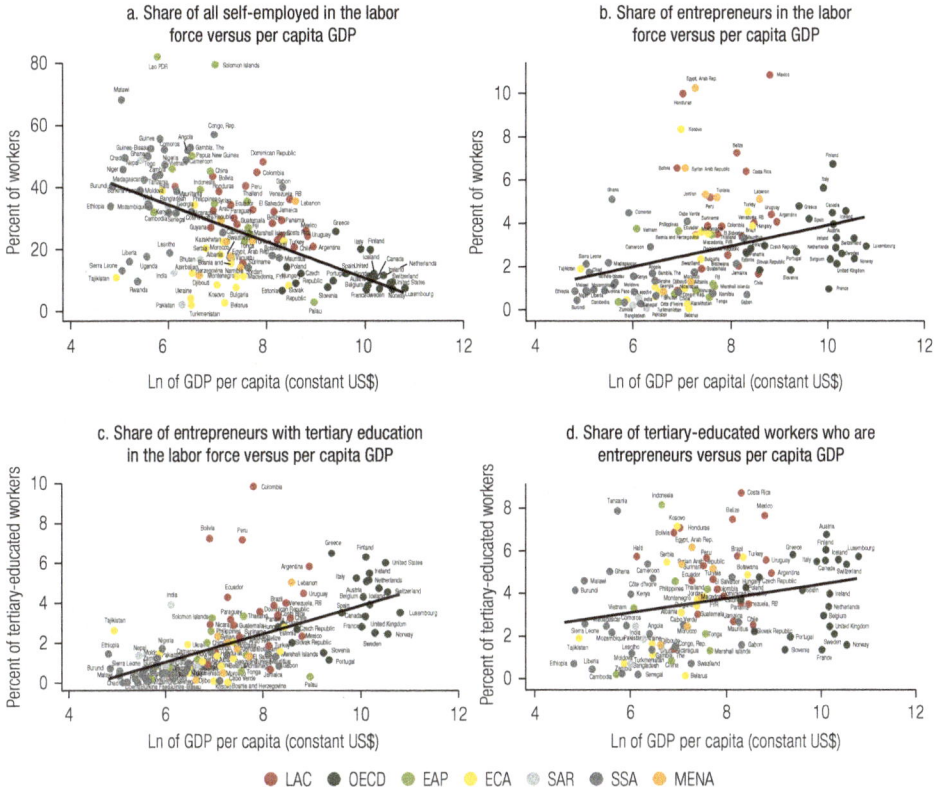

a. Share of all self-employed in the labor force versus per capita GDP

b. Share of entrepreneurs in the labor force versus per capita GDP

c. Share of entrepreneurs with tertiary education in the labor force versus per capita GDP

d. Share of tertiary-educated workers who are entrepreneurs versus per capita GDP

● LAC ● OECD ● EAP ● ECA ● SAR ● SSA ● MENA

Sources: Elaborations using the latest available year of the World Bank's International Income Distribution Data Set (I2D2) and Maloney and Rubio 2018 (all panels); Organisation for Economic Co-operation and Development data (panel d).

Note: EAP = East Asia and Pacific; ECA = Eastern Europe and Central Asia; LAC = Latin America and the Caribbean; MENA = Middle East and North Africa; OECD = Organisation for Economic Co-operation and Development; SAR = South Asia; SSA = Sub-Saharan Africa.

them—those with some tertiary education—also increases with development. This partly reflects lower levels of tertiary education, which, in itself, reduces the pool of possible dynamic entrepreneurs, but also suggests that the very high levels of total self-employment are a function of low levels of education.

However, panel d shows that even among individuals with tertiary education, dynamic entrepreneurship increases with development, arguably reflecting the lack of incentives in the system, or the dearth of more specialized human capital in developing countries, despite the very high expected returns. This suggests that even this more educated pool is not seizing technological arbitrage opportunities as would be expected. In sum, the share of capable entrepreneurs reflects exactly the opposite of what techno-logical gaps would predict, and the great mass of observed self-employment in devel-oping countries is likely to represent "unproductive" churning.

What Explains the Paradox: Operating Environment or Human Capital? Or Both?

Two broad classes of explanations may explain this paradox of scarcity of entrepreneurial energy amidst abundant opportunities. The first is that the economy is characterized by such extreme distortions that even those who could seize arbitrage opportunities do not find it profitable or even possible. The second is that there is a shortage of entrepreneurs with the capabilities to actually start a sophisticated business.

Evidence for the first argument is ever present in, for instance, the Doing Business indicators and myriad interviews with entrepreneurs. The first volume in this series, *The Innovation Paradox* (Cirera and Maloney 2017), precisely argued that distortions and missing markets dramatically reduce the returns to technological adoption, for instance. However, there is also substantial evidence of heterogeneity of entrepreneurial success within the same environment by individuals with distinct human capital. The seemingly disproportionate success of immigrants in the U.S. high tech sector is representative of a large literature (for a recent review, see Kerr 2013).

This is also the case historically, and dramatically so, Maloney and Zambrano (2016) show. Table 4.1 presents the relative contribution to industrialization of locals compared with immigrants in the period of accelerated industrialization during the second Industrial Revolution at the turn of the century. The third column shows that industrialization in

TABLE 4.1 **Immigrants Dominated Industrialization during the Second Industrial Revolution in Latin America**

Country	Year(s)	Percentage of immigrants among business owners	Percentage of immigrants in the population	Overrepresentation of immigrants as business owners
Argentina	1900	80.0	30.00	1.3
Brazil (São Paulo)	1920–50	50.0	16.50	1.5
Brazil (Minas Gerais)	1870–1900	3.6	1.50	1.2
Chile	1880	70.0	2.90	12.1
Colombia (Antioquia)	1900	5.0	4.70	0.5
Colombia (Barranquilla)	1888	60.0	9.50	3.2
Colombia (Santander)	1880	50.0	3.00	8.3
Mexico	1935	50.0	0.97	25.8
United States (5 percent Census sample)	1900	31.0	13.60	1.1
United States (Fortune 500 firms)	Various	18.0	10.50	0.7

Source: Maloney and Zambrano 2016.

Note: The final column shows the percentage of immigrants among business owners divided by the percentage of immigrants in the male population. The local male population is used because women were largely precluded from productive entrepreneurship during the study period.

Latin America, unlike in the United States, was overwhelmingly driven by immigrants and far out of proportion to their share of the population—and, more relevantly, to the male population, given that few entrepreneurs were women in the period.

Whereas in the United States, the influence of immigrants was more or less proportional to locals in the Census sample (1.1) or slightly lower than predicted based on the creation of Fortune 500 companies (0.7) (see also Fairlee 2008; Kerr and Kerr 2011), this is not the case in Latin America, where (with the exception of Antioquia, Colombia, and Minas Gerais, Brazil), the contribution of immigrant entrepreneurs was far out of proportion to their presence in the economy, ranging from 1.5 times in São Paulo, Brazil; to 3.2 times in Barranquilla, Colombia; to 8.3 times in Santander, Colombia; to 12 times in Chile; all the way up to nearly 26 times in Mexico.[2] It is hard to tell a story in which these immigrants were somehow more connected to elites, more fluent in the language, and more familiar with the local geographic and economic terrain. Perhaps they were hungrier than the local elites, but there were plenty of hungry non-elites present as well, and the elites would develop an appetite in the 1950s as they began to dominate the new sectors. Rather, a better story seems to be one of differential human capital of various kinds.

Similarly, in Japan, Odagiri and Goto (1996) document that despite constituting only 5 percent of the population, from 1868 to 1912, former samurai, or *Shizoku*, started 50 percent of new businesses. This makes sense in light of the fact that they were the most traveled and educated individuals of the time and had done much more accounting for the local lords than fighting during the 200 years of the Tokugawa shogunate ending in 1881.[3] Indeed, members of this group who had studied in the United Kingdom were critical private sector and institutional "entrepreneurs" during the formative period of the Meiji restoration that followed (see box 4.1). In any case, the experience serves as a good comparator because it occurred in a context common with other local groups that did not engage as vigorously in the industrialization process.

BOX 4.1

Successful Industrializers "Got Out" Early and Often

In each of the cases that follow, knowledge of frontier industries and supporting institutions was critical to opening new businesses and creating a business culture.

Japan. Under the Tokugawa Shogunate, foreign travel was prohibited until 1866 under penalty of death. Yet some regions understood the dangers of technological inferiority. Five students from Chōshū (1863) and 19 students from Satsuma (1863–65) were smuggled out to study abroad in various universities in the United Kingdom. Upon their return, many would play key roles in the modernization project undertaken by the subsequent Meiji Restoration: head of what would become Tokyo University, Minister of Education, the first Prime Minister, Minister of Foreign Affairs, Minister of Industry, the first Director of Railways, and the head of the stock exchange, what would become the

(Box continues on the following page.)

Successful Industrializers "Got Out" Early and Often *(continued)*

Sapporo breweries, and the Japanese textile industry. In particular, one of the Satsuma students, Godai Tomoatsu, become Japan's leading entrepreneur of the early Meiji period, establishing a textile mill reputed to be Japan's first modern factory. He also negotiated the establishment of a French-Satsuma trading company that attracted French investment into the Satsuma domain to establish a steamship shipyard and textile spinning factories, and to send promising students from Satsuma overseas. Among those from Chōshū was Yozo Yamao, who took classes and worked as an apprentice in shipbuilding in Scotland. On his return to Japan, he helped establish the Imperial College of Engineering (the Faculty of Engineering at the University of Tokyo). Another of the Chōshū Five, Itō Hirobumi, established the cabinet system of government and later became the first Prime Minister of Japan. He recruited the Scotsman Henry Dyer to be the first Principal and Professor of Engineering at the Imperial College of Engineering. Dyer was considered pivotal to the generation of engineering talent and facilitating study abroad.

The United States versus Latin America. The United States was deeply steeped in the industrial project radiating from England. Travel and interchange were frequent, as was industrial espionage. The opposite was true in Latin America. Aspiring Creole merchants were severely constrained by the legal requirement to trade primarily with Spain, a country that came exceptionally late to the Industrial Revolution. Even this trade was prohibited except through peninsular intermediaries. Hence, local entrepreneurs, in contrast to their counterparts in the American colonies, had only distant knowledge of the goings on in foreign business and trade centers like Manchester or of advancing business practices. The demand for greater contact among the incipient entrepreneurial class was keen, however. In the 1720s and 1730s, the merchant classes of Peru and Mexico City, among the most developed in the region, sought direct trade with Spain, but were rebuked. Until the end of the eighteenth century, even the establishment of industries was prohibited by the Portuguese colonial government. However, entrepreneurs appeared, both in a vigorous contraband trade as well as in the emergence of truly protean entrepreneurs. One example was the exiled Colombian Pedro Nel Ospina, who attended the mining school at the new University of California, Berkeley. Upon his return, he established the Antioquia School of Mines, was an entrepreneur in agriculture, and was instrumental in establishing the dominant Antioquian textile industry. As president of the Republic (1922–26), he organized the Departments of Education and Health and the Treasury, secured the creation of the central bank (Banco de la Republica), and greatly advanced critical public works. In 1928, he created the Bogotá stock exchange.

India. Jamsetji Tata, founder of the Tata dynasty and considered one of the fathers of industrialization in India, made frequent trips to England in the mid-1800s in his pursuit of establishing a modern textile plant in India. His interest in iron and steel began when he attended a lecture by Thomas Carlyle in Manchester, where he went to check out new machinery for his textile mill. His interest would take him to the United States (the state of Alabama and the city of Cleveland) and elsewhere to gain expertise. His son Dorabji Tata would complete the project, guiding Tata on its path to becoming one of India's largest conglomerates. He entered Cambridge University in 1877 and also made frequent trips abroad.

In each successful case, being abroad awakened these entrepreneurs to possible industries, ways of operating, and even mindsets that only spending time in the frontier countries can do.

Moving from Opportunity to Entrepreneurship

To explain this paradox of low entrepreneurship amid great opportunity, figure 4.5 presents a simple framework for the entrepreneurial decision and implicitly the elements of the "entrepreneurial ecosystem" needed to redress them. The rest of this chapter discusses the elements of this figure.

Like any investor, an entrepreneur is fundamentally placing a bet, comparing an entrepreneurial project with an expected range of returns and risks against other alternatives, such as "safe" salaried work, which is the opportunity cost of entrepreneurship. As Kerr, Nanda, and Rhodes-Kropf (2014), among others, argue, entrepreneurship is a form of experimentation in which entrepreneurs learn about the viability of a product or process in the local context. This implies both a process of managing risk and a process of learning—about the investment, about running a firm, and about evaluating and managing risk.

Two sets of factors impede this experimentation: operating environment factors (shown in the middle section of figure 4.5), and factors pertaining to entrepreneurs per se—that is, human capital, very broadly construed (shown in the right-hand section of figure 4.5). Without an enabling environment, capable entrepreneurs will not enter the market or thrive if they do (as discussed in chapter 2). Conversely, a pristine experimental environment without capable entrepreneurs will also show limited dynamism.

Operating Environment

Translating Technological Opportunities to Business Opportunities

The ability of an entrepreneur to generate returns from the entrepreneurial "bet" depends, in part, on how supportive the enabling operating environment is and on the costs of experimentation. These factors are explored next and depicted in the top middle section of figure 4.5.

Enabling Operating Environment and Complementary Factors and Markets
The translation of a technological opportunity into a business opportunity that can be exploited by the most able entrepreneur depends substantially on the overall business environment. Clearly, any of the classic frictions in terms of trade distortions, corruption, excessive taxes, and the like will reduce the expected return of a project. However, as *The Innovation Paradox* stresses (Cirera and Maloney 2017), the extremely high returns presumed to characterize Schumpeterian catch-up will not appear if complementary markets are not well developed. If human capital is not available to staff an innovation or necessary machinery cannot be imported, then the actual

FIGURE 4.5 Determinants of Entrepreneurial Experimentation and Productive Entrepreneurial Activity

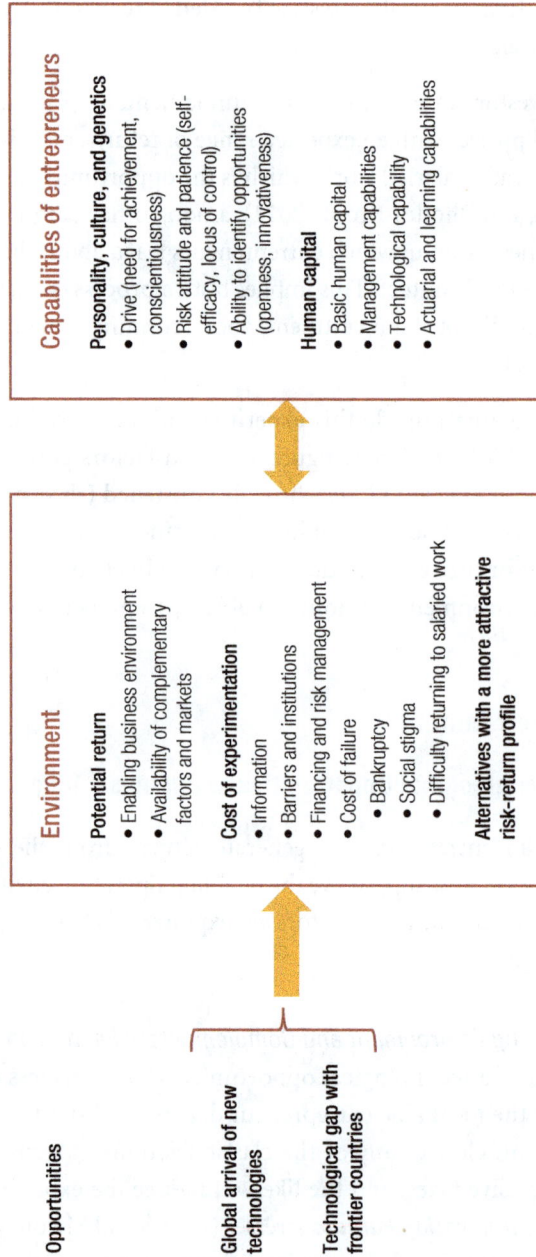

Opportunities

Global arrival of new technologies

Technological gap with frontier countries

Environment

Potential return
- Enabling business environment
- Availability of complementary factors and markets

Cost of experimentation
- Information
- Barriers and institutions
- Financing and risk management
- Cost of failure
  - Bankruptcy
  - Social stigma
  - Difficulty returning to salaried work

Alternatives with a more attractive risk-return profile

Capabilities of entrepreneurs

Personality, culture, and genetics
- Drive (need for achievement, conscientiousness)
- Risk attitude and patience (self-efficacy, locus of control)
- Ability to identify opportunities (openness, innovativeness)

Human capital
- Basic human capital
- Management capabilities
- Technological capability
- Actuarial and learning capabilities

expected return will not materialize. Hence, the traditional concerns with both distortions and market failures remain central.

Costs of Experimentation

Moving down the center section of figure 4.5, the next set of points stresses factors that affect the cost of experimentation to find out whether a project is viable: information, institutions, markets for financing and diversifying risk, and the cost of failure.

Information

The availability and quality of information plays a central role for understanding the likely risk-return profile of a project, or even conceiving of it. As box 4.1 shows, having knowledge about which technologies exist is the clear necessary first step to catching up with the frontier. It is a step that historically the United States achieved by close contact with the mother country and Japan addressed by sending students abroad and then establishing a local engineering university run by a Scottish expert.

More recently, the high-tech clusters in Ireland, India, and Taiwan, China, were all started by bringing home the diaspora from places like Silicon Valley. The impact of immigrants on industrialization shown in table 4.1 also suggest the importance of gathering and processing information—including about the possibility of implementing new technologies in the local context. Figure 4.6 presents an imperfect, although more contemporary, measure of the density of potential entrepreneurs such as the Satsuma and Chōshū students described in box 4.1, who are embedded in global networks and who

FIGURE 4.6   **How Well Plugged In to the Knowledge Frontier Are Developing-Country Students?**
(Number of Foreign Students Studying in the United States as a Percentage of the Overall Home Country Population)

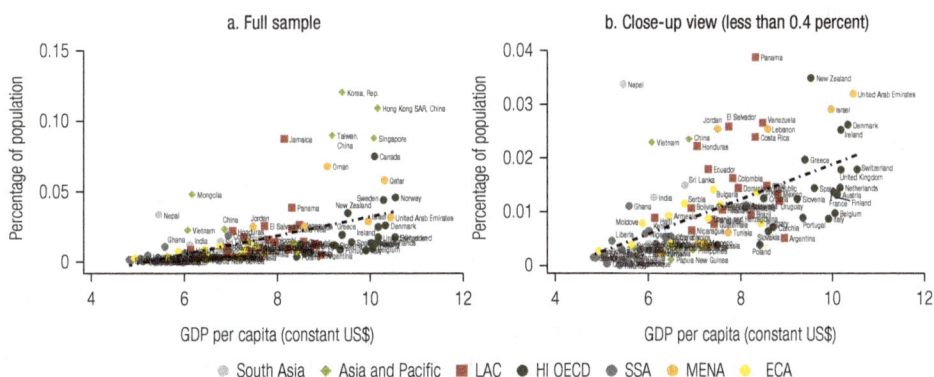

Source: Elaborations based on Open Doors and World Development Indicators.

Note: Data are as of 2015. The close-up view in panel b truncates the *y*-axis scale at 0.4 percent of students studying in the United States. HI OECD = High-income members of the Organisation for Economic Co-operation and Development; LAC = Latin America and the Caribbean; MENA = Middle East and North Africa; SSA = Sub-Saharan Africa.

know from personal experience where the technological frontier is and therefore what opportunities could be cultivated in their home countries. The figure presents the ratio of foreign students studying in the United States, as one possible pole of frontier technology for which data are readily available, to the overall home country population.

There is clearly a positive relationship with GDP, possibly reflecting that advanced economies can afford to send more students. The fact that most of Europe is below trend reflects the presence of excellent universities there. But what is immediately striking is that despite physical and cultural distance, the four Asian miracles are extraordinarily well represented and that even up-and-comers like China, India, Malaysia, and Vietnam are substantially above trend. By contrast, the major Latin American countries historically have been isolated and continue to be below trend and would be even more so if physical and cultural distance were taken into account. Africa, with some exceptions, reflects it lower income levels, but nonetheless its connectivity suffers as a result. In developing countries, to know where the frontier is and what opportunities are available, potential entrepreneurs need to "get out more."

Barriers to Entry and Institutions

Conceptually, lower cost of experimentation raises the value of the project and should stimulate entry (Kerr, Nanda, and Rhodes-Kropf 2014). However, myriad barriers, institutions, and norms can make entry difficult. Dreher and Gassebner (2013), using data for 43 advanced economies and developing countries in the Global Economic Monitor over the period 2003–05, find that more numerous and more onerous procedures required to start a business and larger minimum capital requirements are detrimental to entrepreneurship (see also Djankov 2009). On the legal side, Djankov et al. (2002) offer data for 85 advanced economies and developing countries on the number of procedures, time, and official costs that a startup must bear before it can operate legally. Klapper, Laeven, and Rajan (2006) find that in Europe, costly regulations hamper the creation of new firms, force new entrants to be larger, and cause incumbent firms to grow more slowly. The official costs of entry are extremely high in developing countries (see figure 4.7).

A large literature sees weak institutions working against business dynamism through numerous channels (see, for example, North 1991; Acemoglu, Johnson, and Robinson 2005). For instance, insecure property rights have long been identified as a barrier to commerce and dynamism. The medieval Arab social theorist Ibn Khaldun (1377) noted, "Attacks on people's property remove the incentive to acquire and gain property. People, then, become of the opinion that the purpose and ultimate destiny of (acquiring property) is to have it taken away from them. The extent and degree to which property rights are infringed upon determines the extent and degree to which the efforts of the subjects to acquire property slacken." Johnson, McMillan, and Woodruff (1999) find for five transition economies in Eastern Europe and the former Soviet Union that weak property rights limit the reinvestment of profits in start-up manufacturing firms,

FIGURE 4.7 **Entry and Exit Costs Are Higher in Follower Countries than in Frontier Countries**

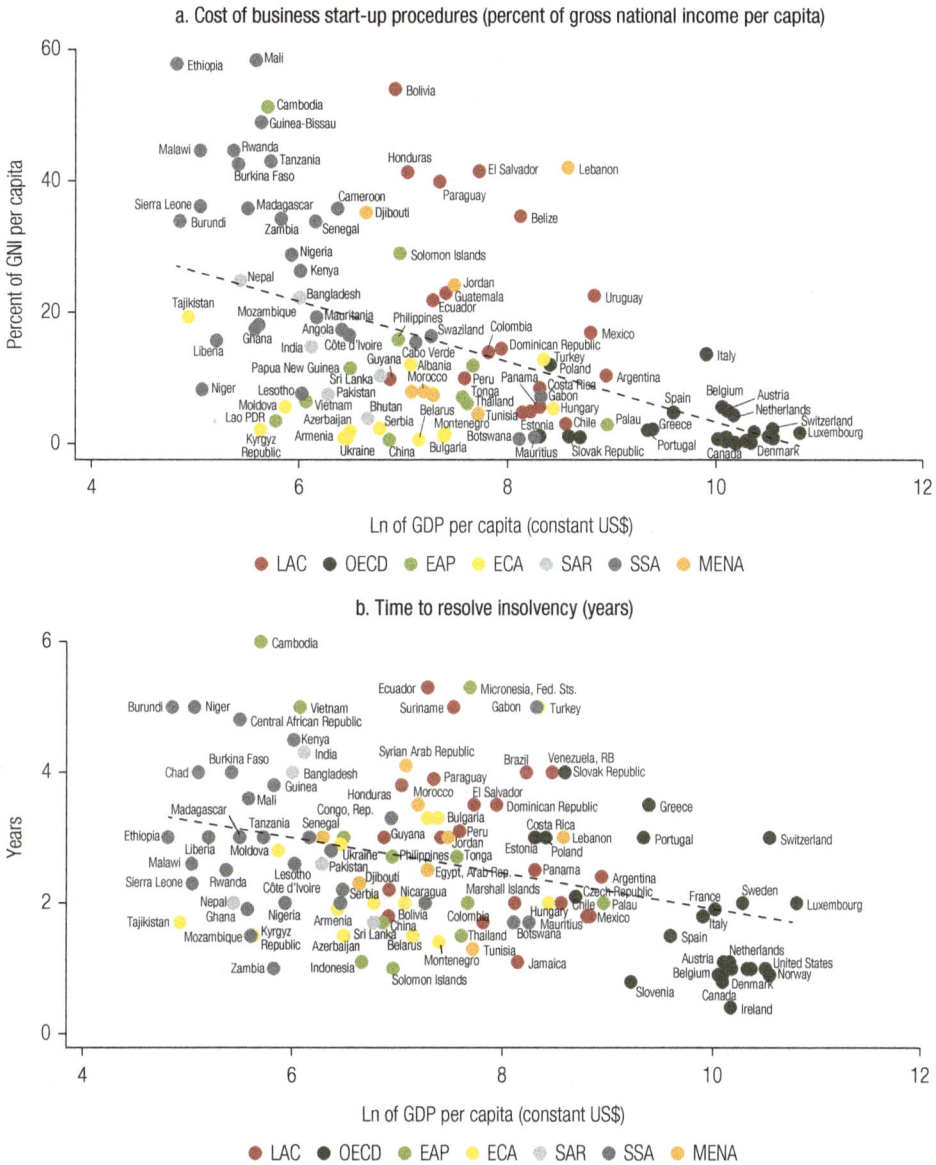

a. Cost of business start-up procedures (percent of gross national income per capita)

b. Time to resolve insolvency (years)

Source: World Bank Doing Business Indicators, 2017.

Note: EAP = East Asia and Pacific; ECA = Eastern Europe and Central Asia; LAC = Latin America and the Caribbean; MENA = Middle East and North Africa; OECD = Organisation of Economic Co-operation and Development; SAR = South Asia; SSA = Sub-Saharan Africa.

while access to credit does not appear to explain differences in investment. Estrin, Korosteleva, and Mickiewicz (2009), using the Global Entrepreneurship Monitor surveys for 42 countries over 1998–2005, find that a strong property rights system is important for high-growth entrepreneurship. Adamopoulos et al. (2017) use household-level panel data from China and find that land institutions in rural China that disproportionately constrain the more productive farmers worsen both the allocation of resources across farmers (misallocation) and the type of farmers who operate in agriculture (selection).

Furthermore, weak property rights or uncertain rules of the game lessen the quality of entrepreneurship by making owners unwilling to hire better professional managers, leading to a decline in firm productivity (figure 4.8). Iacovone, Maloney, and Tsivanidis (2015) show that uncertainty around the rule of law or trust more generally leads to a much higher incidence of family-managed firms, which numerous studies (including Bloom and Van Reenen 2007; Lemos and Scur 2018; Akcigit, Alp, and Peters 2018) have shown to adversely affect the quality of management and productivity.

A wider variety of norms and regulations may also be at play. For instance, Neergaard and Thrane (2011) argue that the ample maternity benefits found in the Nordic welfare model favor employment over entrepreneurship. In Denmark, a sole proprietor is not allowed to work while on maternity leave. If she does so, her maternity allowance is reduced. This may be tantamount to closing the business down if you have a child and may account for the fact that women are generally much older than men when starting a business. Thirty percent of women in the survey perceive the childcare system as a significant barrier to starting a business.

Financing and Managing Risk

Clearly, the ability of entrepreneurs to finance projects across the various stages of starting up a venture is critical. Other studies have dealt in depth with what markets, such as venture capital, are missing in developing countries and how governments can simulate them. Empirically, the evidence is mixed on how much a constraint finance is in early stages. Estrin, Korosteleva, and Mickiewicz (2009), for example, see it as critical; others view it as less so because many start-ups are self-financed initially. And as discussed later in this chapter, the psychological literature is beginning to question how much unavailability of finance is an excuse that more aggressive and resourceful entrepreneurs find a way around. Know-how and mentorship are rated a critical part of most venture capital engagements (De Carvalho, Calomiris, and de Matos 2008). Hence finance is linked to the human capital issues discussed in the next sections.

In addition, however, financial markets are an important way of diversifying risk and limiting liability. As chapter 2 shows, more advanced economies appear to take on more risk—and this is likely to reflect precisely the existence of these kinds of financial markets. Finally, the ease of exiting a successful project enter into the calculations (box 4.2). The existence of private equity markets or stock exchanges makes it easier for entrepreneurs to cash in on their investments and move on to a new project, should they choose to do so.

FIGURE 4.8   **Weak Contracting Mechanisms and Low Trust Diminish Investments in Managerial Capabilities**

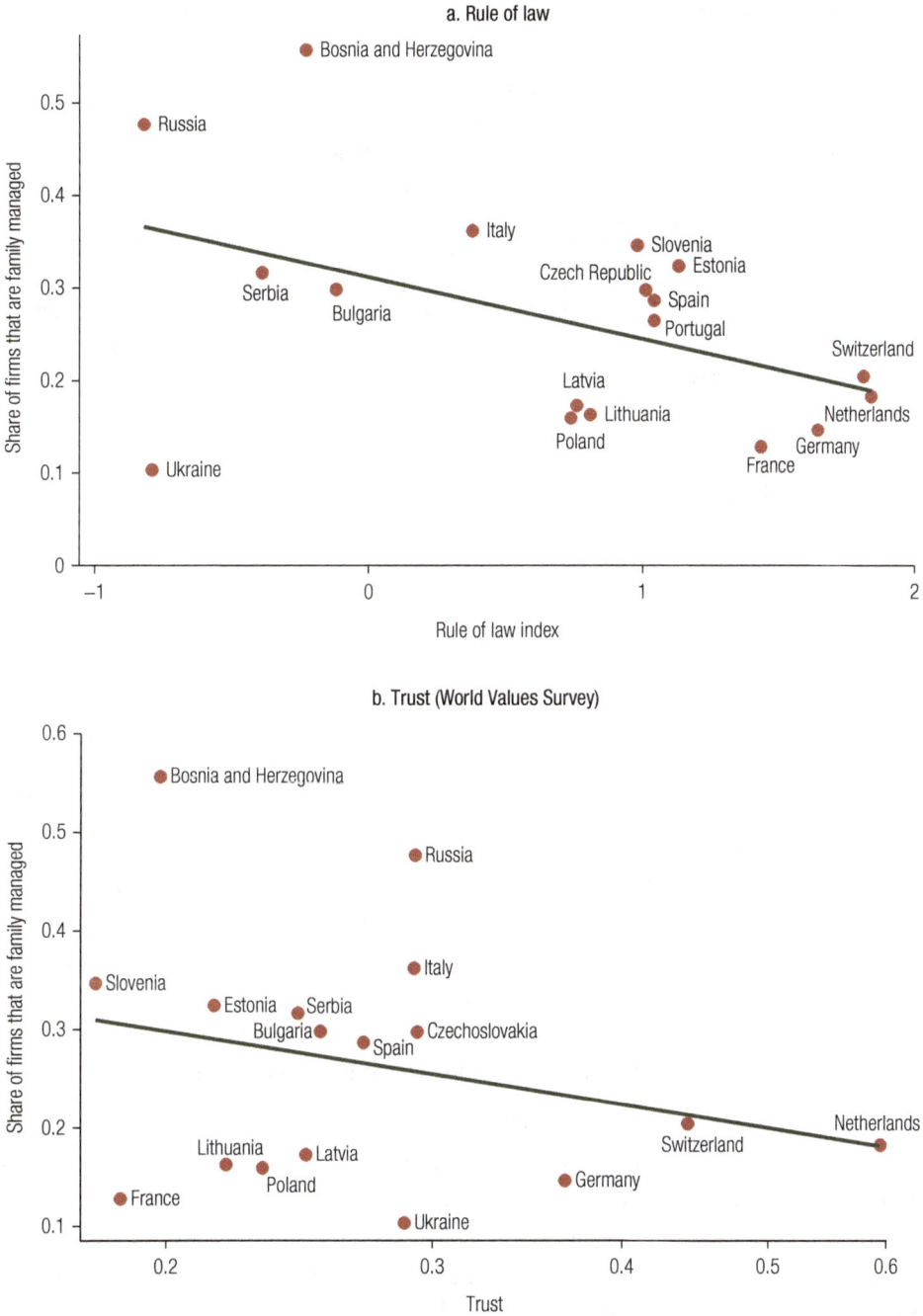

a. Rule of law

b. Trust (World Values Survey)

Source: Iacovone, Maloney, and Tsivanidis 2015.

Note: Panel a plots the share of family firms against measures of the rule of law. Panel b plots the share of family firms against measures of the overall level of trust (from the World Values Survey).

Capital Market Development and the Facilitation of Exit—Novo Mercado in Brazil

Private equity in new ventures eventually needs a way to exit to reap greater returns. Two institutions in Brazil, Novo Mercado and Bovespa Mais, have proven critical to developing Brazil's venture capital market. Brazil has radically increased flows for initial public offerings through its Novo Mercado, a premium listing tier that requires firms to adopt governance standards that are stronger than legally demanded. The increased transparency has helped stimulate Brazil's venture capital and private equity market. In 2007 Novo Mercado celebrated the addition of its 100th company, having hosted 81 of Brazil's 113 initial public offerings since its founding.

Bovespa Mais, which broadly holds to Novo Mercado standards, targets small and mid-cap firms, seeking to host companies with a gradual strategy of gaining access to capital markets. It helps companies improve their transparency, grow their shareholder base, and increase liquidity.

Cost of Failed Experimentation and Exit

In theory, firms decide to exit the market when the present value of the expected future benefits from continuing to operate exceeds the exit costs plus the present value of the best outside option. Several studies find that relatively low productivity, as a contributor to low future returns, helps predict exit (see, for example, Baily, Hulten, and Campbell 1992; Olley and Pakes 1996). Conversely, Eslava, Kugler, and Haltiwanger (2009) find that higher demand, lower input costs, and higher markups reduce the probability that plants exit in Colombia. As firms age, firms' productivity and future profits increase, decreasing the probability of exit (Clementi and Palazzo 2016; Dunne, Roberts, and Samuelson 1988).[4]

Clearly, any barriers to the entry of higher-productivity firms that could challenge low-productivity incumbents will also lower exit. Dunne et al. (2013) find that entry costs faced by potential entrants, fixed costs faced by incumbent producers, and the toughness of short-term price competition are all important determinants of long-term benefits and exit. Also, as the number of firms in the market increases, the value of continuing in the market declines and the probability of exit rises.

Barriers to product market competition are likely to increase markups and reduce the probability of exit, whereas trade liberalization will induce the exit of low-productivity firms. Eslava, Kugler, and Haltiwanger (2009) document the exit of less productive plants after a trade reform in Colombia. Their findings are consistent with the prediction of several models that the productivity threshold required for firms to survive after trade liberalization increases (Melitz 2003; Bernard et al. 2003).

Similarly, while taxes reduce expected future profits, making outside options more attractive and exit more likely, subsidies to incumbent firms have the opposite effect and impede the exit of low-productivity firms. Acemoglu et al. (2013) argue that while policies like research and development (R&D) tax credits to entrants can help and may encourage growth, their impact pales in comparison with removing artificial support for inefficient incumbents. They find for the United States that taxing the continued operation of incumbents can lead to sizable gains (on the order of a 1.4 percent improvement in welfare) by encouraging exit of less productive firms and freeing up skilled labor to be used for R&D by high-productivity incumbents. Subsidies to the R&D of incumbents do not achieve this objective because they encourage the survival and expansion of low-quality firms.

Conversely, what is often overlooked is that the cost of exiting an unproductive firm importantly determines the cost of experimentation. For instance, one explanation that multinationals in Penang, Malaysia, give for their inability to cultivate local suppliers is that Malaysian bankruptcy laws (at the time) were harsh and societal reputational costs of failure are high.[5] Doing Business data on bankruptcy laws across the world show that it takes longer to resolve insolvency in follower countries (figure 4.7, panel b). Furthermore, high bureaucratic costs of closing businesses often lead to the persistence of zombie firms in the enterprise cadasters, distorting inference by showing a large number of very low productivity firm that have, for all intents and purposes, exited.

As is clear, follower countries tend to penalize failure much more than advanced economies, and this makes entrepreneurs carry more of the downside risk. Social stigmas associated with failure compound these costs.

Similarly, highly distorted labor markets that restrict job creation and make reentering the salaried labor market difficult (see, for example, Botero et al. 2004) lower the attractiveness of entrepreneurship. If reentry into a salaried job is difficult, the unemployment becomes part of the downside risk. Together, these imply that the downside costs of entrepreneurship are indeed intimidating and risk, overall, is to be minimized.

These exit costs also affect the approach to risk in important ways. For instance, if an entrepreneur is responsible for the entire downside risk of a failed endeavor, then clearly greater risk is a disincentive to entrepreneurial activity. If, however, bankruptcy laws allow an entrepreneur to walk away from a failed endeavor with minimal debt and easily rejoin the salaried work force, then the decision is best considered as an option problem—more risk implies a possibility for a greater upside without increasing the downside cost of failure. In this situation, a context that heightens the upside risk will encourage more entry. In a sense, the Silicon Valleys of the world approximate this option view. In fact, Manso (2016) argues that the perennial puzzle of why entrepreneurs appear to earn less on average than salaried workers can be explained by viewing the choice in the United States as an option rather than psychological concepts of over-optimism or irrationality or even psychic benefits of entrepreneurship. When the potential upside benefit is correctly calculated, including the fact that, for the most part, U.S. entrepreneurs can get a salaried job if they fail with little social stigma or overhanging debt, entrepreneurs earn significantly more.

Rent-Seeking Alternatives

The final issue with respect to the operating environment is the availability of less productive alternatives with a more attractive risk-return profile—perhaps rent-seeking or corruption, or safe salaried or public sector jobs—that can divert entrepreneurial energy away from productive activities, as Baumol (1990) and Murphy, Shleifer, and Vishny (1991) have stressed. Murphy, Shleifer, and Vishny (1991) argue that the share of talented people who go into law versus engineering captures this trade-off and suggest, using international data, that unproductive entrepreneurship leads to lower economic performance. More generally, safe salaried jobs may seem more attractive; in Penang, Malaysia, talented engineers preferred rotating among the myriad opportunities in the multinational sector than striking out on their own. This can lead to a self-reinforcing bad equilibrium. Acemoglu (1995) argues that the proportion of unproductive agents influences relative rewards. More rent-seeking reduces the return to both entrepreneurship and rent-seeking. Multiple equilibria may arise as a result, where having few entrepreneurs leads to more rent-seeking activities, which, in turn, leads to fewer productive entrepreneurs. In this view, development policy must figure out how to break out of these low-entrepreneurship equilibria.

Capabilities of Entrepreneurs

Beyond the operational environment, individual characteristics that affect the responsiveness to opportunities matter for entrepreneurship to emerge. The final section of figure 4.5 explores two main topics in this regard. The first are psychological, personality, or cultural traits of individual entrepreneurs. The discussion that follows very broadly summarizes a few key strands of the recent work on this topic, with the goal of putting the topic on the productivity reform agenda and introducing some recent policy experiments. The second topic deals with an expanded set of human capital investments, beginning with standard higher education, but then including managerial competencies, technological capabilities, and what we call "actuarial" capability. In fact, with the exception of genetic determinants, this separation between personality traits and human capital may be somewhat arbitrary because increasingly experiments suggest that both family upbringing and deliberate policy interventions can alter even some of the most basic personality characteristics.

Personality, Culture, and Genetic Determinants: Drive, Risk Tolerance and Patience, and the Ability to Identify Opportunities

Economists have tended to resist psychological and cultural explanations for economic outcomes. Too often, the term becomes a hand-wavy residual catch-all for elusive determinants. However, since roughly 2005, psychological perspectives have been reintroduced into the entrepreneurship literature, as Frese and Gielnik (2014) note.

Concurrently, over the last decade, more rigorous explorations have been made possible by the availability of micro data with personal characteristics (Kerr, Kerr, and Xu 2017).[6] The World Values Survey, for example, reveals a great deal of heterogeneity in preferences across individuals, and such heterogeneity has become central in mainstream macroeconomics.

"Culture" has loomed large in the literature on entrepreneurship, most formally in the work of Baumol, but ubiquitous in diagnoses of underdevelopment, for instance, in Latin America (see box 4.3). Guiso, Sapienza, and Zingales (2006) herald the arrival of the "New Cultural Economics," and both empirical and theoretical work now pay more attention to how cultural differences affect economic performance, and their communication across generations.[7] In practice, lines blur. Psychological traits that are malleable, for instance, through training programs, begin to look more like human capital. Culture is hard to separate from more formal institutions,[8] on the one hand, and, on the other hand, as the section argues, can be conflated with certain types of human capital. In addition, in the advanced economies, there is an ongoing debate as to whether at the individual level, entrepreneurs are born or made (Fisher and Koch 2008): that is, how

---

BOX 4.3

Is Inherited Culture Stymying Experimentation?

The Roman empire left a long legacy that potentially worked against entrepreneurship, most particularly in Spain and Latin America. As Baumol (1990) notes, Roman nobility frowned on entrepreneurship and relegated commerce and manufacturing to manumitted slaves. Persons of honorable status had three primary and acceptable sources of income: landholding (not infrequently as absentee landlords), "usury," and what may be described as "political payments" (booty, indemnities, provincial taxes, loans, and miscellaneous extractions).

This attitude was perpetuated through the Middle Ages. As Safford (1976) notes, "The [Spanish] nobility's special position was codified in the thirteenth-century Siete Partidas [the unifying legal code of Spain, based, in some cases verbatim, on the Roman Code of Justinian], which cautioned Spanish nobles against defilement in commerce" (Safford 1976, 6). This attitude remained central to Spanish law into the twentieth century and was transmitted to the Spanish colonies. An overwhelming consensus exists among historians of virtually all countries of Latin America of an attitude of disdain for productive labor, derived from the colonial masters, and mainlined into the emerging societies across the social strata (for an overview, see Stein and Stein 1970; see also Safford 1976 and Maloney and Zambrano 2016). Culture thus plays a large role in one narrative of Latin American development.

In China, on the other hand, Baumol (1990) notes, enterprise was not only frowned upon, ranking very low in the Confucian social order, but was also subjected to impediments deliberately imposed by the officials, at least after the fourteenth century AD. The road to riches ran through the Mandarin bureaucracy that, he argues, allowed for confiscation of rents of others' ingenuity. Yet the dismissive view of enterprise ran throughout many countries and areas influenced by Confucianism, including Japan, the Korean peninsula, the island of Taiwan, and what is now Vietnam, areas that today are or are rapidly becoming very entrepreneurial.

much is inherited genetically and how much is learned and hence malleable. Clearly, at a national level, empirically such factors are hard to distinguish from other slow-moving processes like culture or human capital, broadly considered.[9]

Figure 4.5 identifies three broad entrepreneurial characteristics found in the business and economics literature that have been probed by the recent psychological literature: drive or grit (including aggressiveness and proactivity, autonomy, and innovativeness), risk attitude and patience, and ability to identify opportunities. There are many more characteristics that could be explored, but the point here is only to be illustrative and choose a few that would seem clearly related to exploiting technological opportunities. Underlying these are psychological primitives such as a need for achievement, conscientiousness, openness, and innovativeness.

The literature is just beginning to quantify the contribution to entrepreneurship of different determinants. Though it cannot speak to population-wide characteristics, the literature researching twins (Nicolaou et al. 2008; Nicolau and Shane 2010) provides some support for biological underpinnings arguing that up to 40 percent of variance in entrepreneurship choices is explained by genes. However, Linquist, Sol, and van Praag (2015), comparing biological and adopted children, find that while children of entrepreneurs are 60 percent more likely to become entrepreneurs than others in Sweden, the influence of adoptive parents is twice as large as the influence of biological parents. That is, characteristics related to nurture or environment wind up being more important. Zumbuehl, Dohmen, and Pfann (2013) find that parents who invest more in child-rearing show a greater intergenerational similarity in attitudes toward risk. Nanda and Sørensen (2010) find that Danes are more likely to become entrepreneurs if their coworkers have previously been entrepreneurs.

The source of these parents' and coworkers' beliefs and preferences is often anchored in culture. Spolaore and Wacziarg (2009, 471) show that the distance from the technological frontier captured by genetic characteristics, proxying for "customs, habits, biases, conventions etc. that are transmitted across generations—biologically and/or culturally—with high persistence," is correlated with economic performance. Putterman and Weil (2008) demonstrate that backgrounds of the ancestors migrating to a country are correlated with economic performance.

At a more micro level, Guiso, Sapienza, and Zingales (2006) offer the example of how culture defined by religion and ethnicity affects beliefs about trust and show that entrepreneurship is sensitive to such beliefs. Trustworthy individuals have a comparative advantage in the kinds of incomplete contracts based on handshakes. Trusting others (and being trusted) increased the likelihood of becoming an entrepreneur. More generally, they find that cultural variables, such as agreeing that thriftiness is a value that should be taught to children, can explain half of the cross-country difference in national savings rates.

More specifically, however, the cultural attitudes toward child raising may affect two underlying determinants of attitudes toward risk tolerance, which is often cited as the critical driver of entrepreneurial choice (Kihlstrom and Laffont 1979; Cramer et al. 2002; van Praag and Cramer 2001). "Self-efficacy" describes a person's belief that he or she can perform tasks and fulfill a role. It is directly related to expectations, goals, and motivation (Cassar, Friedman, and Schneider 2009). "Locus of control" is the degree to which people believe that they have control over the outcome of events in their lives, as opposed to external forces beyond their control. As discussed later, there is some evidence that these characteristics are malleable—that is, that policy can affect them. Box 4.4 provides an example of an attempt to inculcate an entrepreneurial culture and entrepreneurial skills that started in Chile and has been replicated in 50 countries around the world.

On the other hand, a recent strand in the behavioral economics literature[10] denies that risk tolerance is, in fact, the distinguishing characteristic of entrepreneurship and focuses rather on nonpecuniary benefits of entrepreneurship, such as preferences for autonomy and control, and overconfidence. For instance, Astebro et al. (2014) cite Holm, Opper, and Nee (2013), who find no clear difference in preferences toward risk between entrepreneurs and non-entrepreneurs in the Yangtze Delta region of China. As an alternative, they explore overconfidence, reflecting the fact that entrepreneurs seem to frequently overstate their chances of success by multiple factors compared to what is objectively the case. The Holm, Opper, and Nee (2013) Yangtze Delta study suggests that entrepreneurs were not biased in their estimation of their abilities relative to others, but did, rather, have a preference for competition. Herz, Schunk, and Zehnder (2014) find that surveyed individuals demonstrate overprecision—an underestimation of the true variance of their information—and hence lowered the perceived option value of exploration and reduced incentives to engage in entrepreneurship.

A much broader literature focuses on the nonpecuniary benefits of entrepreneurship and the fact that these benefits are regularly invoked to explain an apparently recurrent empirical pattern that entrepreneurs earn less than their comparable counterparts in the salaried sector. Frey, Benza, and Stutzer (2004) argue that autonomy and control, aspects of self-employment, raise happiness. Hurst and Pugsley (2011) point out that in the United States most firms start small and remain so, with no new technology and no intention of growing. Most of these self-employed claim nonpecuniary benefits as a first-order motive for self-employment. This is consistent with Lucas's (1978) argument that there is a distribution of entrepreneurial ability or characteristics that imply that both Walmart and mom-and-pop stores will coexist. Bengtsson, Sanandaji, and Johannesson (2017) unpack some of these characteristics, finding that Swedish entrepreneurs, compared with the less dynamic and innovative self-employed, are less averse to risk and ambiguity, more aware of opportunity costs, exhibit greater tolerance of greed, and are less behaviorally inhibited. With the notable exception of risk-aversion, the self-employed do not differ appreciably from wage-earners on most psychological characteristics.

BOX 4.4

Changing Culture, Plugging In: Start-Up Chile and Followers

Start-Up Chile was established in 2010 to increase the incidence of high-potential entrepreneurship in Chile, strengthen the entrepreneurial ecosystem, and position Chile as an innovation and entrepreneurship hub. It has welcomed 1,400 beneficiaries and their start-up teams to Chile since 2010. In total, 76 percent of the entrepreneurs are foreign and 24 percent are Chilean, although the percentage of Chileans has grown to an average of 40 percent, indicating growing interest among Chileans in the benefits of entrepreneurship. The program aims to provide a soft landing for foreign entrepreneurs in Chile, facilitated by a partner in the Chilean business community. Participants receive free office space in downtown Santiago and a $40,000 grant. They also benefit from weekly workshops to learn about start-ups, and training to refine their pitches that is mainly based on peer-to-peer teaching, all in a collaborative environment.

By bringing entrepreneurs to Chile from around the globe, Start-Up Chile seeks not only to connect Chile better to the rest of the world, but to contribute to a cultural change that creates more openness toward entrepreneurship and prepares Chilean entrepreneurs to be competitive globally. Administrators claim this is already happening.[a] The results to date have been mixed. For domestic entrepreneurs, the program has had no clear effect on a variety of economic variables (survival, profitability, exports, employment, future projects of the head of the project). It has, however, led to greater access to funds, suggesting that the process of selection into the program has served as a signal of quality.

Semi-structured interviews with key players suggest that the program had attracted talent. However, concerns about the attractiveness of the investment environment, the relatively low selectivity, and the inability to retain good foreign firms have reduced the impact. The program has contributed to the image of the country as a destination for entrepreneurship and innovation. It also has promoted a culture of entrepreneurship in the country by strengthening the community of entrepreneurs, improving the perception of entrepreneurship, legitimizing it as a career, increasing appreciation of entrepreneurial skills and values, and diffusing new techniques. It has strengthened interactions among agents of the entrepreneurial ecosystem, although in an unsustainable way.

The interviews also revealed some confusion over Start-Up Chile's four goals: attracting and retaining foreign entrepreneurs, strengthening domestic entrepreneurs, strengthening local institutions, and branding the country. The interviews stressed that it is especially necessary to retain foreign start-ups as an anchor to achieve the other goals. It has proven difficult to evaluate the program's impact on establishing a better ecosystem or a country brand. The relatively modest size of the grant has likely led to a modest effect.

The Chilean experience has influenced the creation of 50 entrepreneurship programs across the world. Brazil, the Republic of Korea, Jamaica, Malaysia, Peru, and Puerto Rico have directly replicated the model.

Sources: Melo 2012; Verde 2016.
a. See http://www.startupchile.org/social-impact/.

Self-Employment versus Entrepreneurship

These differences in motivation and goals are arguably central to understanding the contrasting patterns between self-employment and business entrepreneurship seen in figure 4.4. One literature argues that, for instance, the large share of workers in the self-employed sector in developing countries does not reflect labor market distortions, but rather the interaction of the same desire for control and independence combined with low opportunity cost due to the meager remuneration that poorly educated workers can glean in a low-productivity formal salaried sector (see, for example, Maloney 2004 and Perry et al. 2007). This is perhaps the least exotic explanation for the observed downward relationship between the share of the workforce that is self-employed and per capita GDP in panel a of figure 4.4. As examples, Falco et al. (2012) find higher rates of self-reported happiness among those employing at least one individual (a large fraction of the sample) than among those with salaried employment. Workers transiting into informal self-employment from formal salaried employment in Mexico and those informally self-employed interviewed in Brazil report the same valuation of independence and control (Maloney 2004). The now common distinction of "subsistence" versus "entrepreneurial" self-employment is, in this sense, unhelpful because its connotation of being rationed out of formal employment into poverty is not supported by evidence. What is really meant by "subsistence" is "nondynamic," in the same sense discussed by Bengtsson, Sanandaji, and Johannesson (2017).[11] That said, again, these same characteristics dictate that these low-growth firms are not the source of the bulk of productivity gains.

Are Financial Constraints All in Our Mind?

As another example, the psychology literature is also revisiting how much of finance constraints that entrepreneurs declare is really due to failures in the financial markets and how much is really an excuse for other failures. Most U.S. firms start with small amounts of capital; 80–95 percent of founders used some sort of "financial bootstrapping," relying on their own savings or those of family and friends, and did not rely on formal debt from banks or equity from investors. Edelman and Yli-Renko (2010), using longitudinal data on nascent entrepreneurs, argue that entrepreneurs' perceptions of opportunity mediate between objective characteristics of the operating environment and the entrepreneurs' efforts to start a new venture: neither objective evaluations nor perceptions of missing finance affected entrepreneurs' efforts. As Frese and Gielnik (2014) note, median starting capital by founders in the United States was a low $22,700 (Hurst and Lusardy 2004). Bischoff et al. (2013) argue that capital constraints are only binding when nascent entrepreneurs had a mental model common to novice entrepreneurs, but not to experienced entrepreneurs. That is, part of releasing financial constraints in the operating environment may, in fact, be learning entrepreneurship.

Psychological Characteristics Can Be Affected by Policy

A small but emerging literature suggests that personality traits can be changed. In a randomized controlled trial in Togo, for instance, Campos et al. (2017) tested whether teaching personal initiative had a larger impact on entrepreneurship than traditional business training. The former is a psychology-based training approach that teaches a proactive mindset and focuses on entrepreneurial behaviors. The latter tries to teach basic financial and marketing practices. Personal initiative is defined as a self-starting, future-oriented, and persistent proactive mindset. The personal initiative mindset is key to entrepreneurial success because it involves looking for ways to differentiate one's business from others, anticipate problems, better overcome setbacks, and foster better planning for opportunities and long-term preparation.

Campos et al. (2017) find that personal initiative training increased firm profits by 30 percent compared with an insignificant 11 percent for traditional training. They see their results as providing a middle ground between the view that an individual must be born with an entrepreneurial personality and the view that entrepreneurs can be made by learning specific entrepreneurial practices by showing that training can teach people to develop a mindset with attributes such as proactiveness that are often assumed to be innate.

Gertler and Carney (2017) similarly ran a randomized control trial in Uganda of a program to provide youth with traditional hard business skills (such as identifying business opportunities, generating ideas, and using financial statements) versus soft interpersonal and intrapersonal skills (negotiation skills, stress management, self-esteem, risk taking, goal setting, entrepreneurial self-identity). Noncognitive skills were potentially affected by the latter type of training. They found that both types of training, but particularly the soft skills, were significant contributors to finding opportunities for generating business ideas, dealing with the effects of competition, understanding the utility of record keeping, and improving along a hard skills index. Soft skills improved negotiation outcomes, making entrepreneurs more persuasive in selling ideas. Both sets increased total earnings by 30 percent and satisfaction with the quality of life by 16–17 percent. Both, but particularly the hard skills training, increased what are called the "Big 5" personality skills—agreeability, conscientiousness, extroversion, neuroticism, and openness—by significant magnitudes.

Lafortune, Riutortz, and Tessada (2017) tested the impacts of a training program in Chile. Some groups received a visit from a successful ex-student as a role model. Students also received personalized versus group "consulting sessions." Both interventions increase household income one year later, with role models being particularly cost-effective. Role models did not improve knowledge or use of business practices but rather increased motivation, particularly among those with less experience. Consulting benefited experienced and educated entrepreneurs. Similarly, Higuchi, Nam, and Sonobe (2015) establish the importance of motivational aspects to business success in Vietnam.

Bruhn, Karlan, and Schoar (2016) find a positive impact of access to one year of management consulting services on TFP and return on assets for Mexican small and medium enterprises. More interesting, however, owners also increased their "entrepreneurial spirit" (according to an index that measures entrepreneurial confidence and goal setting). Using Mexican social security data, the authors find a persistent large increase (about 50 percent) in the number of employees and total wage bill even five years after the program. They document wide heterogeneity in the specific managerial practices that improved as a result of the consulting, with the most prominent being marketing, financial accounting, and long-term business planning.

Human Capital

Even the entrepreneur most genetically predisposed to be driven, tolerant of risks, and aware of opportunities requires an array of human capital ranging from general analytic and communication skills to sophisticated entrepreneurial and technical training. To recognize a new technological opportunity and make it a business opportunity requires the ability to collect and interpret information, organize the project logistically, analyze the technical feasibility, form the long-term risk-return profile of the project, and compare it to other alternatives, as well as to navigate property rights, financial markets, and government regulation. Various forms of human capital are explored next.

Basic Human Capital
Solid human capital across several dimensions forms the bedrock of entrepreneurial skills.[12] The World Bank has recently developed a Human Capital Index that attempts to capture the basics. Childhood stunting may seem far from high-tech entrepreneurship, but studies show that malnourished children not only perform worse in formal schooling, but also tend to be less energetic and curious, two characteristics associated with entrepreneurs. A recent literature stresses the importance of basic noncognitive skills at the worker level, but this emphasis is applicable to entrepreneurs as well (Cunningham and Villaseñor 2016).

Sophisticated entrepreneurship generally requires general analytical skills at a high level. As Schultz (1980) points out, many agents face and manage risk but are not entrepreneurs. The additional skill required to arbitrage the opportunities arising from the disequilibrium state brought on by technological advance is the ability to make decisions that are neither routine nor repetitive. This is as central to entrepreneurs' success as is their efficiency in acquiring information and in formulating and acting upon their expectations (Schultz 1980) and is likely to involve higher- level generic skills.

Managerial and Technological Capabilities
The emerging literature on managerial quality (Bloom and Van Reenen 2007) clearly stresses the importance of sound basic business strategies and human resources

policies, but also the ability to view a longer horizon. *The Innovation Paradox* (Cirera and Maloney 2017) stresses the need for building managerial capabilities as a critical complement to innovation and hence a productivity strategy. Maloney and Sarrias (2017) further show that raising these capabilities on average is not simply a question of eliminating weak firms. In many cases, it is the best firms that lag the frontier more than the weakest. Furthermore, there seems to be an acute information asymmetry in which managers don't know what they don't know. They believe themselves to be far better informed and skilled than they are, and hence neither realize how they could improve nor the likely returns to doing so. Perhaps for this reason, to address this gap, heavily subsidized management support programs have proliferated throughout the advanced world that encourage firms to benchmark and then upgrade their practices; such programs were central to the productivity policies in Japan and Singapore.

Recent studies find that such management extension services tend to generate very high rates of return. For the United States, Jarmin (1999) finds that firms that participated in manufacturing extension partnership programs in the United States experienced between 3.4 percent and 16 percent higher labor productivity growth between 1987 and 1992 than nonparticipating firms. Giorcelli (2016) has studied the U.S. application of such policies in postwar Italy and finds that management practices had larger and more persistent effects than machinery purchases or technology on productivity, sales, and survival, with effects persisting even 15 years after the program ended. The key channel through which skills improved firm performance was by helping managers make better investment decisions—investing in new plants or new machines, for example—which made their production more efficient.

In a randomized control trial in India in which textile firms were provided management consulting, Bloom et al. (2013) find a dramatic increase in the adoption of good management practices by treated plants, with productivity increasing by 11 percentage points over the treatment group in one year relative to the control group. A similar study in Colombia by Iacovone, Maloney, and McKenzie (2018) finds that locally provided consulting services in a less expensive mode that grouped entrepreneurs have a positive impact on management, firm size, and employment. In general, the small but incipient body of evidence related to management extension and business advisory, much of it randomized control trials and hence the gold standard, appears to be positive across different types of firms (see McKenzie and Woodruff 2014 and What Works Centre for Local Economic Growth 2016 for surveys of this literature).

Another type of intervention supporting business upgrading is the provision of quality-enhancing programs oriented to the adoption of existing quality standards. The available evidence of the impact of quality-enhancement programs and standard-setting is less solid, but also positive (Guasch et al. 2007). Using firm-level surveys, Escribano and Guasch (2005) find that standards (proxied by International Organization for Standardization certification) increased productivity by some 2.4–17.6 percent in four Central American countries, less than 1 percent in four Southeast Asian countries, and 4.5 percent in China.

Many innovative startups and small and medium enterprises have good ideas but do not have these ideas fine-tuned to the stage at which they can attract outside funding. Investment readiness programs attempt to help firms become more prepared to attract and accept outside equity funding through a combination of training, mentoring, master classes, and networking. Cusolito, Dautovic, and McKenzie (2017) conducted a five-country randomized control trial in the Balkans and found that an investment readiness program generated important increases in the investment readiness score.

Technological Capabilities

Being able to recognize technological opportunities requires a minimum level of technological capability that general firm management skills may not offer. Murphy, Shleifer, and Vishny's (1991) comparison of the impact of engineers versus lawyers might be seen as a test of the importance of technological capabilities rather than simply using engineers as a proxy for productive entrepreneurs. Again, history provides dramatic examples of the importance of such a capability. Maloney and Valencia (2017) show that technical capability as proxied by the share of engineers in the population in 1900 is associated with income levels today globally, and at the state and county levels in the United States. Figure 4.9 plots this measure against Comin and Mestieri's (2018)

FIGURE 4.9   There Is a Clear Correlation between Engineering Densities in 1900 and Rates of Adoption of Technologies since 1900

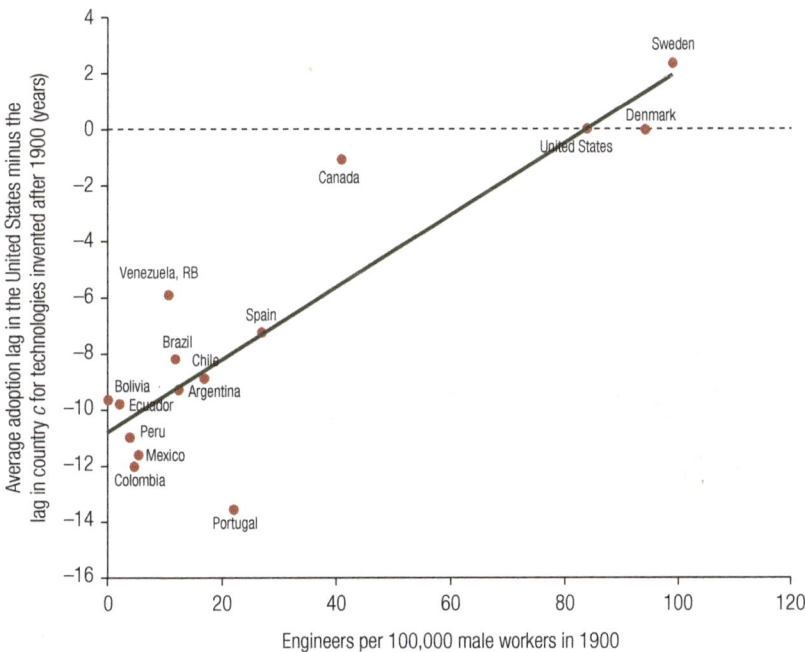

Source: Alfaro and Comin, forthcoming, based on data from Comin and Mestieri 2018 and Maloney and Valencia 2017.

Note: The figure plots the average adoption lag in the United States minus the lag in country *c* for technologies invented after 1900 against the number of engineers per 100,000 male workers in country *c* in 1900.

measures of technological adoption rates and shows a clear correlation. Even though they had the same level of per capita income in 1900 as Chile and Argentina, entrepreneurs in Denmark and Sweden had far faster adoption rates than their Latin contemporaries. This pattern appears even within subnational units in the United States. Counties with higher engineering densities showed higher rates of mechanization, retail activity, and structural transformation across the twentieth century even after controlling for all other types of education, including medical and legal higher education and a vast array of initial economic conditions. Even today, figure 4.10 shows that states with higher engineering densities in 1900 had higher levels of adoption of home computers in the 1990s.

In a fascinating exercise in "nanoeconomics"—an excruciatingly fine examination of the characteristics of early Meiji-era Japanese firms and their owners—it appears that certain pioneering entrepreneurs had higher levels of strategic ability, which led to a stronger international outlook and led them to forge more international connections (see box 4.5). They also hired more engineers than their more insular competitors. Both their strategic ability and the engineering prowess led to more sophisticated production mechanisms and higher total factor productivity that launched Japan's industrialization process. Both managerial and technical capabilities appear central to successful entrepreneurship.

FIGURE 4.10   U.S. States with Higher Engineering Densities in 1900 Had Higher Rates of Adoption of Home Computers in the 1990s

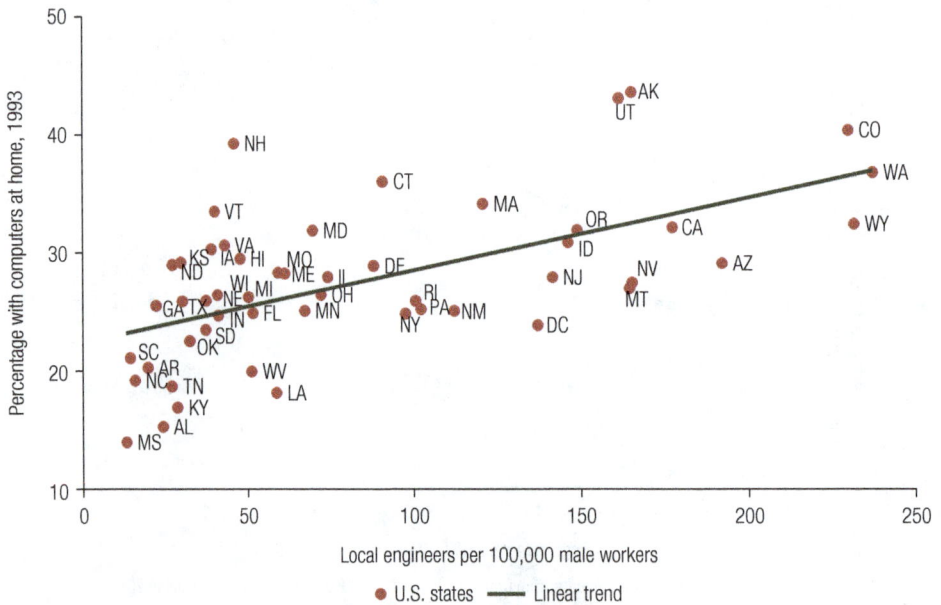

Source: Maloney and Valencia 2017, using data supplied by Skinner and Staiger (2005).

BOX 4.5

The Nanoeconomics of Entrepreneurial Strategy in Meiji-Era Cotton Spinning: Evidence from Japan's First Manufacturers

From 1880 to 1920, Japan's cotton spinning industry went from negligible to a global player, adopting ring spinning frame technologies faster than any other country, starting the Industrial Revolution in Japan and taking the first step in what became known as the Japanese miracle. In contrast to most other latecomers to industrialization, this success happened under a highly competitive open economic regime, without government protectionist measures.

To understand the variation of success of firms in Japan's first giant manufacturing industry, Braguinsky and Hounshell (2016) compiled a detailed "nano"-level database that captures information such as firm founders and key employees, their educational and employment histories, professional networks, the institutions and organizations they interacted with, and intellectual property. Important strategic choices diverged from the outset.

Indeed, low-quality government efforts to diffuse technology actually hurt early textile firms. The dominant firms that adopted the latest technologies and that subsequently dominated the industry association that disseminated them received no government assistance. Only the Osaka Spinning Company, which engaged international expertise, entered at necessary scale. Meanwhile, the government technology specialist who advised 20 plants had no training as an engineer, had not studied abroad, and had no experience in cotton spinning. He led numerous government-sponsored mills into technological blind allies. Meanwhile, Osaka Spinning Company recruited Takeo Yamanobe, who had studied mechanical engineering at Kings College, Cambridge, and then worked at Rose Hill Mill in Lancashire. Contacts in Lancashire allowed him to draw on a different (globally connected) knowledge base from that of government-aided mills. Yamanobe worked with Platt Brothers of Oldham to adapt the technologies to local conditions. Yamanobe would also head Boren, the industry association that disseminated the latest technologies. New entrants, working with Boren and Osaka, introduced ring spinning frames and developed new major sources of supply of longer-staple cotton from India and the United States. The chief engineers of the three most progressive firms were sent by their respective employers to England for training. All were graduates of Imperial College of Engineering. Diffusion of ring spinning technology was the fastest in the world. Attention to product quality during the early years of industry development meant first and foremost having competent trained engineers in charge of production facilities. This was not the case in most firms, and many firms did not choose to follow the leaders. The superior strategic management of the leading firm, as well as its stronger engineering capabilities, led to better performance and survival.

In sum, the story of Japan's first industry was not one of government support, but rather of several leading private entrants powered by visionary entrepreneurs and guided by the first generation of educated engineers whose technical knowledge stemmed from direct contact with frontier firms in England. They "broke the spell of backwardness" and put the Japanese cotton spinning industry on the path to global competitiveness.

The nanoeconomic database assembled by Braguinsky and Hounshell shows that the worst technological choices were made by firms that received government subsidies and technical assistance, challenging the view that government efforts played a vital role in steering Japan's first manufacturing giant. While Taiwan, China, appears to have been more successful in the semiconductor industry, "the vast majority of efforts by the public sector to target particular industries seem to have been far less successful" (Lerner 2009, 132). The nanoeconomics data illustrate the extreme heterogeneity in entrepreneurial quality that permitted some firms to invest in developing

(Box continues on the following page.)

The Nanoeconomics of Entrepreneurial Strategy in Meiji-Era Cotton Spinning: Evidence from Japan's First Manufacturers *(continued)*

demand and sales networks, improving quality, diversifying, and upgrading the product mix. "Perhaps the most surprising takeaway from our study of the Japanese Meiji Era cotton spinning industry is that individual vision and volition mattered so much," Braguinsky and Hounshell (2016, 62) conclude.

Sources: Braguinsky and Hounshell 2016; Ohyama, Braguinsky, and Murphy 2004.

Clearly, establishing a capability to generate such technological expertise is necessary. Importing engineers helps in the short run but does not develop an indigenous innovative capability. The United States, through the Morrill Land Grant program, launched in 1862, created land-grant colleges in U.S. states using the proceeds of federal land sales. Starting out as institutions for teaching agricultural and mechanical expertise, some of these colleges eventually morphed into some of the most important engineering departments in the country, among them the Massachusetts Institute of Technology (MIT) and the University of California (UC) Berkeley. Pedro Nel Ospina, on return to Colombia from studying at UC Berkeley, established the Antioquia School of Mining, which provided managerial and technical expertise for one of the three most important centers of industrialization in Latin America. One of the students from Chōshū, Japan, returned from studies in Scotland to establish what would become the Imperial College of Engineering in Japan (box 4.1). Again, figure 4.6 crudely captures the fact that the Asian miracles send far more students per capita abroad at every level of income than other developing regions.

Government attempts to disseminate technological knowledge have a mixed record. Low-quality government efforts include the British government's use of unskilled agents in attempting to replicate German success in dyestuffs, the unsuccessful technology transfer in the Ghana aluminum industry (Easterly 2001), and the failed Skolkovo (Silicon Valley) project in Russia (Lerner 2009). In Japan, misguided government efforts hurt early textile firms. The firms that adopted the latest technologies and that subsequently dominated the industry association that disseminated them were firms that had no government assistance. The engineer in charge of the program was not up to date and distributed dated information (box 4.5). Again, this is an argument for maximizing private sector participation in the design of all types of programs to support technology transfer and innovation.

Actuarial Capabilities: Learning to Experiment
General higher-order human capital, managerial capabilities, and technical capabilities are all necessary types of human capital for successful entrepreneurship. However, the

framing of entrepreneurship as a process of experimentation (Kerr, Nanda, and Rhodes-Kropf 2014; Manso 2016) highlights the question of how entrepreneurs manage information, how they learn from the experimentation process, and how they become better learners over time. Development is about placing informed bets. Getting the necessary information to place the right bet is only half the battle; entrepreneurs must also be able to process it in a way that allows rigorous cost-benefit analysis and comparison against other options. We term this skillset "actuarial capabilities." In a microcosm of R&D investment, Roberts and Weitzman (1981), Bolton and Harris (1999), and Moscarini and Smith (2001) discuss how entrepreneurs invest in information arising from the process of experimentation to decide whether to continue experimentation or whether to stop. Key to the discussion is that the process of experimentation itself leads to increased precision in detecting the signals of how profitable a project is and hence how much should be invested.

Good analogs are found in the process of adopting new "disruptive" technologies about whose impact little is known. Investors need to form an opinion not only about the likely returns and risks associated with any particular industry or technology in the local context, but historically of the viability of the entire industrialization process itself. Maloney and Zambrano (2016) push the R&D literature further in this context to explore investment not only in regard to the precision of evaluating arriving information, but also in regard to the precision of evaluating prior expectations about the relative payoffs of different projects. For example, two individuals may receive identical information about the increasing use of steam engines globally, but one may lack the technical and business background to confidently undertake an evaluation of the profitability of using steam engines in a particular local context. As shown in box 4.6, Chilean entrepreneurs established a vast copper industry in the mid-1800s and a thriving nitrate industry and proved very agile in responding to demand shocks in the agricultural sector affecting nitrate sales. However, at the dawn of the twentieth century when industries become more technically and managerially complex, Silva Vargas (1977) observes "the surprising ignorance of established merchants' techniques, accepted and in common usage in Europe for centuries, like letters of exchange, double entry bookkeeping, or banking operations, as well as the lack of a basic theoretical knowledge of credit, simple and compound interest, amortization, capitalization, banks." That is, Chilean entrepreneurs lacked the basic knowledge about discounted present value, let alone the ability to price out the likely risk inherent in a complex project.

Furthermore, entrepreneurs' prior beliefs about likely profitability may not only prevent entry into new sectors but may also discourage investing in the ability to weigh the import of new information—that is, learning how to assess new opportunities. This leads to a new information-driven development trap: The entrepreneur cannot see the potential in the industrialization project and hence does not invest in the ability to interpret the associated new "signals" surrounding its benefits—and hence stays with safe traditional activities. This may mean underinvesting precisely in the kinds of

BOX 4.6

Industrial Retrogressions: Insights from Chile and Brazil into the Relative Roles of Learning and the Culture and Business Climate

The local elite in Chile exhibited plenty of entrepreneurial mettle in the mid-1800s. As soon as Spanish restrictions on trade were lifted after independence, exports from Chile—and Latin America more generally—boomed. Chilean entrepreneurs were the second largest presence in Peruvian nitrate fields, ahead of the British, and pioneered copper mining in their home country. They proved responsive to global price movements in commodities. When the price of copper rose mid-century, production by Chileans quadrupled from 1844 to 1860. When demand for foodstuffs skyrocketed during the gold rushes in California and Australia, Chilean wheat exports rose ten-fold in value from 1848 to 1850. Southern *hacendados* borrowed heavily to clear lands, tripling acreage from 1850 to 1870 (Conning 2001). The early nitrate economy in the Norte Grande had global links that elicited a strong and dynamic response from Chilean entrepreneurs throughout the economy, Cariola and Sunkel (1985) argue. As many as 50,000 Chileans sailed to San Francisco to search for gold and brought mining technologies to their Anglo counterparts (Monaghan 1973).

However, the decline in entrepreneurship at the end of the nineteenth century demands explanation. Mac-Iver (1900, 10–11) notes that "Chilenos didn't lack either an entrepreneurial spirit, nor the energy to work, characteristics which are incarnate in the first railroads and telegraphs, in ports and piers, the irrigation canals in the central valley. But these qualities have been lost." Writing in 1911, Encina concurs, but notes that the Chilean had an "obsession for fortune at one blow (*ganada de un arretazo*), or in one-off adventure (*extraña aventura*)" and lacked the technical and managerial skills to enter modern sectors (Encina 1911, 195). Silva (1977, 50) notes the lack of "the basic theoretical knowledge of credit, simple and compound interest, amortization, capitalization, banks, etc. which the principle newspaper, *El Mercurio de Chile*, sought to explain to its readers in 1822." Furthermore, Maloney and Valencia (2017) show that Chile and Latin America had perhaps one-third of the engineering and scientific capacity of even the U.S. South at the time available to evaluate the new technologies in mining and industry. This missing entrepreneurial and technological capital would have been essential to moving from the customary high-return, short-horizon projects to the evaluation and planning of more complex projects with longer gestations emerging from the Second Industrial Revolution.

By contrast, the foreign entrepreneurs arriving in Valparaiso after independence had precisely this capital. Villalobos and Beltran (1990, 99) note that "the empresarial spirit united with the motivation to apply new techniques was almost always the result of initiatives on the part of foreigners who came to Chile and saw opportunities to develop or solutions to problems based on practical experience. They brought a greater tradition of information, spirit of action, attention to detail, and urgency to capitalize on the results or resources generated; these were not common traits of the average inhabitant of the country, whose nature of work was little developed beyond the artesenal level." Explicit is the emphasis on the role of practical experience based on having managed industries beyond the artisanal level previously, that is, the capability to manage information and see opportunities.

Minas Gerais, the other self-starting region highlighted in table 4.1, offers another example of backsliding that also suggests the importance of entrepreneurial capital. Largely financed by the traditional landed elites, the textile and iron industries grew significantly in the nineteenth century. However, in contrast to the northern U.S. colonies, which engaged in a sustained process of learning by doing and innovation in both iron and steel from the early eighteenth century on

(Box continues on the following page.)

BOX 4.6

Industrial Retrogressions: Insights from Chile and Brazil into the Relative Roles of Learning and the Culture and Business Climate *(continued)*

(Swank 1965), from 1830 to 1880 Brazil experienced a "retrogression in technique"(Rogers 1962, 183). Birchal (1999) argues that the underlying problem was difficulty in selecting new technologies (in our model, evaluating a new project). Success in the productive process was affected by variation in resource inputs in ways that could not be predicted or understood, given the limits in metallurgy at the time. The best mix of resource inputs was found by trial and error and depended on the knowledge of workers, entrepreneurs, or managers. Therefore, not surprisingly, the most successful Mineiro foundries in the first three-quarters of the century were set up by foreigners with extensive knowledge of metallurgy. Birchal's (1999) description corresponds tightly to the learning process we model: success in the iron industry required experimentation to learn about processes and this, in turn, required the accompanying human capital.

Similarly, in the 1880s there was potential for Minas to enter the electrical industry before foreigners moved the frontier too far to catch up. However, as in Chile, there was insufficient investment in entrepreneurial capital, in this case of both managerial and technical bent. Birchal (1999, 183) concludes, "Mineiro firms relied strongly on foreign technologies and skilled personnel. . . . The existing informal and spontaneous technological innovation system was not developed enough to take the process of technological assimilation farther in the direction of a profound modifcation of existing foreign technologies or to create a more complex indigenous technological alternative." As in Chile, local entrepreneurs were active but were unable to evaluate and adopt the new technologies that would keep them competitive and abandoned industries to foreigners.

The seeming loss of entrepreneurial zeal, but the subsequent regaining by the end of the twentieth century by local elites in Chile, who became major industrial players, and Brazilians, who became major producers of steel, cast some doubt, for instance, on the view that cultural attitudes toward entrepreneurship, or even the operating environment, are the binding constraints on entrepreneurship. The lack of preparation in both entrepreneurial and technical skills as the technological frontier moved forward seems a more likely explanation.

higher-order business skills as well as the technical capabilities discussed previously. Finally, without such investment, as modernization proceeds and new projects become more complex, locals' skills in interpreting these signals will deteriorate, potentially leading entrepreneurs and countries to abandon established industries as they become more sophisticated. Box 4.6 shows that this is precisely what happened in both Chile and Brazil. This view suggests another source of multiple growth paths: It may not be the case, as Murphy, Shleifer, and Vishny (1991) and Baumol (1990) argue, that potential entrepreneurs allocate their talents between productive and rent-seeking activities based on the incentives. Rather, to the degree that entrepreneurs in a country are unable to evaluate productive projects, they may decide to *create* less sophisticated but potentially relatively unproductive ones. That is, the incentives to pursue rent-seeking or productive paths may emerge endogenously from the presence or absence of advanced entrepreneurial skills, as side effects.

Given such development traps, the question arises, How much can culture and personality be modified to avoid or break out of them? Here, two anomalies of the Latin American experience are again informative. First, table 4.1 showcases two regions (Antioquia, Colombia, and Minas Gerais, Brazil) fully steeped in the Spanish-Portuguese traditions, where locals nonetheless embraced and drove the industrialization project. In both cases, tradition proved malleable.

Both phenomena suggest that something more than culture or institutional context is at work. As prominent observers remarked at the time, it was the loss of entrepreneurial spirit that was notable, not its absence. For example, Chilean entrepreneurs completely established the copper industry during the Golden Era from 1850 to 1880, and entrepreneurial zeal was evident in the nitrate and wheat industries. Yet the copper industry, as with mining industries across the continent, was ceded to the modern U.S. firms, and industrialization was led by immigrants. Such rapid changes in entrepreneurial presence cannot be easily explained by a sudden resurgence of Roman influence, or even a worsening business climate, since this is precisely when immigrants were arriving and thriving.

Concluding Remarks

The entry of more productive firms and the exit of less productive firms in a period of "normal" economic activity is an important contributor to productivity growth. It also is the central player in structural transformation: ideas for new industries must be identified, and entrepreneurs must start and run them. Counter to the U.S. evidence, declining dynamism of this type does not seem to be the key driver of slower growth in the follower countries for which we have data, although Chile does seem to show some decrease in responsiveness to technological shocks. In fact, the factors driving the slowdown may differ substantially by income level. Financial constriction arising from the crisis may be more binding in countries with less developed markets than the advanced economies, but perhaps the slower arrival of technological advances at the frontier affect the latter more.

The greater mystery this chapter began with is why, given the vast potential for the adoption of existing technologies in follower countries, there are not cadres of entrepreneurs pursing these vast opportunities. The chapter shows that the masses of self-employed in developing countries are generally very low-skilled workers who lack the skillset needed for entrepreneurship. Even among workers with a tertiary education, who are most likely to be able to launch and manage sophisticated firms, the share of entrepreneurs decreases with the distance from the frontier, both as a share of the population and as a share of tertiary graduates.

This is the *entrepreneurial paradox* that accompanies the innovation paradox. To probe it, the chapter digs more deeply into what the new wave of analysis is saying about the characteristics of an ecosystem that can support experimentation, as well as the skillset the experimenter must have. The discussion urges revisiting the idea that all countries have a cadre of capable entrepreneurs just waiting for the right framework conditions.

Beyond basic education, technological know-how, managerial capabilities, and a kind of "actuarial" capital that enables evaluating and managing the risk attendant to sophisticated projects are also needed.

In addition, the chapter sketches recent research on psychological and cultural predispositions that underlie successful entrepreneurship. Among the most important are drive, tolerance for risk, and openness to new ideas. How malleable these characteristics are and the appropriate policies to instill and support them are frontier questions in this agenda. But it is increasingly clear that parenting and early childhood development, social interactions with other entrepreneurs and inventors, a culture that promotes risk and experimentation and does not penalize failure, and framework conditions that set the right incentives are crucial to fostering the creation of an entrepreneurial society.

Notes

1. To understand why firm turnover is more important for some countries than others, Asturias et al. (2017) explore this question in the context of fast-growth and slow-growth episodes. Their results for Chile and the Republic of Korea show that net entry plays a relevant role during periods of fast growth. Clementi and Palazzo (2016) show that entry and exit play a major role in shaping aggregate dynamics, in the sense that they propagate the effects of aggregate shocks. The authors find that a positive shock to the common productivity component increases the number of entrants because it makes entry more appealing. However, entrants are smaller than incumbents and they exhibit lower average idiosyncratic efficiency than incumbent firms.

2. Fairlee (2008), for the United States, finds that immigrants start more firms, but as a share of firms, they are broadly in line with their share of the population. Relatedly, Akcigit, Grigsby, and Nicholas (2017) document a disproportionate contribution of immigrants to innovation, but they do not document their share in high tech start-ups. They examine the relationship between immigration and innovation in the United States and show that technology areas in which immigrant inventors were prevalent between 1880 and 1940 experienced more patenting and citations between 1940 and 2000. They find that the contribution of immigrant inventors to U.S. innovation was substantial and that immigrant inventors were more productive than native-born inventors.

3. Odagiri and Goto (1996) note that nearly half of managers (those born before 1869) were low-class *Shizoku*, who accounted for only 5 percent of the population. Stead (1904) also shows that at the turn of the century, they were roughly 35 percent of those accepted into the best institutions of higher education, again, despite being less than 5 percent of the population. The former samurai also became some of the earliest foreign exchange students, not directly because they were *Shizoku*, but because many were literate and well-educated scholars. Some of these exchange students started private schools for higher education. Many became reporters and writers, setting up newspaper companies, while others entered government service (see box 4.1).

4. Hopenhayn's (1992) framework shows how firm size affects the exit rate. In his model, there exists a "size threshold" below which firms decide to exit. Similarly, in Jovanovic's (1982) noisy selection model, firms remain in business as they receive positive news each period about their continued productivity. Hence, in general, longer-lived firms are less likely to leave unless challenged by new technologies.

5. Interviews by authors with enterprises in Penang.

6. See Zhao, Seibert, and Lumpkin 2010 for a meta review of literature on personality and entrepreneurship.

7. Cultural factors are also thought to be a determinant in the overall level of the accumulation of human capital. Botticini and Eckstein (2005) find that Jewish religious beliefs led to accumulation

of human capital and choices of specialization in occupations with high return to literacy. Becker and Woessmann (2009) find that in nineteenth century Prussia, Protestant counties were more prosperous than Catholic ones because of differences in literacy and education. A substantial literature studying the behavior of immigrants documents that immigrants share attitudes toward living with parents (Giuliano 2008), female work, and fertility decisions (Fernández and Fogli 2006), or petty corruption (Fisman and Miguel 2007). At one level, Max Weber's (1905) assertion of a link between religious belief or religiosity and entrepreneurial qualities is revived by McCleary and Barro (2006) and Becker and Woessmann (2009), who argue that the economic consequences of the emergence of Protestantism have lasted centuries, although through its impact on human capital accumulation (literacy), rather than through a work ethic and thrift.

8. Doepke and Zilibotti (2008) further argue for a mutual determination of institutions and values, which give rise, as with Acemoglu (1995), to different growth paths.

9. On a grand historical scale, Galor and Michalopoulos (2009) take a genetic point of view that the failure of the landed aristocracy to lead the risky process of industrialization could be attributed to the effect of Darwinian selection on the low representation of entrepreneurial, risk-tolerant individuals within the landed gentry, and the prevalence of risk-tolerant individuals among the middle and even the lower classes.

10. For a survey, see Astebro et al. (2014).

11. Subjective responses, for instance, from the Global Entrepreneurship Monitor data, show that those reporting being own-employed "Out of Necessity" are a minority (roughly 43 percent) in Latin America. In Croatia, Hungary, and Slovenia, the share is only 29 percent, which is not distinguishable from the levels in Japan (26.3 percent) or Germany (26.5 percent). Furthermore, it would be interesting to know how formal salaried workers with comparable education responded to being asked whether they were employed "out of necessity."

12. See vander Sluis, van Praag, and Vijverberg (2004) for a meta-analysis of education and entrepreneurship.

References

Acemoglu, D. 1995. "Reward Structures and the Allocation of Talent." *European Economic Review* 39 (1): 17–33.

Acemoglu, D., U. Akcigit, H. Alp, N. Bloom, and W. R. Kerr. 2013. "Innovation, Reallocation and Growth." Working Paper 18993, National Bureau of Economic Research, Cambridge, MA.

Acemoglu, D., S. Johnson, and J. A. Robinson. 2005. "Institutions as a Fundamental Cause of Long-Run Growth." In *Handbook of Economic Growth*, Vol. 1A, edited by P. Aghion and N. Durlauf, 385–472. Amsterdam: Elsevier B. V.

Adamopoulos, T., L. Brandt, J. Leight, and D. Restuccia. 2017. "Misallocation, Selection and Productivity: A Quantitative Analysis with Panel Data from China." NBER Working Paper 23039, National Bureau of Economic Research, Cambridge, MA.

Akcigit, U., H. Alp, and M. Peters. 2018. "Lack of Selection and Limits to Delegation: Firm Dynamics in Developing Countries." NBER Working Paper 21905, National Bureau of Economic Research, Cambridge, MA. Issued in January 2016, revised in April 2018.

Akcigit, U., J. Grigsby, and T. Nicholas. 2017. "Immigration and the Rise of American Ingenuity." *American Economic Review* 107 (5): 327–31.

Alfaro, L., and D. Comin. Forthcoming. *Macroeconomics*. Oxford: Oxford University Press.

Astebro, T., H. Herz, R. Nanda, and R. A. Weber. 2014. "Seeking the Roots of Entrepreneurship: Insights from Behavioral Economics." *Journal of Economic Perspectives* 28 (3): 49–70.

Asturias, J., S. Hur, T. Kehoe, and K. Ruhl. 2017. "Firm Entry and Exit and Aggregate Growth." Research Department Staff Report 544, Federal Reserve Bank of Minneapolis.

Baily, M. N., C. Hulten, and D. Campbell. 1992. "The Distribution of Productivity in Manufacturing Plants." *Brookings Papers on Economic Activity: Microeconomics* 4: 187–249.

Baumol, W. J. 1990. "Entrepreneurship: Productive, Unproductive, and Destructive." *Journal of Political Economy* 98 (5, Part 1): 893–921.

Becker, S. O., and L. Woessmann. 2009. "Was Weber Wrong? A Human Capital Theory of Protestant Economic History." *Quarterly Journal of Economics* 124 (2): 531–96.

Bengtsson, O., T. Sanandaji, and M. Johannesson. 2017. "The Psychology of the Entrepreneur and the Gender Gap in Entrepreneurship." In *Gender and Entrepreneurial Activity*, edited by A. N. Link, 6–45. Cheltenham, U.K.: Edward Elgar.

Bernard, A. B., J. Eaton, J. B. Jensen, and S. Kortum. 2003. "Plants and Productivity in International Trade." *American Economic Review* 93 (4): 1268–90.

Birchal, S. d. O. 1999. *Entrepreneurship in Nineteenth-Century Brazil: The Formation of a Business Environment.* New York: St. Martin's.

Bischoff, K. M., M. M. Gielnik, M. Frese, and T. Dlugosch. 2013. "Limited Access to Capital, Start-Ups, and the Moderating Effect of an Entrepreneurship Training: Integrating Economic and Psychological Theories in the Context of New Venture Creation (Summary)." *Frontiers of Entrepreneurship Research* 33 (5): 3.

Bloom, N., S. Bond, and J. Van Reenen. 2007. "Uncertainty and Investment Dynamics." *Review of Economic Studies* 74 (2): 391–415.

Bloom, N., B. Eifert, A. Mahajan, D. McKenzie, and J. Roberts. 2013. "Does Management Matter? Evidence from India." *Quarterly Journal of Economics* 128 (1): 1–51.

Bloom, N., C. I. Jones, J. Van Reenen, and M. Webb. 2017. "Are Ideas Getting Harder to Find?" NBER Working Paper 23782, National Bureau of Economic Research, Cambridge, MA.

Bloom, N., and J. Van Reenen. 2007. "Measuring and Explaining Management Practices across Firms and Countries." *Quarterly Journal of Economics* 122 (4): 1351–408.

Bolton, P., and C. Harris. 1999. "Strategic Experimentation." *Econometrica* 67 (2): 349–74.

Botero, J. C., S. Djankov, R. La Porta, F. Lopez-de-Silanes, and A. Shleifer. 2004. "The Regulation of Labor." *Quarterly Journal of Economics* 119 (4): 1339–82.

Botticini, M., and Z. Eckstein. 2005. "Jewish Occupational Selection: Education, Restrictions, or Minorities?" *Journal of Economic History* 65 (4): 922–48.

Braguinsky, S., and D. A. Hounshell. 2016. "History and Nanoeconomics in Strategy and Industry Evolution Research: Lessons from the Meiji-Era Japanese Cotton Spinning Industry." *Strategic Management Journal* 37 (1): 45–65.

Brandt, L., J. Van Biesebroeck, and Y. Zhang. 2012. "Creative Accounting or Creative Destruction? Firm-Level Productivity Growth in Chinese Manufacturing." *Journal of Development Economics* 97 (2): 339–51.

Bruhn, M., D. Karlan, and A. Schoar. 2016. "The Impact of Consulting Services on Small and Medium Enterprises: Evidence from a Randomized Trial in Mexico." Policy Research Working Paper 6508, World Bank, Washington, DC.

Campos, F., M. Frese, M. Goldstein, L. Iacovone, H. C. Johnson, D. McKenzie, and M. Mensmann. 2017. "Teaching Personal Initiative Beats Traditional Training in Boosting Small Business in West Africa." *Science* 357 (6357): 1287–90.

Cariola, C., and O. Sunkel. 1985. "The Growth of the Nitrate Industry and Socioeconomic Change in Chile, 1880–1930." In *The Latin American Economies*, edited by I. R. C. Condre and S. J. Hunt. Teaneck, NJ: Holmes and Meier.

Cassar, A., D. Friedman, and P. H. Schneider. 2009. "Cheating in Markets: A Laboratory Experiment." *Journal of Economic Behavior & Organization* 72 (1): 240–59.

Cirera, X., and W. F. Maloney. 2017. *The Innovation Paradox: Developing-Country Capabilities and the Unrealized Promise of Technological Catch-Up.* Washington, DC: World Bank Group.

Clementi, G. L., and B. Palazzo. 2016. "Entry, Exit, Firm Dynamics, and Aggregate Fluctuations." *American Economic Journal: Macroeconomics* 8 (3): 1–41.

Comin, D., and B. Hobijn. 2010. "An Exploration of Technology Diffusion." *American Economic Review* 100 (5, December): 2031–59.

———. 2011. "Technology Diffusion and Postwar Growth." *NBER Macroeconomics Annual* 25 (2011): 209–59.

Comin, D., and M. Mestieri. 2018. "If Technology Has Arrived Everywhere, Why Has Income Diverged?" *American Economic Journal: Macroeconomics* 10 (3): 137–78.

Conning, J. 2001. "Latifundia Economics." Unpublished, Department of Economics, Williams College.

Cramer, J. S., J. Hartog, N. Jonker, and C. M. van Praag. 2002. "Low Risk Aversion Encourages the Choice for Entrepreneurship: An Empirical Test of a Truism." *Journal of Economic Behavior & Organization* 48 (1): 29–36.

Cunningham, W. V., and P. Villaseñor. 2016. "Employer Voices, Employer Demands, and Implications for Public Skills Development Policy Connecting the Labor and Education Sectors." *World Bank Research Observer* 31 (1): 102–34.

Cusolito, A. P., E. Dautovic, and D. McKenzie. 2017. "Can Government Intervention Make Firms More Investment-Ready? A Randomized Experiment in the Western Balkans." Policy Research Working Paper 8541, World Bank, Washington, DC.

De Carvalho, A. G., C. W. Calomiris, and J. A. de Matos. 2008. "Venture Capital as Human Resource Management." *Journal of Economics and Business* 60 (3): 223–55.

Decker, R. A., J. C. Haltiwanger, R. S. Jarmin, and J. Miranda. 2018. "Changing Business Dynamism and Productivity: Shocks vs. Responsiveness." NBER Working Paper 24236, National Bureau of Economic Research, Cambridge, MA.

Djankov, S. 2009. "The Regulation of Entry: A Survey." *World Bank Research Observer* 24 (2): 183–203.

Djankov, S., R. La Porta, F. Lopez-de-Silanes, and A. Shleifer. 2002. "The Regulation of Entry." *Quarterly Journal of Economics* 117 (1): 1–37.

Doepke, M., and F. Zilibotti. 2008. "Occupational Choice and the Spirit of Capitalism." *Quarterly Journal of Economics* 123 (2): 747–93.

Dreher, A., and M. Gassebner. 2013. "Greasing the Wheels? The Impact of Regulations and Corruption on Firm Entry." *Public Choice* 155 (3/4): 413–32.

Dunne, T., S. D. Klimek, M. J. Roberts, and D. Y. Xu. 2013. "Entry, Exit, and the Determinants of Market Structure." *RAND Journal of Economics* 44 (3): 462–87.

Dunne, T., M. J. Roberts, and L. Samuelson. 1988. "Patterns of Firm Entry and Exit in US Manufacturing Industries." *RAND Journal of Economics* 19 (4): 495–515.

Easterly, W. 2001. *The Elusive Quest for Growth.* Cambridge, MA: MIT Press.

Edelman, L., and H. Yli-Renko. 2010. "The Impact of Environment and Entrepreneurial Perceptions on Venture-Creation Efforts: Bridging the Discovery and Creation Views of Entrepreneurship." *Entrepreneurship Theory and Practice* 34 (5): 833–56.

Encina, F. A. 1911. *Nuestra Inferioridad Economica, sus Causas, sus Consequencias.* Santiago: Coleccion Imagen de Chile.

Escribano, A., and J. L. Guasch. 2005. "Assessing the Impact of the Investment Climate on Productivity Using Firm-Level Data: Methodology and the Cases of Guatemala, Honduras, and Nicaragua." Policy Research Working Paper 3621, World Bank, Washington, DC.

Eslava, M., M. Kugler, and J. Haltiwanger. 2009. "Trade Reforms and Market Selection: Evidence from Manufacturing Plants in Colombia." NBER Working Paper 14935, National Bureau of Economic Research, Cambridge, MA.

Estrin, S., J. A. Korosteleva, and T. Mickiewicz. 2009. "Better Means More: Property Rights and High-Growth Aspiration Entrepreneurship." IZA Discussion Paper 4396, Institute for the Study of Labor, Bonn.

Falco, P., W. F. Maloney, B. Rijkers, and M. Sarrias. 2012. "Heterogeneity in Subjective Wellbeing: An Application to Occupational Allocation in Africa." Policy Research Working Paper 6244, World Bank, Washington, DC.

Fairlee, R. 2008. "Estimating the Contribution of Immigrant Business Owners to the U.S. Economy." Office of Advocacy Report, U.S. Small Business Administration, Washington, DC.

Fernald, J. 2014. "Productivity and Potential Output before, during, and after the Great Recession." Chapter 1 in *NBER Macroeconomics Annual 2014*, edited by J. A. Parker and M. Woodford, vol. 29, 1–51. Cambridge, MA: MIT Press.

Fernández, R., and A. Fogli. 2006. "Fertility: The Role of Culture and Family Experience." *Journal of the European Economic Association* 4 (2-3): 552–61.

Fisher, J. L., and J. V. Koch. 2008. *Born, Not Made: The Entrepreneurial Personality.* Santa Barbara, CA: Praeger.

Fisman, R., and E. Miguel. 2007. "Corruption, Norms, and Legal Enforcement: Evidence from Diplomatic Parking Tickets." *Journal of Political Economy* 115 (6): 1020–48.

Foster, L., J. C. Haltiwanger, and C. J. Krizan. 2001. "Aggregate Productivity Growth: Lessons from Microeconomic Evidence." In *New Developments in Productivity Analysis*, edited by C. R. Hulten, E. R. Dean, and M. J. Harper, 303–72. Chicago: University of Chicago Press.

Frese, M., and M. M. Gielnik. 2014. "The Psychology of Entrepreneurship." *Annual Review of Organizational Psychology and Organizational Behavior* 1 (1): 413–38.

Frey, B. S., M. Benz, and A. Stutzer. 2004. "Introducing Procedural Utility: Not Only What, but Also How Matters." *Journal of Institutional and Theoretical Economics* 160 (3): 377–401.

Galor, O., and S. Michalopoulos. 2009. "The Evolution of Entrepreneurial Spirit and the Process of Development." The Carlo Alberto Notebooks 111, Collegio Carlo Alberto.

García, Alvaro. 2018. "Job Reallocation and the Productivity Slowdown in Chile." Background paper for *Productivity Revisited*, World Bank, Washington, DC.

Gertler, P., and D. Carney. 2017. "Making (Great) Entrepreneurs: The Return to Teaching Youth Hard versus Soft Entrepreneurial Skills from an At-Scale Experiment." Presentation, World Bank.

Giorcelli, M. 2016. "The Long-Term Effects of Management and Technology Transfer: Evidence from the US Productivity Program." SIEPR Discussion Paper No. 16-010, Stanford Institute for Economic Policy Research, Stanford University.

Giuliano, P. 2008. "Culture and the Family: An Application to Educational Choices in Italy." *Rivista di Politica Economica* 98 (4): 3–38.

Gordon, R. 2015. "Secular Stagnation: A Supply-Side View." *American Economic Review: Papers and Proceedings* 105 (5): 54–59.

Gort, M., and S. Klepper. 1982. "Time Paths in the Diffusion of Product Innovations." *Economic Journal* 92 (367): 630–53.

Guasch, J. L., S.-L, Racine, I. Sanchez, and M. Diop. 2007. *Quality Systems and Standards for a Competitive Edge.* Washington, DC: World Bank.

Guiso, L., P. Sapienza, and L. Zingales. 2006. "Does Culture Affect Economic Outcomes?" *Journal of Economic Perspectives* 20 (2): 23–48.

Haltiwanger, J. 2015. "Top Ten Signs of Declining Business Dynamism and Entrepreneurship in the U.S." Paper written for the Kauffman Foundation New Entrepreneurial Growth conference, June.

Haltiwanger, J., R. Decker, R. Jarmin, and J. Miranda. 2014. "The Secular Decline in Business Dynamism in the U.S." Working paper, University of Maryland.

Haltiwanger, J., H. Hyatt, L. B. Kahn, and E. McEntarfer. 2017. "Cyclical Job Ladders by Firm Size and Firm Wage." NBER Working Paper 23485, National Bureau of Economic Research, Cambridge, MA.

Hausmann, R., and D. Rodrik. 2003. "Economic Development as Self-Discovery." *Journal of Development Economics* 72 (2): 603–33.

Herz, H., D. Schunk, and C. Zehnder. 2014. "How Do Judgmental Overconfidence and Overoptimism Shape Innovative Activity?" *Games and Economic Behavior* 83: 1–23.

Higuchi, Y., V. H. Nam, and T. Sonobe. 2015. "Sustained Impacts of Kaizen Training." *Journal of Economic Behavior & Organization* 120: 189–206.

Holm, H. J., S. Opper, and V. Nee. 2013. "Entrepreneurs under Uncertainty: An Economic Experiment in China." *Management Science* 59 (7): 1671–87.

Holmes, T. J., and J. A. Schmitz Jr. 1990. "A Theory of Entrepreneurship and Its Application to the Study of Business Transfers." *Journal of Political Economy* 98 (2): 265–94.

Hopenhayn, H. A. 1992. "Entry, Exit, and Firm Dynamics in Long-Run Equilibrium." *Econometrica* 60 (5): 1127–50.

Hurst, E., and A. Lusardy. 2004. "Liquidity Constraints, Household Wealth and Entrepreneurship." *Journal of Political Economy* 112 (1): 319–47.

Hurst, E., and B. W. Pugsley. 2011. "What Do Small Businesses Do?" NBER Working Paper 17041, National Bureau of Economic Research, Cambridge, MA.

Iacovone, L., W. Maloney, and D. McKenzie. 2018. "Improving Management with Individual and Group-Based Consulting: Results from a Randomized Experiment in Colombia." Working paper.

Iacovone, L., W. Maloney, and N. Tsivanidis. 2015. "Family Firms and Contractual Institutions." Working paper. LACEA 2016 Papers, Latin American and Caribbean Economic Association.

Jarmin, R. S. 1999. "Evaluating the Impact of Manufacturing Extension on Productivity Growth." *Journal of Policy Analysis and Management* 18 (1): 99–119.

Johnson, S., J. McMillan, and C. M. Woodruff. 1999. "Property Rights, Finance and Entrepreneurship." Conference Paper for The Nobel Symposium in Economics—The Economics of Transition, Stockholm; CESifo Working Paper No. 212, Center for Economic Studies and Ifo Institute (CESifo).

Jovanovic, B. 1982. "Selection and the Evolution of Industry." *Econometrica* 50 (3): 649–670.

Kerr, S. P., and W. R. Kerr. 2011. "Economic Impacts of Immigration: A Survey." NBER Working Paper 16736, National Bureau of Economic Research, Cambridge, MA.

Kerr, S. P., W. R. Kerr, and T. Xu. 2017. "Personality Traits of Entrepreneurs: A Review of Recent Literature." Working Paper 24097, National Bureau of Economic Research, Cambridge, MA.

Kerr, W. R. 2013. "US High-Skilled Immigration, Innovation, and Entrepreneurship: Empirical Approaches and Evidence." NBER Working Paper 19377, National Bureau of Economic Research, Cambridge, MA.

Kerr, W. R., R. Nanda, and M. Rhodes-Kropf. 2014. "Entrepreneurship as Experimentation." *Journal of Economic Perspectives* 28 (3): 25–48.

Khaldun, I. 1377. *The Muqaddimah: An Introduction to History*. Princeton, NJ: Princeton University Press. 2015 edition.

Kihlstrom, R. E., and J. J. Laffont. 1979. "A General Equilibrium Entrepreneurial Theory of Firm Formation Based on Risk Aversion." *Journal of Political Economy* 87 (4): 719–48.

Klapper, L., L. Laeven, and R. Rajan. 2006. "Entry Regulation as a Barrier to Entrepreneurship." *Journal of Financial Economics* 82 (3): 591–629.

Lafortune, J., J. Riutortz, and J. Tessada. 2017. "Are Micro-entrepreneurs Constrained by Their Lack of Knowledge or Motivation? Lessons from a Randomized Experiment in Chile." https://www.pov ertyactionlab.org/sites/default/files/publications/651_Are-micro-entrepreneurs-constraineds -by-their-lack-of-knowlwdge-or-motivation_February2017.pdf.

Lee, Y., and T. Mukoyama. 2015. "Entry and Exit of Manufacturing Plants over the Business Cycle." *European Economic Review* 77 (July): 20–27.

Lemos, R., and D. Scur. 2018. "All in the Family? CEO Choice and Firm Organization." Working Paper, University of Oxford.

Lerner, J. 2000. "Small Businesses, Innovation, and Public Policy in the Information Technology Industry." In *Understanding the Digital Economy: Data, Tools, and Research,* edited by E. Brynjolfsson and B. Kahin, 201–14. Cambridge, MA: MIT Press.

———. 2009. *Boulevard of Broken Dreams. Why Public Efforts to Boost Entrepreneurship and Venture Capital Have Failed—And What to Do about It.* Princeton, NJ: Princeton University Press.

Lindquist, M. J., J. Sol, and M. van Praag. 2015. "Why Do Entrepreneurial Parents Have Entrepreneurial Children?" *Journal of Labor Economics* 33 (2): 269–96.

Lucas Jr., R. E. 1978. "On the Size Distribution of Business Firms." *Bell Journal of Economics* 9 (2): 508–23.

Mac-Iver, E. 1900. *Discurso sobre la Crisis Moral de la Republica.* Santiago, Chile: Imprenta Moderna.

Maloney, W. F. 2004. "Informality Revisited." *World Development* 32 (7): 1159–78.

Maloney, W. F., and M. Rubio. 2018. "Self-Employment and Entrepreneurship across the Life Cycle and Level of Development." Background paper for *Productivity Revisited,* World Bank, Washington, DC.

Maloney, W. F., and M. Sarrias. 2017. "Convergence to the Managerial Frontier." *Journal of Economic Behavior & Organization* 134 (C): 284–306.

Maloney, W. F., and F. Valencia Caicedo. 2017. "Engineering Growth: Innovative Capacity and Development in the Americas." Working paper, World Bank, Washington, DC.

Maloney, W. F., and A. Zambrano. 2016. "Entrepreneurship, Information and Learning." World Bank, Washington, DC, and Universidad de los Andes, Bogotá, Colombia.

Manso, G. 2016. "Experimentation and the Returns to Entrepreneurship." *Review of Financial Studies* 29 (9): 2319–40.

McCleary, R. M., and R. J. Barro. 2006. "Religion and Economy." *Journal of Economic Perspectives* 20 (2): 49–72.

McKenzie, D., and C. Woodruff. 2014. "What Are We Learning from Business Training and Entrepreneurship Evaluations around the Developing World?" *World Bank Research Observer* 29 (1): 48–82.

Melitz, M. J. 2003. "The Impact of Trade on Intra-industry Reallocations and Aggregate Industry Productivity." *Econometrica* 71 (6): 1695–725.

Melo, H. 2012. "Prosperity through Connectedness (Innovations Case Narrative: Start-Up Chile)." *Innovations: Technology, Governance, Globalization* 7 (2): 19–23.

Monaghan, J. 1973. *Chile, Peru, and the California Gold Rush of 1849.* University of California Press.

Moscarini, G., and L. Smith. 2001. "The Optimal Level of Experimentation." *Econometrica* 69 (6): 1629–44.

Murphy, K. M., A. Shleifer, and R. W. Vishny. 1991. "The Allocation of Talent: Implications for Growth." *Quarterly Journal of Economics* 106 (2): 503–30.

Nanda, R., and J. B. Sørensen. 2010. "Workplace Peers and Entrepreneurship." *Management Science* 56 (7): 1116–26.

Neergaard, H., and C. Thrane. 2011. "The Nordic Welfare Model: Barrier or Facilitator of Women's Entrepreneurship in Denmark?" *International Journal of Gender and Entrepreneurship* 3(2): 88–104.

Nicolaou, N., and S. Shane. 2010. "Entrepreneurship and Occupational Choice: Genetic and Environmental Influences." *Journal of Economic Behavior & Organization* 76 (1): 3–14.

Nicolaou, N., S. Shane, L. Cherkas, J. Hunkin, and T. D. Spector. 2008. "Is the Tendency to Engage in Entrepreneurship Genetic?" *Management Science* 54 (1): 167–79.

North, D. C. 1991. "Institutions." *Journal of Economic Perspectives* 5 (1): 97–112.

Odagiri, H., and A. Goto. 1996. *Technology and Industrial Development in Japan: Building Capabilities by Learning, Innovation, and Public Policy.* Oxford, U.K: Oxford University Press.

Ohyama, A., S. Braguinsky, and K. M. Murphy. 2004. "Entrepreneurial Ability and Market Selection in an Infant Industry: Evidence from the Japanese Cotton Spinning Industry." *Review of Economic Dynamics* 7 (2): 354–81.

Olley, G. S., and A. Pakes. 1996. "The Dynamics of Productivity in the Telecommunications Equipment Industry." *Econometrica* 64: 1263–97.

Perry, G. E., O. Arias, P. Fajnzylber, W. F. Maloney, A. Mason, and J. Saavedra-Chanduvi. 2007. *Informality: Exit and Exclusion.* Washington, DC: World Bank.

Pugsley, B. W., and A. Şahin. 2015. "Grown-Up Business Cycles." *Review of Financial Studies.* https://doi.org/10.1093/rfs/hhy063.

Putterman, L., and D. Weil. 2008. "Post-1500 Population Flows and the Long-Run Determinants of Economic Growth and Inequality." NBER Working Paper 14448, National Bureau of Economic Research, Cambridge, MA.

Roberts, K., and M. L. Weitzman. 1981. "Funding Criteria for Research, Development, and Exploration Projects." *Econometrica* 49 (5): 1261–88.

Rogers, E. 1962. "The Iron and Steel Industry in Colonial and Imperial Brazil." *Americas* 1 (2): 172–84.

Safford, F. 1976. *The Ideal of the Practical: Colombia's Struggle to Form a Technical Elite.* Austin, TX: University of Texas Press.

Schmitz Jr., J. A. 1989. "Imitation, Entrepreneurship, and Long-Run Growth." *Journal of Political Economy* 97 (3): 721–39.

Schultz, T. 1980. "Investment in Entrepreneurial Ability." *Scandinavian Journal of Economics* 82 (4): 437–48.

Silva Vargas, F. 1977. "Notas sobre la evolucion empresarial chilena en el siglo xix." *Empresa Privada*, 73–102.

Skinner, J., and D. Staiger. 2005. "Technology Adoption from Hybrid Corn to Beta Blockers." NBER Working Paper 11251, National Bureau of Economic Research, Cambridge, MA.

Spolaore, E., and R. Wacziarg. 2009. "The Diffusion of Development." *Quarterly Journal of Economics* 124 (2): 469–529.

Stead, A. 1904. *Japan by the Japanese—A Survey by Its Highest Authorities.* Portsmouth, NH: Heinemann.

Stein, S. J., and B. H. Stein. 1970. *The Colonial Heritage of Latin America*, vol. 10. New York: Oxford University Press.

Swank, J. M. 1965. *History of the Manufacture of Iron in All Ages, and Particularly in the United States from Colonial Times to 1891*, 2nd ed. New York: B. Franklin.

vander Sluis, J., M. van Praag, and W. P. Vijverberg. 2004. "Education and Entrepreneurship in Industrialized Countries: A Meta-analysis." Working Paper 51-04, Amsterdam School of Economics Research Institute (ASE-RI). https://pure.uva.nl/ws/files/2107544/35537_wp51_04.pdf.

van Praag, C. M., and J. S. Cramer. 2001. "The Roots of Entrepreneurship and Labour Demand: Individual Ability and Low Risk Aversion." *Economica* 68 (269): 45–62.

Verde. 2016. "Evaluación del Programa Start-Up Chile de Corfo, Resumen Ejecutivo." Santiago, February 19. http://www.economia.gob.cl/wp-content/uploads/2016/08/Res-Ejecutivo-START -UP-CHILE.pdf.

Villalobos, S. R., and L. Beltran. 1990. *Historia de la Ingeniera en Chile.* Santiago: Hachette.

Weber, M. 1905. *The Protestant Ethic and the Spirit of Capitalism.* Routledge. 2013 ed.

What Works Centre for Local Economic Growth. 2016. *Evidence Review 2: Business Advice,* Updated June 2016. London.

Zhao, H., S. E. Seibert, and G. T. Lumpkin. 2010. "The Relationship of Personality to Entrepreneurial Intentions and Performance: A Meta-Analytic Review." *Journal of Management* 36 (2): 381–404.

Zumbuehl, M., T. J. Dohmen, and G. A. Pfann. 2013. "Parental Investment and the Intergenerational Transmission of Economic Preferences and Attitudes." IZA Discussion Paper 7476, Institute of Labor Economics, Bonn.

5. Productivity Policies

The new wave of thinking about productivity presented in previous chapters has attendant consequences for the design of productivity policies. The disciplining principle for policy design and implementation should be the same as in the first wave of analysis and reforms. That is, government interventions are justified by the need to remove distortions, establish the right framework of economic incentives, redress missing markets, or correct other market failures that can be found in many aspects of the economy.

However, the analysis of previous chapters shows that many of the approaches commonly used to identify which of these are critical in the realm of productivity rest on weak conceptual or analytical foundations or use databases that lack the requisite information. Hence, there is a risk of erroneous policy prescriptions, mistakes in the inferences of welfare implications and distributional effects from policy reforms, and in the end, an inability to prioritize the policy reform agenda. This is critical since governments have limited capabilities and attention spans (bandwidth) and must choose among policies with the most potential impact. Furthermore, the findings stress that there are complementarities across broad areas of policy that need to be treated in integrated ways. This makes both policy and policy making more complex.

Both the need to prioritize amid policy uncertainty and the need to address complementarities amplify a central theme of the previous volume in this series, which can be updated as the *Productivity Policy Dilemma*: for developing countries, the greater magnitude of the market failures to be resolved and distortions to be removed and the multiplicity of missing complementary factors and institutions increase the complexity of productivity policy, yet government capabilities to design, implement, and coordinate an effective *policy mix* to resolve and coordinate them are weaker.

This dilemma dictates a need for progress along two fronts. For starters, there is a need to reduce the dimensionality of the policy mix by setting priorities broadly guided by two questions. First, how certain is it that the identified distortion or market failure is, in fact, a major barrier to productivity growth relative to others? Second-wave analysis clearly increases the uncertainty surrounding some traditional recommendations. At the same time, it offers important new findings and new tools for the analytical agenda ahead.

Second, how likely is it that the government can successfully redress the distortion or market failure? The classic concerns here are the analytical capabilities of the government, the ability to design and evaluate appropriate policies, and then the ability to execute across several policy dimensions. Here, enhancing *the productivity of the state*—the number of tasks it can execute and coordinate given its finite resources, and the quality of those tasks—becomes a critical dimension of productivity policy.

The sections that follow summarize the main lessons from the second wave of analysis and discuss their major implications for evidence-based policy making and prioritization.

Summary of Main Lessons from the Second Wave of Productivity Analysis

1. Toward a New Toolkit of Productivity Diagnostics and Analytics

The question about whether resolving a particular distortion or market failure should be a priority can only be answered by careful analytical work that will progressively establish with some certainty the efficacy of interventions and the mechanisms through which they work. This volume has so far explained that when output and input prices at the firm level are not observed, then the productivity measure conflates both demand- and supply-side factors—and therefore the usual productivity residual is a measure of firm performance instead of efficiency. Furthermore, the chapters have discussed that even when output and input prices at the firm level are observed, the productivity measure captures both efficiency and quality, unless the quality measure is observable. Identification problems linked to the lack of acknowledgment of demand factors embedded in the productivity residual can have nontrivial consequences for "evidence-based" policy making.

- *Revenue-based productivity measures are a flawed diagnostic of efficiency.* One concern is to mistakenly infer efficiency gains from the reallocation of resources toward the most productive firms while the effect of such reallocation is to increase market concentration. If variations in productivity at the firm level are mainly driven by variations in output prices (instead of technical changes), then a higher covariance between productivity and employment, which is often the measure used to infer the degree of (mis)allocation in an industry or economy, will indicate higher market concentration instead of aggregate productivity gains. A similar problem arises when exploring structural transformation issues. In this case, large differences in labor productivity among sectors can suggest that efficiency can be gained by transferring workers to more productive sectors. To the degree that labor productivity is capturing rents due to barriers to entry, this approach amounts to arguing for transferring workers to the more distorted and inefficient parts of the economy.
- *Productivity analysis that does not account for market structure and market power may lead to false inference about the impact of policy reforms and the channels through which they work.* As an example, evidence from India suggests that trade liberalization led to larger declines in input prices than output prices and hence

a rise in firm markups and a decrease in competitive pressures. In contrast to what standard trade models would have predicted, the benefits from the trade reform were not passed through to consumers. In Chile, increased Chinese competition led to a fall in markups and a concomitant fall in innovation and productivity because financially constrained firms did not have the revenues needed to cover the fixed costs of innovating. Thus, the second wave of analysis asks for a serious reevaluation of a long list of productivity diagnostics that document broad gains from policy reforms when those studies rely on simple assumptions or weak data.

- *Productivity analysis that does not take into account demand factors may lead to ineffective policies for fostering firm growth over the life cycle.* Identification problems about the type of growth model, whether supply-driven or demand-driven, that helped a country move forward along the development path may affect the effectiveness of economic policies geared toward expanding the private sector and may imply a waste of public resources when policies target the wrong objectives. For instance, the evidence here shows that productivity is more important at early stages of the life cycle, while cultivating demand matters more at a mature age. Furthermore, there may be trade-offs between developing "efficiency" comparative advantages and "quality" comparative advantages. Moreover, not taking into account quality aspects when analyzing firm productivity may lead to false inferences that high-quality firms are the unproductive firms in a sector.

- *The commonly used metric of dispersion of revenue-based productivity is not a reliable measure of distortions or barriers to the efficient allocation of resources in an economy.* Conceptually, dispersion may depend on assumptions that are shown to be unsupported by the data. Dispersion can be driven by technology, quality, risky investment, adjustment costs, and markup differences without necessarily implying a bad outcome at the aggregate level. Indeed, dispersion can have a positive implication for aggregate productivity if it is the result of technological differences, quality upgrading, innovation, and entrepreneurial experimentation. New evidence for a sample of 12 developing countries shows that heterogeneity in production technologies (that is, firm-level differences in output elasticities of capital and other inputs in the production function) can potentially account for between about one-quarter and one-half of dispersion. This is an important result, as it suggests that a nonnegligible portion of observed dispersion may not entail a "misallocation" at all. Furthermore, inferences about misallocation prove to be empirically highly sensitive to how data are processed and cleaned, rendering cross-country comparisons unreliable. For example, just using the raw U.S. data to calculate dispersion instead of the Census-cleaned data reverses the relationship between the calculated "gains from reallocation" and GDP, showing that the most advanced economies have the most to gain from reallocation.

- *Entrepreneurs cannot be assumed to be similar in basic human capital, including basic numeracy, managerial skills, or psychological traits.* Traditionally, economics has shied away from opening the black box of the entrepreneur—the individual who combines factors of production or decides to launch a firm. However, the recent research on management quality and on culture and an emerging psychological literature on the characteristics of successful engineers suggest that these dimensions are central to understanding productivity differences. The vast share of the workforce in both formal employment and informal self-employment in developing countries is characterized by low basic human capital and low modern sector productivity. Hence the opportunity cost of being self-employed is low, and the reserve of entrepreneurs who can manage sophisticated enterprises is limited. In an important sense, total factor productivity differences are, in fact, managerial capability differences, which can be thought to include basic abilities to combine capital and labor, technological literacy, and what this volume calls actuarial capability—the ability to learn about, quantify, and manage the risks involved in a project. Finally, a new literature suggests that issues of personality with respect to identifying opportunities, having the energy to push a project forward, and tolerating risk are also important. A nascent literature suggests that these traits are malleable.

Overall, although we now know much more about how to approach the measurement of productivity and its correlates, much of what we thought we knew needs to be reviewed. In each case discussed, a rejuvenated analytical agenda is needed to isolate the true impact of proposed policy reforms and the necessary supporting contexts. In addition, the volume draws on a new generation of data to support this agenda. Chapter 2 emphasizes the need for firm-level data on prices, marginal costs, product quality, worker qualifications, and risk.

Generating the necessary empirical base in the productivity realm requires more analytical rigor and more detailed firm-level data. Thus, access to firm-level census data that gather that type of information and expansion of the coverage of existing databases to incorporate these key dimensions of firm performance are crucial to providing new insights for the second wave of policy reforms. In the end, strong analytical work combined with a second generation of industrial surveys are essential to making productivity policies more effective.

2. A Comprehensive Approach toward Productivity Growth and the Role of the "Within" Component

The productivity (physical total factor productivity, TFPQ) decompositions presented in this volume confirm that all three components (within-firm, between-firm, and selection) are relevant for explaining productivity growth and dictate a reweighting of the elements in the productivity policy mix. Though the tractability of the Hsieh-Klenow approach has moved the (mis)allocation agenda to the center of many policy discussions, the recent criticisms on both conceptual and empirical levels suggest that the static focus is not fully justified.

The TFPQ decompositions in chapter 1 suggest that all margins of productivity growth are important and, in fact, the within-firm margin, which is related to firm upgrading (through innovation, technology adoption, and managerial practices, among others) is relatively more important than the between-firm margin. The within-firm margin explains at least half of productivity growth in China, Ethiopia, and India, consistent with a renewed focus on technology adoption and good managerial practices as explaining productivity and income differences between advanced economies and emerging markets. In Chile and Colombia, the entry and exit of firms is the largest contributor. Reallocation is arguably equal in contribution to the within dimension only in the Indian case, broadly following that country's far-reaching trade liberalization.

This said, this volume shows that these three components are inextricably linked. The small red arrows in figure 5.1 capture this interdependency: On the one hand, as chapter 3 establishes, impediments to reallocation of resources driven by distortions, such as trade barriers, poor regulation, and the presence of informal firms or overbearing state-owned enterprises, can have negative dynamic effects on the within margin, as they may discourage firm upgrading or prevent the exit of unproductive firms and the entry of high-productivity firms.[1] On the other hand, without the arrival of new innovation shocks as incumbent and new firms introduce new products and processes and compete for resources, even the cleanest, least distorted economic system will cease to reap gains from reallocation.

3. The Operating Environment and Human Capital: Critical Complements across All Three Productivity Margins

The last point highlights that, cutting across the three margins in figure 5.1 is the essential complementarity of both environmental factors and a range of types of human capital: personality, as well as managerial, entrepreneurial, and technological capabilities. Productivity growth requires progress on all these fronts.

FIGURE 5.1   Drivers of Productivity Growth

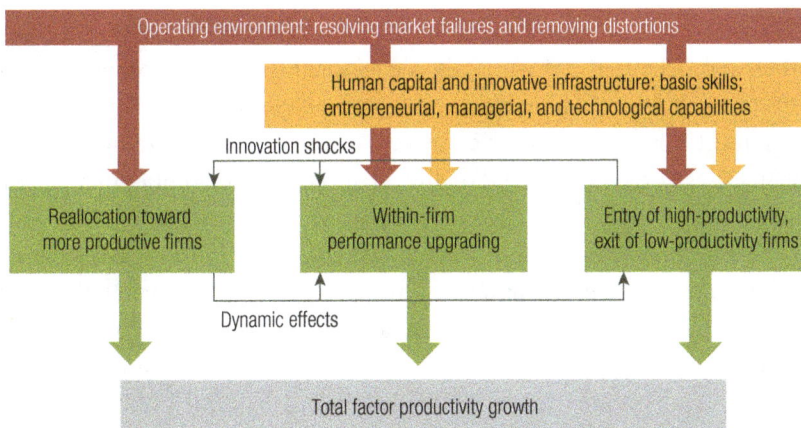

Chapter 2 notes a long literature that shows the positive impact of competition policy on productivity working through the reallocation channel by facilitating the transfer of resources to more productive firms—the within-firm component; by stimulating incumbents to invest in productivity-enhancing innovation; and in entry and exit by permitting the entry of more productive firms and encouraging the exit of less productive ones. Hence opening markets to international trade, exposing state-owned industries to competition, and reducing their ability to prevent the emergence of competitors is of central importance to ensuring that managers are on their toes and looking at opportunities to bring new techniques and technologies from the frontier. Here, the insistence from industrial organization economists that productivity policy and market structure be approached in an integrated fashion becomes a critical agenda for understanding both the channels through which policy changes affect firm incentives and how they respond.

However, though the overall system may be crystalline—undistorted and with all market failures resolved—if there are no entrepreneurs with the necessary human capital to take advantage of it, there will be no growth. The centrality of this point and the need for better measurement of human capital are highlighted in the World Bank's recently launched Human Capital Index. The Human Capital Project includes a program of measurement and research to inform policy action, and a program of support for country strategies to accelerate investment in human capital.[2] As noted, entrepreneurship without at least numeracy and literacy is likely to lead to the non-productivity-increasing churning seen in much of the developing world's self-employed sectors. If the managers of established firms or incipient start-ups lack the managerial capabilities to recognize or respond to new technological opportunities or domestic and foreign competition, there will be no impetus to upgrade their firms or enter the market.

The evidence presented here and elsewhere on immigrants makes this case. Some kind of human capital—whether world experience, business training, risk appetite or tolerance, or openness to seeing the viability of a project—permitted them to thrive in the same imperfect business climate and institutional setup in which locals did not.

Furthermore, chapter 2 documents a heterogeneity of responses to increased competition, such as trade liberalization, that depend on firms' ability to develop a strategy to meet competition, to diversify into other products, or to upgrade to a different market—all of which depend on higher-level firm capabilities that rest on core managerial competencies that developing countries lack. Attracting foreign direct investment is an initial way of transferring technology and driving reallocation, but over the longer term, the enhancement of human capital along several dimensions—capabilities in management, technological adoption, and risk evaluation, for example—becomes central for both within-firm performance upgrading and new firm entry.

4. Beyond Efficiency: Policy Needs to Adopt a Broader View of Value Creation in the Modern Firm

The firm is the main creator of value added and the ultimate driver of aggregate economic growth. Breaking apart revenue-based productivity into its constituent parts in chapter 2, while confirming the centrality of efficiency improvement, fortuitously opened the door to identifying other dimensions of *firm performance* that also contribute to the generation of value added but that require a broader policy focus. However, from a policy perspective, all determinants of firm performance should not be taken as interchangeable. New evidence shows that advantages in marginal costs matter relatively more at early stages of a firm's life cycle, while demand factors such as quality upgrading, advertising, marketing, and brand name have a relatively larger effect on firm performance at later stages.

Raising the quality of a product may require some of the same kinds of investments needed to increase efficiency—and suffer from similar market failures.[3] In this regard, all the considerations discussed in *The Innovation Paradox* (Ciera and Maloney 2017) are relevant, and its discussion about improving the functioning of the innovation system by improving firm capabilities, facilitating technology transfer and adoption, and enhancing the enabling environment are germane.

Policy in these areas can be justified largely in terms of information asymmetries of multiple types. First, firms don't know what they don't know. Self-evaluations of management quality at even the most basic level reveal that entrepreneurs are generally wildly optimistic about their own abilities. The kinds of managerial extension programs that offer subsidized benchmarking and improvement plans help make such self-evaluations more realistic. Second, weak information about the quality of private sector services offered makes firms reluctant to contract them and hence support a market for such services. There are important barriers to technology adoption for both managers and workers. Financial constraints impede managers from covering the fixed costs of acquiring the latest technologies, even when they are available in the countries where their firms operate. Resistance to learning, adapting, and changing, and misalignment of incentives within firms between employers and workers have been highlighted by the literature as important reasons for the lack of adoption and use of new technologies.

From a policy perspective, establishing the right framework of economic incentives to encourage firms to make those investments is crucial to increasing firm performance. This centers the competition policy agenda as a core pillar of the productivity policy agenda.

The importance of competition policy has been widely recognized, although its effectiveness with respect to trade reforms can be easily questioned. Inherent in the promise of the first wave of structural reforms was the assumption that competitive markets would emerge if the right regulatory framework were established and therefore consumers would benefit from the procompetitive effects of these reforms. However, evidence has shown that product market competition has decreased in several advanced economies, while the degree of product market concentration has remained stubbornly high in emerging ones (De Loecker and Eeckhout 2018), raising the priority of product market competition policies in the productivity agenda.

Experimental methods have the potential to test new instruments for both real or digital markets, address market failures from a nonregulatory standpoint, and solve key identification issues, such as the fact that entry and exit are also endogenous responses to market conditions that may have independent effects. Busso and Galiani (forthcoming), for example, analyze the effects of a randomized expansion of retail firms serving beneficiaries of a cash transfer program in the Dominican Republic by certifying more firms as providers for the program. Six months after the intervention, product prices decreased by about 5 percent while service quality perceived by consumers improved. However, Bergquist (2017) produced less expected results in her analysis of the competitiveness of rural agricultural markets. She implemented three different incentive experiments to induce traders to enter randomly selected markets for the first time. Entry in this case did not enhance competition and had negligible effects on prices, documenting a high degree of market power of intermediaries, with large implied losses to consumer welfare and market efficiency. Again, understanding the underlying market structure seems essential to ensuring that policies have their predicted impact.

Scaling up demand. The issue of quality elides into a broader agenda of how the new importance of demand highlighted in chapter 2 matters for firm growth. Here, additional policies may be considered. The findings that most firms enter with higher productivity than incumbent firms and that most firm growth in the United States and a large fraction of that in Chile, Colombia, Malaysia, and Mexico after entry is due to increased demand suggest a range of programs focused exactly on creating and expanding that demand. Policies to support firm growth should therefore focus on building firms' client base, mainly through innovative solutions that reduce buyer-seller transaction costs due to searching, matching, and informational frictions.

Examples of those policies include digital platform development or connection, business intermediation, and links to global value chains. Reducing matching costs has been highlighted as a major objective of export promotion agencies to facilitate access to foreign markets (Lederman, Olarreaga, and Payton 2010). A recent intervention for rug producers in the Arab Republic of Egypt—where a group of academics partnered with a U.S. nongovernmental organization and an Egyptian intermediary to secure export orders from foreign buyers through trade fairs and direct marketing channels— shows that demand-side interventions can be a powerful tool to boost firm growth

(Atkin, Khandelwal, and Osman 2017). They help build a self-sustained customer base, generate learning-by-exporting effects, increase product quality, and reduce production costs. Business support services that help firms develop the necessary quality standards to get access to global value chains by supplying intermediate inputs to multinational companies can also have an important effect, as can managerial consulting services on marketing to develop brand recognition.

5. Creating Experimental Societies

Chapters 3 and 4 highlight that investments, either by ongoing firms to upgrade efficiency or quality, or by newly entering firms, are fundamentally wagers under uncertainty. Firms cannot know how much a new technology or marketing plan will increase their profitability. New firms cannot know whether their new idea, or firm, or sector is viable until they enter and then learn from experience. The finding of a risk-return frontier in investments in quality, and the further finding that advanced economies place big risky bets while less developed countries do not, suggest that societies need to learn to quantify, tolerate, and manage risk to accelerate the process of productivity catch-up. As also discussed in chapter 3, such risk or uncertainty can reduce the rapidity with which firms make the investments needed to adjust to shocks. Fundamentally, we need to create experimental societies in which individuals are encouraged to place well-researched bets and reduce the penalties for failure.

Here again, both the environment and the human capital of the individuals who populate it are central to facilitating the large-scale entry of firms that can bring ideas from the frontier and test them out in the local context—a process that will lead to many failures, but some major successes that drive growth. Chapter 3 shows that the advanced economies appear to be more able to take on more risk and reap larger growth rates. Increasing the willingness and ability of entrepreneurs to experiment, while reducing the cost of experimentation, is thus critical to the strategy for long-term productivity growth. In addition, the providers of inputs, such as financing, also need high levels of actuarial capabilities to identify and gauge risk.

At the most basic level, there must also be mechanisms in the financial sector precisely to diversify risk of various types. It may be that the inability to diffuse risk is as much a barrier to upgrading and innovation as credit restrictions per se. The finding that financing innovation is difficult, especially for start-ups and young firms, is not news, but sustainable solutions have been elusive, especially for developing countries. Imperfect information about borrowers and difficulties monitoring their activities have long been known to lead to credit rationing or costly borrowing.[4] Innovation is risky and produces both intangible assets that typically are not accepted as collateral to obtain external funding and intangible assets that are easily "expropriated" by other firms. Early stages of the innovation process are typically more difficult to finance because both uncertainty and intangibility are high, while at the later stage much of the uncertainty may have been resolved and investments are focused on tangible assets. Poorly designed regulation compounds these issues.[5] On the other side, it is possible that developing-country bankers lend short term and to safe customers because they lack the capabilities to effectively evaluate new products.

Governments often try to support innovative start-ups and high-growth firms with direct public support programs through such means as grants, royalties, and tax breaks. However, public servants are often not the best qualified people to select innovative projects to be financed. The longer-term goal is the development of a self-sustaining risk capital ecosystem. This requires supporting framework conditions that permit the financing of seed and venture funds and the accumulation of managerial expertise to staff them, as well as the development of a pipeline of high-quality projects supported by investment readiness programs.[6]

More generally, the process of experimentation with new processes and new products is affected by the standard appropriability externalities. Because knowledge is easily used by others, an innovator is likely to be copied and lose some of the potential rents. The social benefit is higher than the private benefit; thus, there will be underinvestment in experimentation. Hence government subsidies, tax write-offs, and patents are long-accepted remedial policies. The same logic supports public foundations that search out and test for the viability of new practices or products and then disseminate them through such means as agricultural extension programs, public research institutes, and university departments specializing in basic research. A long-standing literature stresses the coordination failures among such nonmarket institutions in National Innovation Systems (see, among others, Freeman 1995; Lundvall 1992; Nelson 1993; Soete, Verspagen, and Weel 2010; and Edquist 2006) and stresses failures surrounding the acquisition of firm capabilities.

However, it is not always clear that such common market failures are the most critical barrier to experimentation. Numerous countries, for example, have established subsidies or tax write-offs for R&D expenditure with little to show for it, despite the success of these policies elsewhere. But the key failure may not be in the accumulation of innovation (knowledge capital) per se, but rather there may be a more pressing problem in accumulation more generally—in capital markets, barriers to entry and exit, labor restrictions, or especially management quality, as discussed earlier (see Maloney and Rodriguez Clare 2007 and Cirera and Maloney 2017). Likewise, the process of self-discovery highlighted by Hausmann and Rodrik (2003) may be hampered not by market failures, but by a shortage of capable discoverers and may reflect the inability of local entrepreneurs to recognize productive opportunities in the first place.

The insights of second-wave analysis have profound implications for policy. Box 5.1 explores how the fundamental process of structural transformation can be rethought in terms of these insights.

BOX 5.1

Structural Transformation: What Are the Conclusions for Policy?

Moving from evidence to effective policy demands keeping all three components of total factor productivity (reallocation, innovation, and selection) in mind. This is particularly true for policies to promote structural transformation.

McMillan and Rodrik (2011) and McMillan, Rodrik, and Verduzco-Gallo (2014) offer some suggestive causal channels driving structural transformation. Slow structural transformation can be seen as reflecting barriers to reallocation; McMillan and Rodrik (2014) identify rigid labor markets as a possible candidate. To the degree that such rigidities imply segmentation, the available measures of average productivity are not adequate to confirm it on conceptual grounds. As they note, efficiency requires calculation of marginal product, but data are readily available only for average labor productivity. They also correctly note that different production technologies (among other factors) across sectors can lead to different corresponding average products across sectors (see Rogerson 2017), even if marginal products are equalized. If agriculture is more labor intensive than manufacturing, its average productivity will be lower, even if no distortions exist.

This gap between concept and measurement may be more important than McMillan and Rodrik acknowledge. Figure B5.1.1 presents Rogerson's calculations for this volume, showing the average productivity for manufacturing relative to agriculture over time. If removing barriers to movement were facilitating structural transformation, average productivities would be expected to converge if, in fact, they are a good proxy for marginal products. However, as figure B5.1.1 shows, they do not. This result is more consistent with differing production technologies driving

FIGURE B5.1.1   Average Productivity Gaps between Manufacturing and Agriculture Persist over Time, Suggesting That Segmenting Labor Market Distortions Are Probably Not the Main Barrier to Structural Transformation

(Log sectoral productivity relative to agriculture, by country)

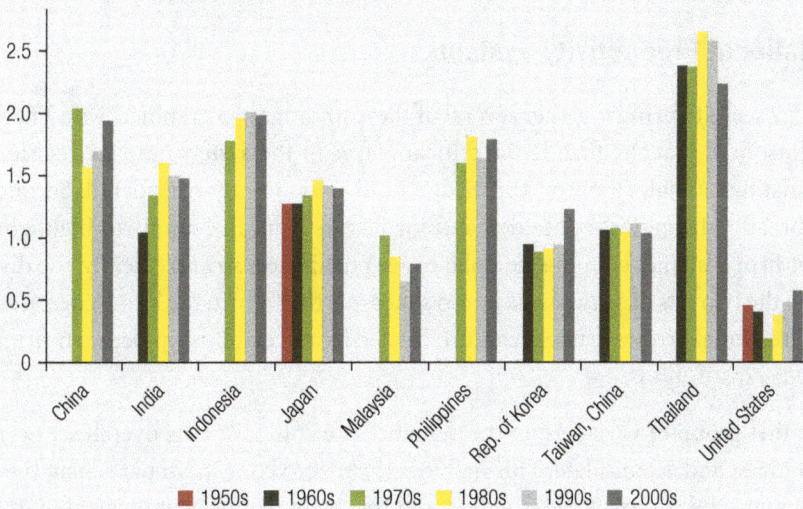

Source: Rogerson 2017, for this volume.

(Box continues on the following page.)

Structural Transformation: What Are the Conclusions for Policy? *(continued)*

average productivity gaps than with distortion-driven segmentation. Furthermore, as a forthcoming volume on agricultural productivity will discuss, the measurement of agricultural productivity is difficult; hence permanent gaps between measurement and reality are likely.

One possible takeaway is that removing distortions is not the major driver of transformation. Rather, the question that needs to be asked is, Who or what creates the underlying opportunities in new sectors that drive structural transformation? As chapters 2 and 4 discuss, and as the Melitz decompositions in chapter 1 suggest, weaknesses in the process of upgrading existing firms or in entrepreneurship may merit as much focus in explaining the pace of structural transformation as distortions.

In fact, both elements may be salient at different moments in the development process. Chile, for instance, was Latin America's growth miracle from 1986 to 2006. Much of Chile's productivity growth is thought to have arisen from the unwinding of the vast distortions accumulated over the previous 50 years. However, productivity has leveled off over the last 15 years, turning attention to the weaknesses along the other two dimensions. Figure B5.1.1 similarly suggests that the importance of reallocation diminishes with level of income, accounting for very little in more advanced economies. In the United States, structural transformation never accounts for more than 0.1 percent of growth, while in Japan; Taiwan, China; and the Republic of Korea, the contribution is low or negative, despite having been important during their miracle periods. Such a negative contribution may be optimal, for example, if demand increases for nontraded services that require shifting work away from more productive manufacturing. The increasing role of lower productivity growth in services as societies get richer is known as the Baumol Effect: it may be the best for society, but it slows growth. More generally, the findings suggest that the importance of the between-sector reallocations versus the within-sector improvements depends on the stage of development.

The National Productivity System

Figure 5.2 seeks to bring together several of these findings in a graphical way. The figure highlights, first, that the firm is the critical player in the system, and its decisions on accumulating capital, labor, or knowledge need to be jointly considered. Second, the figure broadly distinguishes the demand for factors from the supply to highlight that without firm demand, supply-side policies are pushing on strings. Clearly, the division between the two sets of variables is not so sharp, particularly in the knowledge area, and the bidirectional arrows crudely capture the feedback relationship between firms and knowledge institutions.

The first group of variables on the demand side comprises the overall set of incentives to invest and accumulate. This includes the macro context: in particular, the volatility of sales, the competitive structure, and the trade regime that determine whether firms seek to enter or grow. In addition, as chapter 2 stresses, demand-related initiatives such as the development or connection to digital platforms that reduce searching,

FIGURE 5.2 The National Productivity System

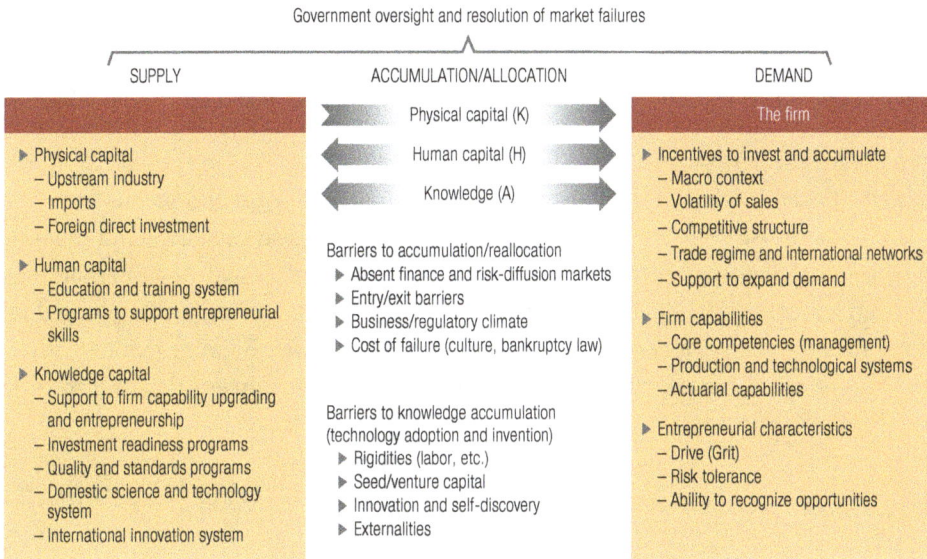

Government oversight and resolution of market failures

SUPPLY	ACCUMULATION/ALLOCATION	DEMAND
	Physical capital (K)	The firm
	Human capital (H)	
	Knowledge (A)	
▶ Physical capital – Upstream industry – Imports – Foreign direct investment		▶ Incentives to invest and accumulate – Macro context – Volatility of sales – Competitive structure – Trade regime and international networks – Support to expand demand
▶ Human capital – Education and training system – Programs to support entrepreneurial skills	Barriers to accumulation/reallocation ▶ Absent finance and risk-diffusion markets ▶ Entry/exit barriers ▶ Business/regulatory climate ▶ Cost of failure (culture, bankruptcy law)	▶ Firm capabilities – Core competencies (management) – Production and technological systems – Actuarial capabilities
▶ Knowledge capital – Support to firm capability upgrading and entrepreneurship – Investment readiness programs – Quality and standards programs – Domestic science and technology system – International innovation system	Barriers to knowledge accumulation (technology adoption and invention) ▶ Rigidities (labor, etc.) ▶ Seed/venture capital ▶ Innovation and self-discovery ▶ Externalities	▶ Entrepreneurial characteristics – Drive (Grit) – Risk tolerance – Ability to recognize opportunities

matching, and informational transaction costs; the establishment of domestic or international commercial networks; or even procurement policies are also included here.

The second set of variables captures firm capabilities: the core managerial competencies, production systems, and higher-end capabilities for technological development or absorption and innovation that enable a firm to recognize an opportunity and mobilize itself to take advantage of it. Of particular salience is what chapter 4 calls actuarial capabilities, the ability to quantify and manage the risk intrinsic to any project. As discussed throughout the volume, development is, by nature, a process of placing a series of bets on opportunities with uncertain returns. Entrepreneurs need to develop the capabilities to quantify and manage the associated risk.

The third set of variables are those characteristics discussed in chapter 4 that relate to the process of entrepreneurship: drive or grit, risk tolerance, and openness to recognizing new opportunities.

There are clear interactions between the three sets of variables. As chapter 2 documents, the ability to participate in a large international market increases the likely benefits of upgrading and innovating and informs about entrepreneurial opportunities, while better capabilities permit established and new firms to take advantage of these markets. Higher macro volatility will lead to less firm entry and upgrading, while low growth may lead governments to experiment with unsustainable macro policies.

On the supply side are all the sources of knowledge that support firm demand. On the physical capital side are efficient domestic industries and easy access to imported intermediate goods. On the human capital side is the entire set of institutions ranging from primary school to technical institutes to universities, as well as whatever programs can teach the skills that feed into higher worker, managerial, and entrepreneurial efficacy.

The second set are institutions that support firms, including the kinds of productivity and quality extension services found around the world, services to disseminate new technologies or best practices, and higher-end consulting services in specialized topics as well as more advanced skills for risk evaluation. The science and technology and quality systems (see box 5.2) specifically facilitate technological transfer, adapt existing knowledge, or generate new knowledge for the use of firms. Finally, the international innovation system generates most new knowledge; therefore, being firmly plugged in along manifold dimensions is key for technological transfer. Because many of these institutions are nonmarket (government research institutes, universities, and so on),

---

BOX 5.2

The Role of a Modern and Efficient Quality Infrastructure Ecosystem in Enhancing Competitiveness and Increasing Productivity

Over the long run, raising product quality may increase a firm's profitability and its demand for better skilled workers. Hence quality-upgrading programs have been commonplace in advanced economies such as the United States and Japan. Furthermore, as countries develop or become more integrated with the international market, firms that serve consumers are looking for a higher quality of goods and services. At a very practical level, a firm's ability to demonstrate quality and safety of goods and services, and to comply with international standards, is often necessary to enter desirable export markets. Demonstrating such compliance requires a sound quality infrastructure (QI) ecosystem.

This system comprises the organizations (public and private) together with the policies, relevant legal and regulatory framework, and practices needed to support and enhance the quality, safety, and environmental soundness of goods, services, and processes. It relies on scientific measurement (metrology), standardization, accreditation, and conformity assessment.

For *governments*, a QI ecosystem serves as a mechanism for supporting relevant trade and industrial policies and for ensuring enforcement of mandatory technical regulations. A recent study from the United Kingdom argues that more than €6.1 billion of U.K. exports per year can be attributed to meeting standards (Hogan, Sheehny, and Jayasuriya 2015). For *businesses*, a modern and efficient QI ecosystem helps firms adopt new technologies and innovation in their production processes. A survey of British companies found that more than 60 percent of product and process innovators used standards as a source of information for innovation, while 37.4 percent of the productivity growth can also be attributed to use of standards. For *consumers*, a QI ecosystem ensures public health and safety and environmental and consumer protection. Technical regulations play an important role in this regard, together with effective enforcement mechanisms such as market surveillance. These mechanisms ensure that fraudulent and counterfeit products are not traded in the marketplace.

The World Bank Group and the National Metrology Institute of Germany have partnered to develop the *first comprehensive QI diagnostic and reform toolkit* (World Bank, forthcoming). It is designed to help development partners and country governments analyze the QI ecosystem and

(Box continues on the following page.)

The Role of a Modern and Efficient Quality Infrastructure Ecosystem in Enhancing Competitiveness and Increasing Productivity *(continued)*

put together a coherent offering to support QI reforms and capacity development. The focus of such reforms could be any one or a combination of the following:

- Improve the legal and institutional framework for efficient and effective QI
- Enhance trade opportunities by removing unnecessary nontariff barriers and technical barriers to trade through harmonization of technical regulations and mutual recognition of conformity assessments
- Better integrate into global value chains
- Enhance the overall quality of products and services
- Encourage innovative products to enter high value added markets
- Increase productivity and efficient use of scarce resources
- Provide for better consumer protection

The analysis of QI ecosystems is done across four pillars: (1) legal and institutional framework, (2) administration and infrastructure, (3) service delivery and technical competency, and (4) external relations and recognition. Each pillar scores the level of QI development on a number of relevant indicators. The toolkit is an important analytical tool that not only identifies gaps in national QI systems but facilitates benchmarking to the best international practices. It also complements firm-level analyses of productivity and analysis of trade dynamics to identify constraints and identify opportunities to increase the export competitiveness of firms.

the question about what mechanisms and incentives link them to one another is prominent in the National Innovation System literature.[7]

The upper part of the center panel of figure 5.2 captures barriers to accumulation of all factors: absent finance and risk mitigation markets, entry and exit barriers, poor regulatory measures, and for start-ups, the cost of failure and the burden of bankruptcy, as discussed in chapter 4. It is essential to make the point, highlighted in chapter 2, that all types of barriers to accumulation and reallocation affect within-firm upgrading and innovation as well: first, because physical and human capital are complements to knowledge; and second, because the accumulation of knowledge capital is subject to all the same accumulation barriers as physical capital (capital markets, business climate, ability to diversify risk, and so on).

Clearly, innovation-specific issues are still important, and they are captured in the next group down. For instance, there may be an absence of seed or venture capital that would enable new innovative start-ups to emerge and existing firms to place new innovative bets. In addition, there may be specific restrictions on the workforce restructuring required for the adoption of new technologies (see Levy 2018 for Mexico). Finally, there are all the standard information-related market failures discussed earlier: those related to the appropriation of knowledge that have given rise to R&D subsidies and tax incentives and to intellectual property rights systems.

Obviously, this figure and discussion merely sketch the interactions that theory and the empirics suggest are potentially important to increasing productivity. Furthermore the importance or configuration may vary across sectors and some types of firms, such as microenterprises, which have little interaction within this formal system at all (see box 5.3). However, the challenge for an individual country, as outlined in the introduction, is to identify where the most binding distortions or constraints lie. The role for government is discussed next.

Government Productivity and Policy Making

As shown at the top of figure 5.2, government has a role in overseeing the National Productivity System (NPS) and resolving a broad set of potential market failures or distortions. Like firms, government makes policy under uncertainty: in this case, about which market failures are really the most critical to redress or which distortions to reduce, and what the likely impact of any corresponding policy will be. Also, like firms, governments and government agencies differ in their productivity and quality of output. This "output" can be measured along at least four dimensions: (1) rationale and design of policy, (2) efficacy of implementation, (3) coherence of policies across the actors in the NPS, and (4) policy consistency and predictability over time.[8]

Chapter 2 establishes that firms in poorer countries tend to have lower efficiency and produce lower-quality products, both arising from low investments in firm capabilities and innovation. Figure 5.3 confirms that, unsurprisingly, the same is true of public organizations as well. The measure of *bureaucratic effectiveness* in the figure captures perceptions of the quality of public services, the quality of the civil service and the degree of its independence from political pressures, the quality of policy formulation and implementation, and the credibility of the government's commitment to such policies. As shown in figure 5.3, bureaucratic effectiveness declines with GDP.

Hence governance capabilities diminish with distance from the frontier precisely as the number of missing markets and market failures become larger.[9] Thus, on the one hand, given finite resources, including the government's attention span (or bandwidth) and capacity, governments need to identify some rough ranking of the policy space— based on the likelihood that a distortion or market failure is important and the probability that it can be redressed successfully—to prioritize productivity policies. On the other hand, increasingly the productivity of government allows government both to take on more tasks and to do them better and in more coordinated ways and thus becomes a critical element of the productivity agenda. This chapter does not go into detail on the vast topic of governance reform: a substantial literature exists, and ongoing work by the World Bank Bureaucracy Lab and others lays out the contours of the current debates. But several themes emerging from the analysis of the private sector are salient for the public sector, as well.

BOX 5.3

How Do Microenterprises and Informal Firms Unplugged from the National Productivity System Affect Overall Productivity?

In many low-income countries, self-employment can reach 80 percent of the workforce. This percentage decreases linearly with development. The self-employed and microenterprises that employ a handful of additional workers are usually of low productivity, are not covered by labor protections, lack access to finance, and are disconnected from large firms. They are unplugged from the National Productivity System. How do we think about their impact on overall productivity?

Barriers to reallocation. One view is that distortions are preventing the transfer of these workers and associated capital to more productive, larger firms. Levy (2018), for instance, argues that in Mexico, the fact that large firms need to pay health insurance, taxes, and the like offers an implicit subsidy to microenterprises and leads to an excessive investment in low-productivity projects. Relatedly, very high minimum wages may prevent workers from transiting to more productive sectors. This is probably an overstatement. Falco et al. (2015) and Perry et al. (2007) note that in Brazil, Ghana, and Mexico, self-employment is for the most part a choice—often an option out of formal employment—not a survival modality. Even without segmented labor markets, however, the distortions highlighted by Levy can lead to significant misallocation, even if workers consider themselves indifferent between the two sectors. Hence, designing social protection legislation that is not de facto a subsidy to less productive firms becomes an important productivity policy.

Barriers to within-firm growth. Firms not registered with authorities often lack access to capital, risk-mitigating mechanisms, or new technology. Hence policies to facilitate formalization are often considered a key to productivity growth within the sector. It is important, however, to also think of formalization as a choice variable and that firms with little desire to expand may not see the benefits of interaction with government institutions.

Put differently, low modern sector productivity combined with a large mass of poorly educated workers makes the opportunity cost for very poor entrepreneurs very low: they will not grow, no matter how much access to finance they have. This said, recent randomized control trials (Bruhn, Karlan, and Schoar 2018; Anderson, Chandy, and Zia 2017; Brooks, Donovan, and Johnson 2017; McKenzie and Puerto 2017) suggest that microentrepreneurs often do have the potential to improve their managerial quality and strengthen performance and hence raise the incomes of the generally poorer workers. Over the long run, however, it is unlikely that many Steve Jobs or Bill Gates will emerge from a sector of extremely poorly educated workers.

In the end, it is not possible to say whether the association with high employment shares of microenterprises is a cause or merely a result of low national incomes. However, research to date suggests that policy proceed on three fronts:

1. Improve the productivity in the modern sector that is the focus of this volume, raising the opportunity cost of opening or continuing low-productivity microenterprises
2. Eliminate the implicit subsidies toward unproductive firms in often poorly designed social legislation and barriers to worker mobility (such as minimum wages)
3. Improve the quality of entrepreneurship and facilitate access of microenterprises to the formal National Productivity System

FIGURE 5.3 **More Developed Countries Have More Effective Bureaucracies**

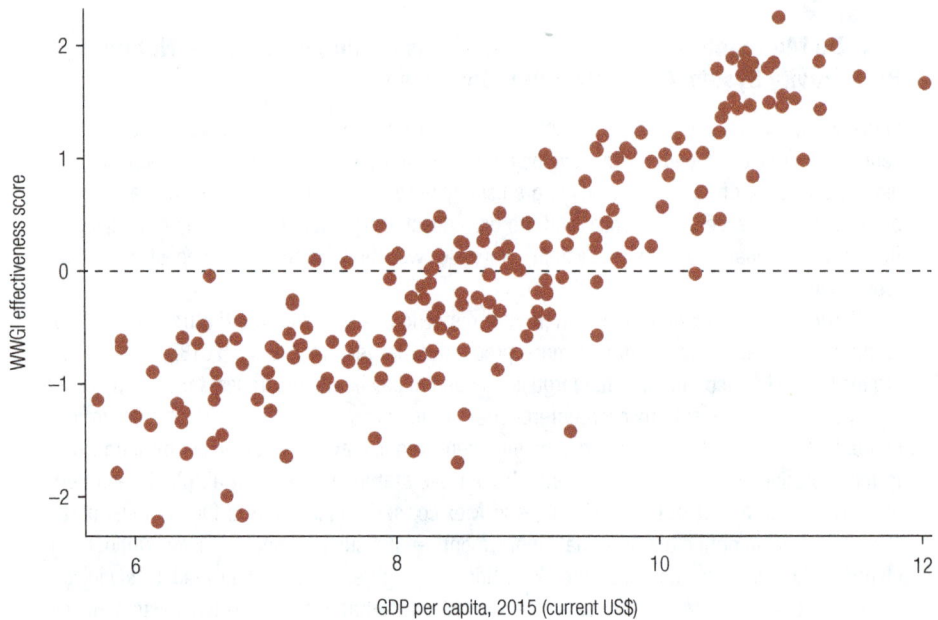

Source: World Bank 2017.

Note: WWGI = World Bank Worldwide Governance Indicators.

1. Identifying, Designing, and Implementing Policies: The Importance of Second-
   Wave Analysis

The limited productivity of the public sector dictates improving the ability of governments to identify truly critical failures in the NPS and then design and implement feasible
policies to remedy them. In approaching this, policy makers need to quantify the importance of a given market failure or distortion and weigh it against others.[10] The second-
wave analysis discussed in this volume, on the one hand, has increased the uncertainty
around some of the impacts of some traditionally recommended policies and made the
analysis to identify critical policy areas more demanding. For instance, reliable inferences
on the impact of reforms requires that we have reliable prices at the firm level, and that
we are able to discuss the market structure that reforms will work within. On the other
hand, second-wave analysis has opened the black box of firm performance: total factor
productivity. It has also expanded the menu of policy options—not only to policies dealing with efficiency, but also to policies related to quality and demand, and necessary com-
binations (such as trade reform coupled with access to finance and capability upgrading).
As this volume explains, this analysis requires a "second generation" of more detailed
firm-level data on prices, marginal costs, intangible assets, quality, and management.
Hence an effort at the global and country levels to collect such data is necessary.

Such analytical work benefits from other complementary sources of information
but cannot be substituted for it. For instance, discussions with entrepreneurs help

Productivity Revisited

suggest areas for investigation, validate findings, and give them context,[11] although this source of information is not without caveats. We know that firms and industries with weak management often don't know what they don't know and hence will offer incorrect self-diagnostics. Industry associations may not be widespread enough to distill quality information in a representative way. Finally, large business associations may be involved in quasi-corporatist relationships with government in which representatives may be closely linked to political parties or families, for example, and their combined objective may not necessarily be the growth rate of the economy. In this case, concrete evidence from solid evaluations helps: When reforms addressing market failures are presented as "good things to do" because they are "removing inefficiencies," governments often resist—partly because they are not sure of the potential benefits of implementing politically sensitive reforms. But when presented with hard evidence of concrete benefits in terms of employment, for example, it is easier to make the case for the reforms (Devarajan 2012).

2. Strengthening Executive Capability

As with capability building in the private sector, there are long-standing efforts to increase executive capabilities through traditional methods, such as personnel policies that attract the right talent, competitive salaries to retain that talent, promotion policies that reward performance and technical skills, and good training programs (IDB 2014). Here again, this volume does not summarize the emerging literature, but draws a few parallels to the firm literature discussed in this and other chapters.

First, output quality depends on inputs and, as shown in chapter 2, better inputs tend to cost more. A randomized control trial by Dal Bó, Finan, and Rossi (2013) finds that for Mexico's public sector, higher wages attract not just more able workers but also those who report having greater motivation for public service. This last characteristic echoes the research on the role of psychological characteristics in entrepreneurship, and expands the discussion of what makes government functionaries effective and optimizes the design of incentives. As Dal Bó, Finan, and Rossi (2013) note, for instance, because markets are not used to value outputs in the public sector, it is difficult to price outputs, and hence financial remuneration such as bonuses may not work. Consistent with their focus on public service–mindedness, Besley and Ghatak (2018), moving beyond a narrow notion of *homo economicus*, argue for better understanding how functionaries derive their status and self-worth. They note that there is potential for incorporating the pursuit of nonpecuniary goals in the make-up of incentives, talent selection, and organization design. One possibility is to put decision making in the hands of those who are most motivated to behave honestly and help beneficiaries of those services. Consistent with this, Rasul and Rogger (2018) in Nigeria show that when management practices are more geared toward autonomy, project completion and quality improve and agency problems are diminished.

3. Developing Experimental Governments

As with the rest of society, in the absence of all the desired information on diagnostics and policies, governments must also become more experimental in searching for the appropriate solutions. Continuous well-designed evaluation of implemented policies, both as rapid follow-up and sophisticated program evaluation, should be a central feature of every relevant government strategy to deal with a problem, because it both reveals information on what interventions work and develops a performance and accountability mindset.

Such experimentation requires nimbleness in adjusting to lessons learned and flexibility in measuring performance, including a tolerance for failure. Policies to support start-ups, for instance, will necessarily involve many "failed experiments." However, the need for governments to take risks and learn from mistakes runs immediately into programs to reduce corruption: it is often difficult to distinguish between a functionary who placed a reasonable bet and lost versus one who is incompetent or corrupt. Hence, like the firms in chapter 2 who slowed their adjustments to shocks or investments as they faced more sales uncertainty, the frequent combination of unclearly defined public sector rules and draconian punishments can lead to paralysis where, far from taking risks, functionaries do not want to be responsible for anything. As with changing social attitudes toward failure and bankruptcy laws, reducing penalties for taking informed risks is necessary. Khemani et al. (2016), in *Making Politics Work for Development: Harnessing Transparency and Citizen Engagement,* focus on two forces—citizen engagement and transparency—as strategies to reduce corruption that are less likely to create such paralysis.

On the other side of the table, experimentation also needs to be balanced against the fourth dimension of quality government: the consistency of policy across time that firms face. Frequent policy reversals or priority changes with alternations of administrations add to firm uncertainty about the operational environment. Box 5.4 discusses how regulatory uncertainty can depress investment and productivity growth and how developing a well-designed regulatory system can reduce it.

Both consistency over time and the third dimension—coherence of policies across the NPS—can be partly mitigated by overarching productivity councils that span elected administrations, have legitimacy and weight within the public debate, and oversee the overall functioning of the various parts of the system (see box 5.5). Many areas of government are directly or indirectly involved in the design and execution of policies to promote productivity. Trade tribunals, competition authorities, and individual bureaus inside finance ministries and different line ministries (education, labor, agriculture, trade), for example, are incidentally or directly engaged in crafting policies to promote productivity. However, the potential of these policies to translate into productivity growth is diminished by the lack of coordination between different government agencies, which may have conflicting mandates and policy goals. Not only does each

Regulatory Uncertainty: A Barrier to Productivity Growth

As noted in chapters 1 and 2, the uncertainty firms face impedes investment and productivity growth, as well as how quickly they adjust to shocks. Research has recognized that increased risk arising from regulatory uncertainty can depress investment (World Bank 2018). Regulatory uncertainty can arise from unclear or inconsistent regulations; poor delivery of what could be robust regulations, including discretionary behavior by various players along the regulatory value chain; or both.

A good regulatory management and governance system—sometimes referred to as *good regulatory practices*—is critical for regulatory efficiency and predictability. In addition to good-quality regulations, this includes high-quality and effective regulatory institutions, timely public consultation, systematic assessment of impacts of new regulation, and regular "fit-for-purpose" checks of the regulatory stock, leading to reduced perceptions of risk, sustainable investments, and growth. The recent World Bank *Global Investment Competitiveness Report, 2017–2018* (World Bank 2018), which surveyed executives in nearly 750 companies, found that the "legal and regulatory environment" was the second most important consideration of senior executives when making investment decisions, superseded only by "political stability and security." They also identified regulatory uncertainty as the second most important constraint to investment and growth.

Good regulatory practices are complementary to regulatory efficiency reforms. Research has found that countries with relatively good regulatory governance practices stand to gain more from efforts to streamline regulations and procedures affecting business than countries that embark only on reductions of regulatory costs and procedures. Scores on the World Bank's Global Indicators for Regulatory Governance also show strong correlations between regulatory governance and many indexes for lower corruption and stronger rule of law.

The World Bank Group has, in recent years, developed an approach to improving regulatory management and governance and increasing regulatory predictability. A strong focus on institutions and regulatory delivery, user engagement and feedback, and strong interagency coordination are increasingly providing some evidence that regulatory predictability can reduce the perception of risk for investors and enhance innovation and investment.

bureau cater to a distinct constituency, but the fragmentation creates information silos within each government area, limiting the quality and potential economic gains of a productivity-enhancing policy. For example, a regulatory overhaul in a particular sector might not serve to increase productivity if the main productivity bottleneck for firms is access to credit.

Increasingly, governments across both emerging market and advanced economies are addressing these problems through innovative institutional frameworks to promote productivity. Although the shape of such institutions might vary depending on existing institutional arrangements, the most effective institutions share a number of necessary characteristics, including "independent governance, transparent processes, solid research capacity, an economy-wide frame of reference and linkages to policy-making mechanisms within government" (Banks 2015, 24). At a

Examples of National Productivity Agencies: Ensuring Coherence across the National Productivity System

National productivity agencies require technical expertise, a comprehensive overview of the system (policy reach), and transparency to be effective. Examples of special advisory councils are the Australian Productivity Commission, created in 1998; the New Zealand Productivity Commission, created in 2010, based on the Australian model; and the Mexican National Productivity Commission (CNP), created in 2013.

The Australian Productivity Commission is housed in the Treasury. Among its core functions are the preparation of studies and public inquiries at all levels of government and across all economic sectors, performance monitoring of other government bodies, annual reporting and research on productivity, and the assessment of competitive neutrality complaints (Australian Government Productivity Commission 2014). Overall, the commission has been prized for its "independence, transparency, and community-wide perspective" (Dougherty 2015, 33).

In contrast to the Australian model—a purely governmental advisory council—the Mexican CNP is a tripartite body chaired by the Ministry of Finance that comprises other relevant ministries and representatives of business associations, labor unions, universities, and technical training institutions (Mexico, Secretaría de Hacienda y Crédito Público 2015). The CNP is an advisory body to the executive (who is also the commission's honorary president) in matters related to economic growth and productivity. The economy-wide mandate of the CNP is "to generate structural change in the economy, expanding the most productive sectors and transforming traditional sectors" through the implementation of sector-specific productivity policies (López-Córdova and Rebolledo Márquez Padilla 2016). The Secretariat of the CNP, housed in the Ministry of Finance, provides technical expertise and coordination support for the design and implementation of the commission's long-term policies. Tripartite bodies such as the Mexican CNP are exceptionally well suited to "build awareness of current policy problems among key stakeholders and the potential gains from change" (Banks 2015, 13).

Source: López-Córdova and Soria 2018.

minimum, pro-productivity institutions should have the technical capacity to produce high-quality information and analysis, and a channel to connect this information to the policy-making process (Banks 2015). Existing institutions—such as think tanks, departmental bureaus, and research units inside government agencies—meet one or more of these characteristics to varying degrees. More recently, governments have created institutional arrangements expressly designed to promote productivity policies, often in the form of advisory councils or ad hoc task forces (Banks 2015) (see box 5.5).

In addition, productivity systems often show evidence of undisciplined experimentation over many years that leads to fragmentation of programs and duplication of mandates in many different ministries without evaluation of the efficacy of the programs or location within the system. In the realm of innovation policy, the Public

Expenditure Reviews (PERs) for Science, Technology, and Innovation (STI) offer a first step by generating a map of government programs and documenting the flow of resources (Correa 2014). These can be enhanced to take a broader view of government productivity programs that can incorporate all three margins of productivity growth. The PERs for STI already cover much of the territory of within-firm upgrading (innovation) and start-ups. A Productivity Public Expenditure Review (P-PER) would more explicitly integrate the regulatory angle: Not only would governments understand what resources are being spent on, for instance, start-ups, but they could also see what regulatory barriers to experimentation, or excessive costs of failure, are working at cross-purposes. Not only would they see the implicit costs of tax write-offs or subsidies for R&D in existing firms, but they could map the industry and competitive structure that those firms face, or the degree of regulatory uncertainty in the system. Annex 5A explores the potential for P-PERs in more detail.

4. Making Do with Limited Information: Integrating Industrial Policy in Productivity Policy

Industry-specific externalities feature prominently in the growth and trade literatures. Various studies suggest that positive externalities lead productivity to rise with the size of the industry. They may arise for numerous reasons—local industry-level knowledge spillovers, input-output links, and labor pooling, for instance—but they are not captured by the market price of a good, which is therefore underproduced. Historically, these externalities have been thought to justify quite large interventions aimed at removing trade distortions, and to justify subsidizing and directing credit. Often such "vertical policies" are dismissed on the grounds that government will implement them badly. However, government failures also affect more "horizontal" policies—witness dysfunctional public education systems and corruption in infrastructure provision around the world—yet governments continue to enter these areas.

The real problem is that such industry-related externalities have proved extremely difficult to document and quantify, let alone permit a ranking of goods by their potential for productivity growth.[12] The persistent empirical gaps on these points has led the literature to develop shortcuts to identifying potentially good sectors. For instance, natural resources are thought to have negative growth externalities; high technology goods are thought to have more knowledge spillovers; "complex" products are thought to stimulate capabilities that allow moving to more sophisticated industries—yet the evidence on these assumptions is mixed at best (see Maloney and Nayyar, forthcoming, for details; see also box 5.6).

However, the same overall questions laid out at the beginning of the chapter apply here: Should policy focus on this market failure, or are there other distortions, market failures, or considerations that are more important? The evidence presented in chapter 2 suggests there may well be. First, even if we knew for sure that on average a particular good offered important positive externalities, the tremendous heterogeneity in the way in which even very narrowly defined goods are produced across countries, as documented in chapter 2, should give policy makers pause. The vast differences in productivity and quality reflect differences in the enabling environment, access to inputs, managerial capabilities, design capacity, human resource organization, and marketing—and may correspondingly lead to very different levels of spillovers to the rest of the economy.[13] This supports concerns that expanding a sector with potential positive externalities does not necessarily imply that they automatically will occur (see Baldwin 1969; Rodriguez Clare 2007; and Lederman and Maloney 2012). Box 5.6 argues that presumably low-externality industries, such as mining, helped lay the foundation for industrialization in the United States and Japan, while high-tech industries in Mexico have not led to growth miracles.

These examples raise the fundamental question of whether the heterogeneity in productivity and quality within products swamps any differences between goods in

---

BOX 5.6

Industrial or Productivity Policies? Natural Resource Blessings and High-Tech Disappointments

Particular goods are often thought to have externalities, such as learning spillovers, that enhance overall productivity beyond what their price would reflect and justify industry-specific support in what can be called "industrial policies." However, the vast heterogeneity of development experiences around specific goods suggests that the focus should instead be on productivity policies of the kinds described in this volume. To cite two examples:

Extractive natural resource industries are often thought of as having few or even negative externalities, yet, at the beginning of the twentieth century, copper mining in the United States led to a knowledge network in chemistry and metallurgy that laid the foundations for subsequent diversification and industrialization. Japan was the second largest exporter of copper in the mid-nineteenth century, and two of the six dominant industrial conglomerates (*zaibatsu*)—Furukawa and Sumitomo—started as copper extraction companies before becoming prominent in computers (Fujitsu) and manufacturing and banking (Sumitomo). At the same time, the largest exporter of copper, Chile, saw its industry nearly die by 1900, as was the case with indigenous mining throughout Latin America. Copper is a highly homogeneous product, yet the development outcomes were vastly different.

Similarly, electronics are thought to have strong learning externalities. Both Mexico and the Republic of Korea began assembling electronics in the early 1980s, yet only Korea has produced a truly indigenous electronic device in the Galaxy and there is no Mexican Samsung.

Both examples suggest the importance of a deliberate focus on raising firm and sectoral productivity and quality performance in any sector, and that this focus on the "how" may be more important than the "what" that is produced.

Source: Lederman and Maloney 2012.

Productivity Revisited

terms of development impact: that is, whether *how* a good is produced is potentially more important than *what* is produced (see Lederman and Maloney 2012). This volume strongly suggests that the overall framework for productivity growth is a necessary complement to sectoral policies: attention probably should be focused more on the market failures and distortions attending more horizontal considerations such as education, managerial quality, institutions, or entrepreneurship, the overall innovation system, and the competitive environment than the production basket itself.

Concluding Remarks

Productivity has again moved to center stage in the debates surrounding two growth-related puzzles: the slowdown in global economic dynamism in the midst of spectacular technological advances and the frustratingly slow catch-up of developing countries to the technological frontier. The tremendous effort behind recent analytical advances dedicated to understanding these puzzles and raising productivity across the globe suggests that Ibn Khaldun's early appreciation of productivity's centrality to societal progress is widely shared. And in the same way that his *Muquddimah* shifted paradigms of social organization in its time, the literature grouped here as "second wave" has importantly shifted the approach to pivotal productivity issues. This volume pulls together these insights and, using new data sets from multiple countries, extends the analysis and grounds it in the developing-country reality.

This last chapter has attempted to summarize some of the lessons emerging from these new approaches and offer guidance for policy. In the first instance, from a purely empirical point of view, it flags that many existing diagnostics and analytical approaches need to be reconsidered. This includes, in particular, using dispersion as a measure of economic distortions, but extends to a long list of earlier studies exploring the impact of specific interventions on productivity. Central to the latter point is the need to treat market power and productivity analysis in an integrated framework. Furthermore, recent work suggests that exploring the heterogeneity across entrepreneurs and managers is essential to gaining a better understanding of both the determinants of entry of new firms and upgrading among incumbents.

The chapter then stresses the need to approach productivity policy in an integrated way that encompasses all three margins of productivity: the between margin (or reallocation margin), the within margin (or firm-upgrading margin), and the selection margin (or the entry and exit margin). Although the evidence suggests a rebalancing away from the influential focus on static reallocation toward policies to improve within-firm performance, the volume also stresses how the drivers of the individual margins affect the other two in a dynamic sense. Barriers to reallocation may provide a disincentive for firms to upgrade or new entrepreneurs to enter. And symmetrically, factors restricting entry, such as inadequate human capital as broadly construed here, will blunt the force for reallocation over the long run. In looking for these drivers, the volume stresses the need to focus both on the operating environment and on human capital as critical and complementary.

Lifting the hood on the firm, chapter 2 stresses that standard measures of total factor productivity conflate several factors—efficiency, quality, and market power—but that, in fact, growth and jobs policies are interested in more than just efficiency. The average quality of goods rises with development, reflecting the accumulation of many of the same firm capabilities driving efficiency, but also, like efficiency, boosting value added and generating better-quality jobs. Furthermore, for several countries, the analysis confirms that much of firm growth is, in fact, driven by expanding demand rather than increased efficiency. Again, many policies that are important for promoting efficiency remain relevant, but the analysis suggests a shift toward policies focusing on establishment of networks, matching suppliers and clients, connecting firms to global value chains to expand demand, enlarging a firm's customer base by eliminating search and transaction costs, and matching frictions through the development of digital platforms and connections and business skills focused on developing a client base.

Finally, increasing productivity requires the development of experimental societies. Fundamentally, entrepreneurship is a process of experimentation: growth occurs by entrepreneurs placing informed bets. Experimental societies require both an operating environment that encourages and facilitates the mitigation of risk and entrepreneurs who are capable of quantifying and managing it. It also requires a greater tolerance of setbacks and failure, and an understanding that dispersion in total factor productivity measures will be greater, not less, given that the outcomes of investments in efficiency and quality are, by nature, uncertain. The lack of such experimental arrangements is one answer to the *entrepreneurial paradox*: that despite the huge potential gains to be reaped from moving to the technology levels of advanced economies, relatively few entrepreneurs emerge in follower countries who can take advantage of such opportunities.

Together, these various lessons can be broadly captured in the notion of a National Productivity System that highlights the complementarity of a variety of types of human capital and a broad range of critical markets and elements in the operating system. Government also has a role to play in overseeing the overall system, remedying market failures, and removing distortions. Hence, the productivity of government in designing well-founded, well-executed, coherent, and persistent policies becomes a central consideration in overall productivity policy. As with firms, developing-country governments have more limited capabilities at the same time that the market failures and distortions they face are more acute; hence, getting inference right is critical to prioritizing productivity policies. The lessons of second-wave analysis, and a more experimental approach on the part of government, thus become critical elements in this process.

This said, though the volume has sought to distill some key emerging messages, to date, the impact of the new analysis has been less to definitively answer central questions in productivity growth than to reopen many debates and set out the broad outlines of this ambitious analytical and policy agenda going forward. Settling those debates will require greater investment in industrial surveys that collect not only firm-level prices, but also measures of quality, marginal costs, investments in intangible assets, and technology and managerial capabilities across all sectors of the economy, including services. Similarly, the incipient efforts to understand the drivers of productive entrepreneurship will need to be strengthened.

"The Phenomenon of Weightlessness," as depicted by Remedios Varo on the front cover, metaphorically captures the aspirations of this volume. Mankind is by nature bound by gravity and constrained by resources. The miracle of productivity growth is that over two centuries, it has helped lift welfare to levels unimaginable to our ancestors, using the same resources available to them. Continuing this trend is vital in the final push to end global poverty and create fulfilling and challenging jobs for all.

Annex 5A. Policy Coherence and Effectiveness Supporting Productivity Growth: A Proposal for World Bank Productivity Public Expenditure Reviews

Managing the breadth and complexities of policies and regulations with the goal of increasing productivity demands strong processes and capabilities in government. Three areas are key: a good combination of policies to provide incentives for and support productivity growth and coordination across agencies and ministries, effective policies that use robust policy design and implementation, and smart regulatory reform.

The World Bank could address these issues with Productivity Public Expenditure Reviews (P-PERs). Such reviews would attempt to identify the distortions and regulations that are harmful to productivity growth and help countries improve the quality and composition of existing productivity policies. The methodology would build on the existing Public Expenditure Review (PER) on Science, Technology, and Innovation (STI)—an integrated and holistic evaluation of STI policies by the World Bank—and would expand it to cover elements that are specific to productivity policies. The proposed methodology is based on analyzing different stages of the logical framework of public policies: the quality of the policy inputs, the quality of design and implementation, and the efficiency and effectiveness in achieving the policy goals. The proposed country-level P-PER would proceed in five stages:

1. *Diagnostic phase.* This stage would include understanding the evolution of productivity over time, the sources of productivity growth, and the extent of

competition in good markets and misallocation in factor markets in the country. It would involve analytical work to identify the main policy priorities or demand for productivity policies.

2. *General evaluation of the quality and coherence of the policy mix.* Based on the findings of the diagnostic phase and analysis of the existing institutional framework, this stage would evaluate whether existing policies are oriented toward supporting productivity policies, identifying unnecessary overlaps, and finding gaps in terms of public support and inconsistencies in the objective of productivity growth. This stage would examine the portfolio of policies to support the private sector, including innovation policies, export policies, and sector policies. It would assess the coherence of these policies with the priorities identified in stage 1, as well as with general productivity objectives.

3. *Evaluation of the quality of design, implementation, and governance (functional analysis) of existing instruments based on good practices.* This stage would evaluate whether policy design is based on addressing documented market failures, whether the proposed solutions instruments are designed using appropriate policy instruments, and whether solid monitoring and evaluation frameworks are in place. It would also evaluate whether implementation used good management practices in the public sector. It would assess the extent of effective coordination mechanisms in implementing such policies, given the difficulties in coordinating effective policies and regulatory reform.

4. *Evaluation of the efficiency of existing instruments.* This stage would examine the ability of existing instruments to produce the expected outputs with reasonable levels of resources and seek to understand the quality of services that beneficiaries of public policies are receiving.

5. *Evaluation of overall execution of system.* This final stage would focus on documenting the impact of existing policies that support the productive sector in achieving productivity objectives.

In addition to helping build the necessary capabilities for effective policy implementation, the P-PER would prioritize measures to support productivity policies and identify priority areas for regulatory reform. The analysis would also offer suggestions on how to improve coordination in productivity policies.[14]

Notes

1. For example, Adamopoulos et al. (2017) argue that distortionary policies in Chinese agriculture not only lead to misallocation, but also adversely affect the selection of farmers and productive units.

2. See http://live.worldbank.org/building-human-capital.

3. Sutton (1998) terms both types of investment "R&D" (research and development). On the management side, based on the experience of large textile firms in India, Bloom et al. (2013) argue

that investments in managerial upgrading could pay for themselves in a year, yet firms do not undertake them. Bruhn, Karlan, and Schoar (2013) find the same for smaller firms in Mexico. As McKenzie and Woodruff (2013) argue, whether this is a question of information asymmetries, imperfect credit markets, or missing institutions to diversify risk is not clear.

4. Financial market failures also curtail incentives to innovate. Frequently, banks do not know the specific default risk of an individual innovator seeking to borrow funds, so they can price a loan based only on the average default risk. As a result, low-risk borrowers face higher interest rates than they would if there were perfect information and may choose not to seek a loan. In addition, banks cannot perfectly monitor the activities of the innovator after the loan has been approved. As a result, an innovator may be tempted to take on a riskier project than the one originally agreed to because in case of success the innovator gets all of the upside, while in case of failure the loss is capped.

5. Chava et al. (2013) find that banking deregulation facilitates greater risk taking and experimentation by small firms.

6. See Cusolito, Dautovic, and McKenzie 2018 for a World Bank example in the western Balkans.

7. For a more detailed discussion of these and relevant policies, see Cirera and Maloney 2017.

8. See Cirera and Maloney 2017 for greater elaboration of these dimensions.

9. This section draws from Maloney and Nayyar, forthcoming.

10. Andrews, Pritchett, and Woolcock (2013, 2017) propose the approach of "Problem-Driven Iterative Adaption," which combines experimentation with solutions to particular problems with iterative feedback, while engaging a broad set of actors to ensure that reforms are viable and relevant.

11. Rodrik (2004), for instance, refers to "public-private coordination councils," which could seek out and gather information on investment ideas, achieve coordination among different state agencies, push for changes in regulation to eliminate unnecessary transaction costs, and generate a package of relevant financial incentives for new activities when needed.

12. This almost agnostic view is supported by Pack and Saagi (2006) and Harrison and Rodriguez-Clare (2010), who review much of the industrial policy literature per se.

13. The problem is compounded by the fact that as production becomes more fragmented and about half of global trade involves trade in intermediate inputs through global value chains, countries trade tasks, not goods. China does not export the high-tech iPhone but in fact exports low- to medium-skill assembly tasks worth 1–2 percent of the value added of the product. In fact, electronics is one of the lowest value-added sectors in China (Koopman, Wang, and Wei 2008), and there are likely fewer knowledge spillovers that would arise from actually designing the iPhone. Hence, while the focus probably should be on externalities pertaining to tasks, the data available are on final goods.

14. The source for this annex is Cirera 2018.

References

Adamopoulos, T., L. Brandt, J. Leight, and D. Restuccia. 2017. "Misallocation, Selection and Productivity: A Quantitative Analysis with Panel Data from China." NBER Working Paper 23039, National Bureau of Economic Research, Cambridge, MA.

Anderson, S. J., R. Chandy, and B. Husnain Zia. 2017. *Pathways to Profits: Identifying Separate Channels of Business Growth through Business Training.* Finance & PSD Impact Evaluation Note No. 41. Washington, DC: World Bank.

Andrews, M., L. Pritchett, and M. Woolcock 2013. "Escaping Capability Traps through Problem Driven Iterative Adaptation (PDIA)." *World Development* 51(C): 234–44.

———. 2017. *Building State Capability: Evidence, Analysis.* Oxford, U.K.: Oxford University Press.

Atkin, D., A. K. Khandelwal, and A. Osman. 2017. "Exporting and Firm Performance: Evidence from a Randomized Experiment." *Quarterly Journal of Economics* 132 (2): 551–615.

Australian Government Productivity Commission. 2014. "A Quick Guide to the Productivity Commission." Australian Government Productivity Commission.

Baldwin. R. E. 1969. "The Case against Infant-Industry Tariff Protection." *Journal of Political Economy* 77 (3): 295–305.

Banks, G. 2015. "Institutions to Promote Pro-productivity Policies: Logic and Lessons." OECD Productivity Working Paper 2015-01, OECD Publishing, Paris.

Bergquist, L. F. 2017. "Pass-Through, Competition, and Entry in Agricultural Markets: Experimental Evidence from Kenya." PEDL Research Paper, Department of Economics, University of California at Berkeley.

Besley, T., and M. Ghatak. 2018. "Solving Agency Problems: Intrinsic Motivation, Incentives, and Productivity." Working paper, London School of Economics.

Bloom, N., B. Eifert, A. Mahajan, D. McKenzie, and J. Roberts. 2013. "Does Management Matter? Evidence from India." *Quarterly Journal of Economics* 128: 1–51.

Brooks, W., K. Donovan, and T. R. Johnson. 2017. "Mentors or Teachers? Microenterprise Training in Kenya." Unpublished, University of Notre Dame.

Bruhn, M., D. Karlan, and A. Schoar. 2013. "The Impact of Consulting Services on Small and Medium Enterprises: Evidence from a Randomized Trial in Mexico." Policy Research Working Paper 6508, World Bank, Washington, DC.

———. 2018. "The Impact of Consulting Services on Small and Medium Enterprises: Evidence from a Randomized Trial in Mexico." *Journal of Political Economy* 126 (2): 635–87.

Busso, M., and S. Galiani. Forthcoming. "The Causal Effect of Competition on Prices and Quality: Evidence from a Field Experiment." *American Economic Journal: Applied Economics.*

Chava, S., A. Oettl, A. Subramanian, and K. Subramanian. 2013. "Banking Deregulation and Innovation." *Journal of Financial Economics* 109 (3): 759–74.

Cirera, X. 2018. "Towards a Productivity Public Expenditure Review." Background paper for *Productivity Revisited,* World Bank, Washington, DC.

Cirera, X., and W. F. Maloney. 2017. *The Innovation Paradox: Developing-Country Capabilities and the Unrealized Promise of Technological Catch-Up.* Washington, DC: World Bank.

Correa, Paulo. 2014. *Public Expenditure Reviews in Science, Technology, and Innovation: A Guidance Note.* Washington, DC: World Bank Group.

Cusolito, A. P., E. Dautovic, and D. McKenzie. 2018. "Can Government Intervention Make Firms More Investment-Ready? A Randomized Experiment in the Western Balkans." Policy Research Working Paper 8541, World Bank, Washington, DC.

Dal Bó, E., F. Finan, and M. A. Rossi. 2013. "Strengthening State Capabilities: The Role of Financial Incentives in the Call to Public Service." *Quarterly Journal of Economics* 128 (3): 1169–218.

De Loecker, J., and J. Eeckhout. 2018. "Global Market Power." Working paper. http://www.janeeckhout .com/wp-content/uploads/Global.pdf.

Devarajan, S. 2012. "In Defense of Industrial Policy." http://blogs.worldbank.org/africacan/in -defense-of-industrial-policy.

Dougherty, S. 2015. "Boosting Growth and Reducing Informality in Mexico." OECD Economics Department Working Paper 1188, OECD Publishing, Paris.

Edquist, C. 2006. "Systems of Innovation: Perspectives and Challenges." In *The Oxford Handbook of Innovation,* edited by J. Fagerberg and D. C. Mowery, 181–208. Oxford, U.K: Oxford University Press.

Falco, P., W. F. Maloney, B. Rijkers, and M. Sarrias. 2015. "Heterogeneity in Subjective Wellbeing: An Application to Occupational Allocation in Africa." *Journal of Economic Behavior and Organization* 111 (March): 137–53.

Freeman, C. 1995. "The 'National System of Innovation' in Historical Perspective." *Cambridge Journal of Economics* 19 (1): 5–24.

Harrison, A., and A. Rodríguez-Clare. 2010. "Trade, Foreign Investment, and Industrial Policy for Developing Countries." In *Handbook of Development Economics*, Vol. 5, edited by D. Rodrik and M. R. Rosenzweig. Amsterdam: Elsevier B.V.

Hausmann, R., and D. Rodrik. 2003. "Economic Development as Self-Discovery." *Journal of Development Economics* 72 (2): 603–33.

Hogan, O., C. Sheehny, and R. Jayasuriya. 2015. *The Economic Contribution of Standards to the UK Economy.* London: Centre for Economics Research and Business Research for the British Standards Institution.

IDB (Inter-American Development Bank). 2014. *Rethinking Productive Development: Sound Policies and Institutions for Economic Transformation.* New York: Palgrave Macmillan.

Khaldun, I. 1377. *The Muqaddimah: An Introduction to History.* Princeton, NJ: Princeton University Press. 2015 edition.

Khemani, S., E. Dal Bó, C. Ferraz, F. Finan, C. Stephenson, A. Odugbemi, D. Thapa, and S. Abrahams. 2016. *Making Politics Work for Development: Harnessing Transparency and Citizen Engagement.* Washington, DC: World Bank.

Koopman, R., Z. Wang, and S. J. Wei. 2008. "How Much of Chinese Exports Is Really Made in China? Assessing Domestic Value-Added When Processing Trade Is Pervasive." NBER Working Paper 14109, National Bureau of Economic Research, Cambridge, MA.

Lederman, D., and W. F. Maloney. 2012. *Does What You Export Matter? In Search of Empirical Guidance for Industrial Policies.* Latin America Development Forum. Washington, DC: World Bank.

Lederman, D., M. Olarreaga, and L. Payton. 2010. "Export Promotion Agencies: What Works and What Doesn't." *Journal of Development Economics* 91 (2): 257–65.

Levy, S. 2018. *Under-rewarded Efforts: The Elusive Quest for Prosperity in Mexico.* Washington, DC: Inter-American Development Bank.

López Córdova, J. E., and J. Rebolledo Márquez Padilla. 2016. "Productivity in Mexico: Trends, Drivers and Institutional Framework." *International Productivity Monitor* 30 (Spring): 28–42.

López Córdova, J. E., and A. Soria. 2018. "Institutional Arrangements to Boost Productivity Growth: An Overview." Background paper for *Productivity Revisited,* World Bank, Washington, DC.

Lundvall, B-Å, ed. 1992. *National Systems of Innovation: Towards a Theory of Innovation and Interactive Learning.* London: Pinter.

Maloney, W. F., and G. Nayyar. Forthcoming. "Industrial Policy, Information, and Government Capacity." *World Bank Research Observer.*

Maloney, W. F., and A. Rodriguez Clare. 2007. "Innovation Shortfalls." *Review of Development Economics* 11 (4): 665–84.

McKenzie, D., and S. Puerto. 2017. "Growing Markets through Business Training for Female Entrepreneurs: A Market-Level Randomized Experiment in Kenya." Policy Research Working Paper 7993, World Bank, Washington, DC.

McKenzie, D., and C. Woodruff. 2013. "What Are We Learning from Business Training and Entrepreneurship Evaluations around the Developing World?" *World Bank Research Observer* 29 (1): 48–82.

McMillan, M. S., and D. Rodrik. 2011. "Globalization, Structural Change and Productivity Growth." NBER Working Paper 17143, National Bureau of Economic Research. Cambridge, MA.

McMillan, M. S., D. Rodrik, and Í. Verduzco-Gallo. 2014. "Globalization, Structural Change, and Productivity Growth, with an Update on Africa." *World Development* 63: 11–32.

Mexico, Secretaría de Hacienda y Crédito Público. 2015. *Comité Nacional de Productividad* (National Productivity Commision). July 2. https://www.gob.mx/productividad/articulos/comite-nacional-de-productividad-cnp?idiom=es.

Nelson, Richard R., ed. 1993. *National Innovation Systems: A Comparative Analysis.* New York: Oxford University Press.

Pack, H., and K. Saggi. 2006. "Is There a Case for Industrial Policy? A Critical Survey." *World Bank Research Observer* 21 (2): 267–97.

Perry, G. E., O. Arias, P. Fajnzylber, W. F. Maloney, A. Mason, and J. Saavedra-Chanduvi. 2007. *Informality: Exit and Exclusion.* World Bank Latin American and Caribbean Studies 40008. Washington, DC: World Bank.

Rasul, I., and D. Rogger. 2018. "Management of Bureaucrats and Public Service Delivery: Evidence from the Nigerian Civil Service." *Economic Journal* 128 (608): 413–46.

Rodríguez-Clare, A. 2007. "Clusters and Comparative Advantage: Implications for Industrial Policy." *Journal of Development Economics* 82 (1): 43–57.

Rodrik, D. 2004. "Industrial Policy for the Twenty-First Century." John F. Kennedy School of Government, Harvard University, Cambridge, MA, September.

Rogerson, R. 2017. "Structural Transformation and Productivity Growth: Cause or Effect?" Background paper for *Productivity Revisited*, World Bank, Washington, DC.

Soete, L., B. Verspagen, and B. T. Weel. 2010. "Systems of Innovation." In *Handbook of the Economics of Innovation*, edited by B. H. Hall and N. Rosenberg, 1159–80. Amsterdam: Elsevier.

Sutton, J. 1998. *Technology and Market Structure.* Cambridge, MA: MIT Press.

World Bank. 2017. "Worldwide Governance Indicators, 2016 Update." World Bank, Washington, DC. http://info.worldbank.org/governance/wgi/#home.

———. 2018. *Global Investment Competitiveness Report, 2017–2018: Foreign Investor Perspectives and Policy Implications.* Washington, DC: World Bank.

———. Forthcoming. *Assuring Quality to Access Global Markets: A Reform Toolkit.* Washington, DC: World Bank.

Appendix A. Measuring the Productivity Residual: From Theory to Measurement

This appendix explores the measurement of productivity.[1] It focuses in particular on the interpretation of the productivity residual and how it relates to underlying components of producer behavior and consumer demand. The appendix first presents a conceptual framework and discusses how this framework can inform policy, before examining the challenges in measurement and estimation. It contrasts the traditional setup, which considers the production of homogeneous products, and the modern view, which allows for meaningful product differentiation.

Conceptual Framework

To understand the potential problems a researcher may face when working with microdata, consider the case in which we have access to producer-level panel data for an industry.[2]

It is common to consider firm performance (π) as the residual in a regression of sales (s) on input expenditures (e). Assume a log-linear relationship and, for simplicity, labor as the only input, so that

$$s = \beta e + \pi, \qquad (A.1)$$

with s, the log of sales, depending on the log of price and quantity of products sold, $s = p + q$, and e, the log of the total wage bill (input expenditure) defined by the sum of log wage and employment, $e = w + l$.

From a production point of view, a standard production function[3] is given by $q = \alpha l + \omega$, with ω capturing productive efficiency. With few exceptions, the existing literature has viewed the sales-generating equation (A.1) as the empirical analog of the production function and interpreted the residual π as a measure of *total factor productivity* (TFP). But this is true only in a very special case: when $\alpha = \beta$ and $\omega = \pi$. In practice, this will only be identical *if* in fact all producers in the industry face the same output price and wage rate. In any other case, of either output price or input price variation, the term *productivity* would be used too loosely (if not incorrectly).

In general, what we have learned is that standard practices lead to residuals that capture output and input prices, in addition to efficiency (ω), leading to

$$\pi = p - \alpha w + \omega. \qquad (A.2)$$

This is precisely why De Loecker and Goldberg (2014) refer to the residual, π, as *firm profitability*, and why it is probably more appropriate to refer to these residuals as a measure of performance.

The distinction between *physical productivity* ω (often called physical TFP, or TFPQ) and *profitability* π (referred to as revenue TFP, or TFPR) is important; the latter depends not only on physical efficiency, but also on prices, which reflect product differentiation and markups in addition to input costs. To draw conclusions as to how a producer reacts to changes in the operating environment, we need to decompose this residual into its components. This is crucial because the exposure to policy change is not expected to affect these aspects in the same way. Nevertheless, the majority of analyses implemented so far have focused on TFPR without considering that whether a policy affects it through changes in prices or in efficiency has vastly different implications, and this holds at both the micro and macro levels.

Policy Relevance of Decomposing Firm Performance

The framework presented above indicates that TFPR consists of two distinct economic variables of interest: physical efficiency and prices, which reflect product differentiation and markups (in addition to costs). These variables turn out to have very distinct time series patterns in the data and more importantly have different economic interpretations.

As noted by De Loecker and Goldberg (2014), distinguishing between profitability and efficiency is important because this allows the researcher to link improvements in firm performance to specific mechanisms through which globalization affects firms. Understanding these mechanisms is important for assessing the welfare and distributional effects of trade openness. For example, a trade liberalization that improves firm performance by inducing improvements in physical efficiency has different implications from a liberalization that makes firms better off by increasing their profits.

So far, the term "productivity" has been used very loosely, with rather large implications for policy recommendations because there is a risk of prescribing misleading solutions when data do not provide the necessary information to properly identify the contribution of supply and demand factors to firms' profitability. In this respect, the recent consensus on price heterogeneity at the firm level requires researchers to be much more cautious about how to interpret productivity, or what is loosely referred to as TFP. The reason is that, although we can correctly infer productivity from aggregate output and input series when appropriately deflated, we cannot follow the same strategy when relying on micro data unless we observe firms' prices. The bottom line is that markups and production costs play a prominent role. Therefore, performance (and not productivity) is a better definition of the residual of a production function using sales and expenditure data. Nonetheless, there are different approaches that can help address, at least partially, some of the main concerns related to production function estimations.

To organize the discussion that follows, we divide this methodological section into two parts. The first part presents different challenges of estimating the production function in a standard framework of production, which considers single-product firms and perfectly competitive input and output markets. Following the evolution of the literature, we will review the most important approaches to solving for the endogeneity problems: instrumental variables, fixed-effects models, and more recent control variable approaches. The second part, in contrast, presents challenges and recent methodological contributions in a more realistic setup, extending the analysis to imperfectly competitive input and output markets and multiproduct firms.

Traditional Framework (Q, X)

Consider the textbook setup in which a single-product firm, denoted by i, produces a homogeneous good using a Cobb-Douglas production technology:

$$Q_{it} = L_{it}^{\beta_L} \, K_{it}^{\beta_K} \, \Omega_{it}.$$

Assume that we observe physical output (Q) produced using observed inputs, labor (L) and capital (K), and (unobserved) productivity, for a panel of firms in a given industry. Furthermore, this standard framework assumes perfectly competitive input markets, yielding common input prices for all relevant factors of production.

In the discussion that follows, we consider Q to be output generated by capital (K) and labor (L). This is of course a stylized description of (any) production technology. Depending on the data set and the industry under study, a different technology can be specified and as such other inputs can be included, typically intermediate inputs, such as energy. The main choice of specification is, however, whether output is recorded as gross output or value added. Recently the literature has started to become more serious about the difference and under which conditions the value-added production function is in fact formally identified. The reduced-form value-added approach first constructs value added by netting intermediate inputs from output (given that both are expressed in the same units—more on this later) and then proceeds to treat it as output. This of course restricts the underlying production function substantially (for instance, it could come from assuming a coefficient of 1 on the intermediate input bundle). In fact, the traditional motivation for doing this is that intermediate inputs are expected to react the most to productivity shocks, and therefore create a clear simultaneity problem and associated bias. Although this observation is correct, the solution to construct value added is not. The only rationale to not consider intermediate inputs in the production function specification is if the underlying technology is Leontief in these intermediate inputs.[4]

Challenges

The main challenge is that input choices are not random and thought to be a function of the unobserved efficiency term, referred to as productivity. This problem has been discussed and analyzed since at least the 1940s. To make the problem more precise, let us consider the log specification of this production function:

$$q_{it} = \beta_L l_{it} + \beta_K k_{it} + \omega_{it} + \varepsilon_{it}, \tag{A.3}$$

in which lowercases denote logs, and ω_{it} represents shocks that are potentially observed or predicted by the firm when making input choices or TFP, while ε_{it} represents classical measurement error in recorded output, as well as unanticipated shocks to production.

Estimating the production function using ordinary least squares (OLS) will lead to biased coefficients, and subsequently biased productivity estimates.

Simultaneity bias. Firms install capital, purchase intermediate inputs, and hire workers based on their (expected) profitability. In the case of homogeneous goods and common input prices, where all firms receive the same output prices and face the same input prices, this profitability is determined by the efficiency with which firms produce: that is, their productivity. This simply implies inputs are endogenous, and that they are correlated with the unobserved productivity term.

Selection bias. Given that a panel of firms in an industry is tracked over time, attrition will further plague the estimation of the production function. The entry and exit of firms are not random events, and there is a long literature, dating back to Gibrat (1931), on firm growth and selection. In particular, over time, firms with higher values of productivity are expected to, all things equal, survive with a higher probability. This selection bias is expected to mostly plague factors of production that require substantial adjustment cost, be it in a time-to-build or monetary sense. In the standard setup, this is the case for capital. Firms with a higher capital stock can therefore absorb lower-productivity shocks, given that their option value of remaining active in the market is higher. This would lead to a downward bias in the capital coefficient.

Measurement error in inputs. Labor is usually measured in man-hours or simply number of full-time employees, while it would be more appropriate to control for the type of labor, education, experience, and specific skills. For materials, specific information on discounts or quality differences in inputs may be lacking. For capital, it is usually necessary to aggregate investment over various categories of capital such as equipment, machinery, land, and buildings and correct for the appropriate depreciation. There are basically two ways of measuring capital: either directly via book value (not free from problems) or through the investment sequence using the perpetual inventory method, which requires making some assumptions about the initial stock of capital.[5]

Approaches

In the last decade, several approaches have been proposed to control for the problems just presented. In this section, we provide a brief description of the main methodological contributions, their advantages and weaknesses, together with econometric programs and commands developed for their implementation. We refer the reader to the overview by Ackerberg et al. (2007) for a detailed discussion.

Historically, the two traditional approaches adopted to face such problems were instrumental variables and fixed effects.

Instrumental variables. The logic behind the instrumental variables approach is to find appropriate instruments (that is, variables) that are correlated with the endogenous inputs but do not enter the production function and are uncorrelated with the production function residuals. Researchers have mainly used input prices (such as capital cost, wages, and intermediates prices) or lagged values of inputs. While input prices clearly influence input choices, the critical assumption is that input prices need to be uncorrelated with ω_{it}. Whether this is the case depends on the competitive nature of the input markets in which the firm is operating. If input markets are perfectly competitive, then input prices should be uncorrelated with ω_{it} because the firm has no impact on market prices. If this is not the case, input prices will be a function of the quantity of purchased inputs, which will generally depend on ω_{it}.[6]

Although using input prices as instruments may make sense theoretically, the instrumental variables approach has not been uniformly successful in practice. According to Ackerberg et al. (2007), there are several reasons for this. First, input prices are often not reported by firms, and when firms report the labor cost variable, it is often reported as average wage per worker (which masks information about unmeasured worker quality). The problem is that unobserved worker quality will enter the production function through the unobservable ω_{it}. As a result, ω_{it} will likely be positively correlated with observed wages, invalidating use of labor costs as an instrument. Second, to use input prices as instruments requires econometrically helpful variation in these variables. While input prices clearly change over time, one generally needs significant variation across firms to properly identify production function coefficients. This can be a problem, as we often tend to think of input markets as being fairly national in scope. Third, working with lagged values of inputs requires additional assumptions on the time series properties of the instrument to work.[7] Finally, the instrumental variables approach only addresses simultaneity bias (endogeneity of input choice), not selection bias (endogenous exit).

Fixed effects. A second traditional approach to dealing with production function endogeneity issues is fixed-effects estimation. From a theoretical point of view, fixed-effects models rely on the strong assumption that the productivity shocks are time-invariant: that is, $\omega_{it} = \omega_{it-1}$. If this assumption holds, researchers can consistently estimate production function parameters using either mean differencing, first differencing, or least squares dummy variables estimation techniques.

Unfortunately, this assumption contrasts with the macroeconomic evidence about the productivity dynamics over the business cycle, thus making the entire use of fixed effects invalid. Furthermore, this assumption implies some limitations in the analysis, because researchers are usually interested in exploring the evolution of the residual when there is a change in policy variables (such as deregulation, privatization, or trade policy changes). Typically, these changes affect different firms' productivities differently, and those firms that the change affects positively will be more likely to increase their inputs and less likely to exit.

The fixed-effects estimator also imposes strict exogeneity of inputs. This is an assumption that is difficult to validate empirically, because a profit-maximizing firm will change the optimal use of inputs when facing a productivity shock. Finally, a substantial part of the information in the data is often left unused because fixed effects exploits only the within-firm variance, which in micro-data tends to be much lower than the cross-sectional variance. Often it is not even enough to allow for proper identification, leading, therefore, to weakly identified coefficients.

Thus, even if fixed-effects approaches are technically (fairly) straightforward and have certainly been used in practice (usually delivering unrealistically low estimates for β_k), they have not been judged to be all that successful at solving endogeneity problems in production functions, given the issues just discussed.[8]

Control function. A third approach, the control function approach, was introduced by Olley and Pakes (1996) and has become a popular approach to dealing with the simultaneity and selection bias. This approach was modified and extended by various authors, notably Levinsohn and Petrin (2003) and Ackerberg, Caves, and Frazer (2015).[9] The main insight and critical assumptions are discussed below.

The Control Function

The control function approach relies on two main assumptions: one about firm behavior, and the other about the statistical process of the time series of productivity.

Optimality condition. The behavioral assumption is that firms maximize profits, and this generates an optimal "input" demand equation, directly relating each input to the firms' productivity and relevant state variables of the firm. The latter enter the modeling environment due to the explicit notion of entry and exit and modeling the industry's equilibrium in the spirit of Ericson and Pakes (1995).

Denote the relevant input demand factor by z. This could be either investment (the case of Olley and Pakes 1996) or a variable input in production, like material inputs (the case of Levinsohn and Petrin 2003). The essential ingredient is that each input will relate directly through an unknown function to the unobserved productivity shock and the other relevant state variables, here simply capital.

This gives $z = h(\omega,k)$. Inverting this equation is the key approach, and the associated assumptions required allowing this inversion, to express productivity as an unknown function of the control variable z, and k:

$$\omega = h^{-1}(z,k).$$

Now simply replace the productivity term by this expression and get

$$q_{it} = \beta_L l_{it} + \beta_K k_{it} + h^{-1}(z_{it},k_{it}) + \in_{it}.$$

The first set of approaches, including those of Olley and Pakes (1996) and Levinsohn and Petrin (2003), suggested estimating the labor coefficient, in a first stage, by projecting output on labor, and a nonparametric function of capital and the relevant control variable: investment in Olley and Pakes 1996, and an intermediate input in Levinsohn and Petrin 2003.

All these approaches, however, are subject to identification concerns. The key concern is that conditional on (a function of) capital and the control variable, it becomes difficult to argue that there is any independent variation left in the labor variable. This is the argument made by Ackerberg, Caves, and Frazer (2016). In particular, Ackerberg, Caves, and Frazer (2015) correctly note that in the model assumed above, featured by a Cobb-Douglas production function in which firms face common input prices and produce a homogeneous good, one can in principle not identify the labor coefficient in the first stage. The reason is simply that the optimal labor choice is a function of the very same variables, capital and productivity. This implies that there is no independent variation in labor, conditional on a function in capital and productivity to identify the labor coefficient.

Illustration of non-identification of the labor coefficient. To highlight the non-identification result of Ackerberg, Caves, and Frazer (2015), consider the (log) optimal labor choice, and invert it to obtain an expression for (log) productivity: in fact, the function $h(\cdot)$:

$$\omega_{it} = c + (1 - \beta_L)l_{it} - \beta_K k_{it},$$

in which c is constant capturing the wage, the output price, and parameters. It suffices to plug this expression into the estimating equation (A.3) to see that the labor coefficient "drops out," highlighting the inability to identify the labor coefficient in a first stage. We refer to Ackerberg, Caves, and Frazer (2015) for a detailed discussion about these non-identification issues, and how one can in principle salvage both Olley and Pakes's (1996) and Levinsohn and Petrin's (2003) methods and achieve identification in the first stage. Although it is fair to say that the conditions under which this identification result is obtained are at best conceptually valid, it is not recommended to launch any productivity analysis using such underlying assumptions—in particular, because Ackerberg, Caves, and Frazer (2015) propose a powerful though simple alternative, by essentially giving up on identifying anything else but predicted output in the first stage.

The main takeaway from this debate, and what is ultimately relevant for empirical work, is that we can abandon the idea of identifying, and hence estimating, any coefficient in this so-called first stage (that is, the semiparametric model).

Instead, the first-stage in Ackerberg, Caves, and Frazer (2015) simply eliminates the measurement error from output by the following projection:

$$q_{it} = \varphi_t(l_{it}, k_{it}, z_{it}) + \epsilon_{it}.$$

This equation in fact immediately generates an expression for productivity, which is known up to the parameters, to be estimated:

$$\omega_{it} = \varphi_{it} - \beta_L l_{it} + \beta_K k_{it}.$$

This relationship will come in handy when generating moment conditions to find the production function parameters. But the estimation crucially relies on the second assumption, regarding the time-series properties of the productivity process.

Productivity process. All control function approaches develop estimators that form moments on the productivity shock ξ_{it}. This shock is the difference between realized and predicted productivity: that is, the so-called news term in the productivity time-series process. The bulk of the literature considers an exogenous Markov process for productivity such that

$$\xi_{it} + \omega_{it} - E(\omega_{it}|\omega_{it-1}),$$

and the familiar AR(1) process is a special case.[10]

From the first stage, this productivity shock can be computed by, for a given value of the parameters (β_L, β_K), projecting productivity on lagged productivity—and in general, this is a nonparametric projection $\xi_{it}(\beta)$. This entails considering a regression of productivity (given parameters) on a nonlinear function in lagged productivity (given parameters). In practice, this is typically done by using a polynomial expansion. The special case would be the AR(1) specification, common in the panel data approach (discussed earlier).

The parameters are then identified, and estimated, by forming moments on this productivity shock. The standard ones used in the literature are

$$E[\xi_{it}(i_L)l_{it-1}] = 0,$$

$$E[\xi_{it}(\beta_K)k_{it}] = 0,$$

in which the very observation of the simultaneity bias is used. Current labor choices do react to productivity shocks, if labor is the standard static variable input used in production, but lagged labor is not. Lagged labor is, however, related to current labor, through the persistent part of productivity; but this is exactly taken out in the procedure discussed above. In the case of capital, both current and lagged capital are valid moments because capital is assumed to face a time-to-build adjustment cost in the standard model. The point is not that these moments always need to be imposed, but that the researcher can adjust the moment conditions depending on the industry and setting and which inputs are thought to be variable or slow to adjust in light of a productivity shock.

If a gross output production function is considered, and one does not assume an underlying Leontief technology, additional parameters need to be estimated.[11] For example, the coefficient on the intermediate input is identified using the same moment condition as used for the labor coefficient. This, however, requires the researcher to state clearly under which conditions lagged materials are valid instruments—especially in light of the standard framework employed in the literature, at least by Ackerberg, Caves, and Frazer (2015) and also recently by Gandhi, Navarro, and Rivers (forthcoming). This framework assumes a neoclassical environment in which firms produce homogeneous products while facing common input prices. This greatly limits the ability to identify purely variable inputs of production (this was, as mentioned, the motivation for constructing value added as a measure of output), because there is no independent variation left to identify these coefficients. However, as soon as this stylized environment is replaced by a more realistic setting, such as the one discussed by De Loecker and Warzynski (2012) and De Loecker et al. (2016), in which firms face different input prices (if anything, due to location and to product differentiation), lagged variable inputs become valid instruments, as long as these firm-specific input prices are, of course, serially correlated. The latter is a very strong fact in a variety of data sets in which input prices (such as wages and price of raw materials) are separately recorded.

Implementation and Discussion

Investment versus intermediate input. The major insight of Olley and Pakes (1996) is to offer an alternative to estimating production functions in the presence of unobserved productivity shocks, which generate biased estimates of both the output elasticities and productivity itself (often the main object of interest). The alternative moves away from panel data techniques (such as fixed effects, discussed earlier), and the search for instruments (also discussed). The control function makes it clear that additional economic behavior is assumed and therefore the validity rests on these assumptions. In particular, Olley and Pakes (1996) heavily rely on investment to be an increasing function in productivity (conditional on a producer's capital stock). Although there is good intuition that more productive firms will invest more, this is of course not always the case, for example, in the case of adjustment cost giving rise to lumpy investment, or complementarities with other (unobserved) factors such as spending on research and innovation, or engaging in global activities (such as foreign direct investment). In addition, firms often do not invest in any given year, which would limit the sample that one can use to estimate the production function.

This is precisely the motivation behind Levinsohn and Petrin 2003. In developing economies, firms often do not invest, and this would yield a systematically different sample of "successful" firms. This is the major attraction of the Levinsohn and Petrin (2003) approach: we can now rely on the same insights of Olley and Pakes (1996), but instead rely on an input, like electricity, materials, or any other input that is deemed to be flexible in production, and easily adjustable by the firm.

There is, however, no golden rule as to which control to use in which application. In fact, carrying out robustness with multiple control variables (either variable input, or investment, or both), is the preferred strategy. The point is that different specifications are valid under different underlying assumptions of economic behavior and underlying market conditions. The productivity residual is computed after estimating the production function, and therefore there is no independent information with which to test the relationship between the control variable and productivity. The best practice is therefore to bring to bear the institutional details and knowledge of the setting under study (particular industry, country, or time frame), and verify whether the underlying assumptions are plausible. Robustness analysis should be done keeping in mind that different results (of the subsequent productivity results) are not necessarily a problem. They might simply imply that different assumptions about firm behavior lead to different conclusions in the productivity analysis of interest.

To summarize, the control function approach relies explicitly on profit maximization to generate a relationship between the unobserved productivity term and observable inputs and a control variable. This is the sense in which the search for "the instrument" is replaced by adding more structure on firm behavior and market structure of output and input markets. In addition, the moment conditions are obtained after specifying a particular productivity process. It is obvious that the parameters obtained, and the subsequent productivity analysis, are subject to the validity of these assumptions. Recent work has relaxed the reliance on a particular exogenous Markov process for productivity (De Loecker 2013; Doraszelski and Jaumaundreu 2013).

Results

Countless papers have applied the control function approaches successfully. As an instructive example, Ackerberg et al. (2007) present the work by Pavcnik (2002) that investigates the effects of trade liberalization on plant productivity in the case of Chile. The results in Ackerberg, Caves, and Frazer (2015) confirm the theoretical predictions mentioned before: the coefficients on variable inputs such as skilled and unskilled labor and materials should be biased upward in the OLS estimation, whereas the direction of the bias on the capital coefficient is ambiguous. Table A.1 displays the results of the production function estimates for plants operating in the food processing industry.

The coefficients from semiparametric estimation in column (3) are lower than the OLS estimates in column (1) for labor and materials. This implies that estimated returns to scale decrease (consistent with a positive correlation between unobserved productivity and input use) with the coefficients on the more variable inputs accounting for all of the decline. Consistent with selection, the capital coefficient rises, moving from OLS to Olley-Pakes. In particular, it exhibits the biggest movement (in relative terms) in the direction that points at the successful elimination of the selection and simultaneity bias. Also considering other industries, semi-parametric estimation by Pavcnik (2002) yields estimates that are from 45 percent to more than 300 percent higher than those obtained in the OLS estimations in industries in which the coefficient increases.

Previous literature has often used fixed-effects estimation that relies on the temporal variation in plant behavior to pinpoint the input coefficients. The fixed-effects coefficients are reported in column (2), and they are often much lower than those in the OLS or the semiparametric procedure, especially for capital. This is not surprising because the fixed-effects estimation relies on the intertemporal variation within a plant, thus overemphasizing any measurement error.

TABLE A.1 **Estimated Input Coefficients: Results of Different Approaches**

	(1) OLS	(2) Fixed effects	(3) Olley and Pakes 1996
Unskilled labor	0.178 (0.006)	0.210 (0.010)	0.153 (0.007)
Skilled labor	0.131 (0.006)	0.029 (0.007)	0.098 (0.009)
Materials	0.763 (0.004)	0.646 (0.007)	0.735 (0.008)
Capital	0.052 (0.003)	0.014 (0.006)	0.079 (0.034)

Source: Pavcnik 2002, p. 259, Table 2—full sample, N = 8,464.

Note: OLS = ordinary least squares.

These results are indicative of those for the other industries in table 2 in Pavcnik's (2002) work. The average of the returns-to-scale estimate across industries when estimated by OLS is 1.13; when estimated by Olley-Pakes, it is 1.09; and when estimated by fixed effects, it is 0.87. The average of the capital coefficients across industries from OLS is 0.066; from Olley and Pakes (1996), 0.085; and from fixed effects, only 0.021 (with two industries generating negative capital coefficients).

In fact, Pavcnik 2002 and hundreds of other papers rely on sales or value added to measure output. Therefore, for the sake of clarity, we should interpret the residual as a measure of sales per unit because researchers estimated a so-called sales-generating production function.[12] Until a few years ago, the focus of researchers was to tackle selection and simultaneity problems. This was clearly an empirical challenge. Pavcnik 2002 represents an excellent example of how these problems should be tackled.

Notable exceptions are Syverson (2004) and Foster, Haltiwanger, and Syverson (2008), who use U.S. data that allow them to separately identify producer-level quantities and prices. In particular, they rely on a selected set of plausibly homogeneous good industries (such as ready-mixed concrete) and exploit output price data to separate out price variation from productivity. An implicit assumption in their framework is that input prices do not vary across firms. This assumption is indeed plausible in the context of the homogeneous product industries they consider; for example, it is plausible to assume that (conditional on region) the input prices ready-mixed concrete producers face are the same. Their results show that there are important differences between revenue and physical productivity. This motivates and introduces the more recent evolution of productivity research.

Modern Framework (*R, E*)

Let's consider now a more realistic setup in which we observe total revenues and sales and a vector of input expenditures. However, we do not observe either the number of goods produced or the quantity used of each input. Using a basic production function with an unobserved productivity term, we can express log sales (s) in the following way:

$$s_{it} = e'_{it}\alpha + \pi_{it} + \epsilon_{it}. \tag{A.4}$$

Equation (A.4) represents a point of departure for the literature that typically utilizes firm- or plant-level data across many different sectors of one or more economies. Such data tend to be readily available based on firms' balance sheet data for a large set of countries and time periods.

However, it is important to review the underlying factors at play in equation (A.4). Relying on the definition of sales, we know that $s_{it} = p_{it} + q_{it}$, assuming a standard Hicks-neutral production function, $q_{it} = \mathbf{x}'_{it}\beta + \omega_{it}$, with β and ω_{it} the vector of production function coefficients and productivity, respectively. Please note that these are theoretically the same coefficients used in equation (A.3). Finally, input expenditures depend on input quantity and input prices, $e_{it} = x_{it} + z_{it}$. In light of this, we can rewrite equation (A.4) as

$$\underbrace{p_{it} + q_{it}}_{s_{it}} = e'_{it}\alpha + \underbrace{p_{it} - z'_{it}\beta + \omega_{it}}_{\pi_{it}} + \in_{it}. \qquad (A.5)$$

In this case, the residual π_{it} contains two more components in addition to productivity: the vector of input prices (z_{it}) multiplied by production function coefficients, and the output price (p_{it}).

As discussed, relying on sales and expenditure data will clearly not deliver an estimate of productivity ω_{it}, nor will it deliver the vector of production function coefficients α. The only exception would be in extreme cases of perfectly competitive input and output markets, in which no output or input price variation across firms is possible (as assumed in the standard approach!). In any other case, α is a vector of coefficients describing the mapping from expenditures to sales.

Challenges

Within this (more) realistic framework, it should not be surprising that researchers face new challenges, which add to those due to selection and simultaneity bias.

Omitted output and input price bias. Estimating the production function would require data on output and inputs, while in fact only sales and expenditures are observed. Lack of data on product and input prices, coupled with the lack of perfectly competitive markets in goods and inputs, implies that important economic variables such as prices and price-cost margins are in fact implicitly absorbed in the productivity residual. Deflating sales by industry-level price indexes will bias downward TFP estimations corresponding to efficient firms that were able to pass through efficiency gains into prices. Deflating input costs by industry-level input indexes will bias upward TFP estimations corresponding to firms that were able to negotiate lower input prices. De Loecker et al. (2016) show that when input price variation is not controlled for, then the coefficients of the production function often seem nonsensical and have the wrong sign.

Multiproduct bias. The estimation assuming the same technology for firms that produce several types of goods will definitively bias the input coefficients. Thus, estimation of production functions for multiproduct firms is usually not possible unless the researcher adopts one of the following three approaches:

- Focus only on single-product firms and eliminate multiproduct firms from the sample. But this approach has its drawbacks since multiproduct firms account for a nontrivial fraction of total output in many sectors.

- Aggregate product prices to the firm level and conduct the analysis at the firm level, but this implies assuming that markups are common across products within a firm (which is a rather restrictive assumption).
- Devise a mechanism for allocating firm input expenditures to individual products and conduct the analysis at the product level (see De Loecker et al. 2016). We will explain the last option at the end of the methodological section.

Approaches

Just as in the standard setting, there are a few ways of dealing with the biases discussed earlier. It is clear, however, that the treatment of the unobserved productivity shocks, discussed above, is not independent from the issues raised in this section. In fact, as we will show below, the framework suggested by De Loecker et al. (2016) combines insights from the control function approach and that of demand estimation from empirical input-output.

Reinterpretation. The first and simplest solution to not observing physical output and input is to reinterpret the residual of the production function as profitability—as discussed in great detail by De Loecker and Goldberg (2014). The change of course calls for a reinterpretation of the findings of any productivity analysis using (deflated) sales and (deflated) expenditures: replace productivity with profitability everywhere, and this of course can have substantial implications for policy and identification of the drivers of efficiency, compared with drivers of markups, or more broadly factors determining pass-through of costs to price.

Add structure on demand. Klette and Griliches (1996) and De Loecker (2011) provide an empirical framework for dealing with the omitted variable bias, focusing uniquely on the unobserved output price component. Sticking to the Cobb-Douglas specification, we now simply recognize that output is measured by sales, leading simply to the following estimating equation:

$$s_{it} = \beta_L l_{it} + \beta_K k_{it} + p_{it} + \omega_{it} + \epsilon_{it},$$

in which s, p denote log sales and log prices, respectively. This equation is referred to as the sales-generating production function, and in fact the residual from the equation ($p_{it} + \omega_{it}$) is referred to as TFPR, and ω_{it} = TFPQ, in Foster, Haltiwanger, and Syverson 2008.

We refer the reader to the two papers—Klette and Grillches 1996 and De Loecker 2011—but the main insight here is that the unobserved output price term can be replaced by a particular functional form for the (inverse) demand function, say $p = p(q,d)$, in which d is an observable demand shifter. This allows the researcher to separate the demand and price variation from the variation in productivity, and the associated relationship with the various inputs. In essence, it allows the researcher to add auxiliary data on demand—in the case of De Loecker (2011), product-level quota and industry output—and thereby isolate the mapping from inputs to physical output, while relying on the insights from the control function literature.

This approach is therefore subject to the validity of the demand system, and moreover relies on additional data that credibly move around demand, and hence prices, independently from production.

Integrate with markups. A recent literature has moved away from the focus on productivity estimation, and instead focuses on estimating markups (price-cost margins) using a production approach. In essence, this approach relies on the production function to obtain output elasticities of variable inputs of production to derive an expression for the markup. Once the markup is estimated, additional prices can be used to recover estimates of marginal costs, which are perhaps more useful when comparing firms producing differentiated products.

In particular, De Loecker and Warzynski (2012) put forward an approach to estimate markups μ_{it} that relies on cost minimization, without specifying the conduct or the shape of the demand function by essentially contrasting the cost share (of a variable input of production) to the revenue share (of that same variable input of production).

The method boils down to applying the following first order condition by firm, time, and product:

$$\mu_{it} = \theta_{it} \, \frac{P_{it} Q_{it}}{E(X)_{it}},$$

in which θ_{it} is the output elasticity of a variable input X—that is, $\frac{\partial q}{\partial x}$,—and $E(X)_{it}$ is the expenditure on input X. Applying the production function techniques discussed earlier could in principle deliver the output elasticity, and the second term is directly observable. An immediate observation is that under a Cobb-Douglas production function, the variation across producers within an industry and over time is determined only by the ratio of sales to variable-input expenditure. If one departs from Cobb-Douglas, and, say, considers a translog production function (as proposed in De Loecker and Warzynski 2012), the variation in markups can also come from variation in the output elasticity. However, both approaches do impose a constant technology over time by keeping the parameters of the production function time-invariant. This can of course be relevant in specific settings where the interest lies in the time-series properties of the markups. See De Loecker and Eeckhout 2018 for such an application.

De Loecker et al. (2016) extend this approach to (1) account for multiproduct firms and (2) explicitly deal with not observing physical inputs, and the fact that products are differentiated, making (observable) quantity variation not immediately useful for identifying technology parameters. Their approach follows two steps.

1. Consider the set of single-product producers in a sector.

De Loecker et al. (2016) observe output prices and therefore consider the mirror image of De Loecker 2011, where now input prices (W) are not observed, and quantities in a given industry cannot be compared immediately, because of, say, quality differences. This means that the estimating equation looks as follows:

$$q_{it} = \beta_L l_{it} + \beta_K k_{it} - \alpha w_{it} + \omega_{it} + \epsilon_{it},$$

in which w is the log input price index. Their approach relies on the notion that unobserved quality differences can be traced back to outcomes in the product market. In particular, De Loecker et al. (2016) provide a flexible approach that relates unobserved input prices to a nonparametric function $D(\cdot)$ of output prices, market shares, and product dummies. This yields an estimating equation that shares many similarities with the standard approach, except for the extra term that controls for the unobserved input price:

$$q_{it} + \beta_L l_{it} + \beta_K k_{it} - D(p_{it}, \cdot) + \omega_{it} + \epsilon_{it}.$$

De Loecker et al. (2016) then provide conditions under which this yields unbiased estimates of the production function and rely on insights from the control function approach (Ackerberg, Caves, and Frazer 2015) discussed earlier.

2. Consider all producers.

Having estimated the technology parameters by sector, we can go back to all firms, including multiproduct firms, and recover the implicit input allocations across products (within a firm). This solves the main problem when estimating multiproduct production functions: we do not know the breakdown of an input by product. While all the details are in De Loecker et al. 2016, and the associated code is posted, the main idea behind the input allocation shares is as follows. We illustrate the approach for a simple production function that consists of just labor, and a producer with two products, each with its respective technology (denoted by 1 and 2, respectively). Let us for simplicity assume away input price heterogeneity such that all workers are paid a common wage w. To keep notation light, consider a firm in a given period of time:

$$q_1 + \beta_{1L} l_1 + \omega;$$

$$q_1 + \beta_{2L} l_1 + \omega.$$

The standard problem is that we do not observe the labor used in each production process, but as in De Loecker et al. 2016, we only have data on production by product (q) and total employment (L) at the firm level. We wish to recover markups and marginal costs for each product-firm-year observation.

First, we obtain the estimates of the technology parameters by considering the set of single-product firms producing products 1 and 2, respectively. This is done as described above, and this makes the parameters (β_{1L}, β_{2L}) known objects. Following De Loecker et al. (2016), we define the expenditure share of employment of a product as $\exp(\rho_{ijt})$, and this simply states how much of, here, the wage bill accrues to product 1 versus product 2. In this simplified setting, the expenditure share is simply given by $L_1/(L_1 + L_2)$, because the wage rate drops out. We can now rewrite the system of equations for the firm producing two products, for a given period:

$$q_1 - \beta_{1L}l = \beta_{1L}\rho_1 + \omega;$$

$$q_1 - \beta_{2L}l = \beta_{2L}\rho_2 + \omega.$$

The crucial insight of De Loecker et al. (2016) is that we are left with three unknowns, but seemingly only two equations. However, the additional restriction is that the sum of expenditures across products must sum to the total recorded expenditure, here the total wage bill. In other words, the shares ρ_{ijt} sum to one across all the products. Paired with the standard assumption in the theory of multiproduct firms that the firm applies its productivity, capability, or management skills to each product line yields a simple solution to this system of equations: solve for the shares, and productivity—which now allows the user to go back to the markup formula and apply this at the level of a firm-product, and with data on prices, marginal costs can be recovered as well.

This procedure is fully general as long as the production function is log additive in the productivity term, and as long as the productivity shock is assumed to be common across products. In addition, the identification of the shares is intuitive: conditional on technology, any variation observed in quantity produced can only come from the use of the input (labor). Productivity is identified simply from the level of average output across products to total employment (here labor productivity).

Results

The realization that measured firm performance captures markups as well as physical efficiency naturally leads to two other sets of literature that were developed in different contexts: the large industrial organization literature on imperfect competition, and the international literature on incomplete (exchange rate) pass-through. The first explicitly investigates the measurement and determinants of markups (such as the role of market structure, product differentiation, and demand elasticities). The second focuses on how a certain type of cost shock (exchange rate changes) is passed through to prices. The role of market power, however, has been traditionally absent in the productivity literature. One can tell many stories as to why this is, but the fact remains that most popular estimators in the literature (Olley and Pakes 2016; Levinsohn-Petrin 2003; and Ackerberg, Caves, and Frazer 2015) are silent about market power and the demand side of the market, which is of course closely related to a producer's market power. A simple way out is to refer to the residual of the production function as a measure of sales per input.[13] This, however, does not help us understand how, for example, trade liberalization affects producers and ultimately consumers, and how firms grow.

Equation (A.2) highlights the relevance that should be given in any productivity analysis to the pass-through of cost to prices. In a more general production function with multiple inputs, this framework will indeed indicate that the performance residual captures, in addition to efficiency, the wedge between the output price and the weighted sum of the various input prices, where weights are in fact the output elasticities.[14]

A robust finding of these literatures is that pass-through is incomplete, which in our setting translates to a situation in which changes in the operating environment that affect production costs will not be perfectly translated into changes in output prices. This implies that it is to be expected that standard productivity analysis will confound efficiency effects with the role of market power and curvature of the demand curve, the two main factors determining the degree of pass-through.

The good news, again, is that micro data sets increasingly contain information on output prices. This means that we can let the data tell us how output prices reacted to changes in the operating environment. Of course, changes in output prices depend on both the markups and cost changes. In this regard, recent developments in the estimation of markups come in handy. De Loecker and Warzynski (2012) and De Loecker et al. (2016) put forward a method to recover an individual producer's markup using standard production panel data. The main premise behind the approach is that the wedge between an input's share of expenditure over sales (such as the wage bill over sales) and input's share of expenditure in total cost (such as the wage bill over total cost) is directly informative about a producer's price-cost margin. Of course, the share of an input's expenditure in total cost of production is not directly observed, or at least we have reasons to doubt the reported numbers on accounting costs because they fail to incorporate opportunity cost. This is where economic theory proves to be useful because cost minimization guarantees that the output elasticity of an input is in fact equal to this share of expenditure in total cost.

With data on prices, and having estimated markups, we can now back out measures of marginal costs to analyze how each of these components is affected by changes in the operating environment. In addition, we can connect these results to the standard productivity regressions, and separately identify the impact on efficiency, cost, and prices.[15]

Let's illustrate this in the case of trade reforms in India, a notable overnight trade liberalization that induced a substantial reduction in tariffs across a wide range of products.

TABLE A.2 **Firm Performance and Trade Reforms: The Case of India**

	(1) Prices	(2) Marginal cost	(3) Markups	(4) Markups
Output tariff	0.15***	0.05	0.10	0.14***
Input tariff	0.35	1.16**	−0.80++	0
Marginal cost	—	—	—	Yes

Source: De Loecker et al. 2016.

Note: Each column refers to a regression of the component of firm performance on output and input tariffs. All regressions include firm-product fixed effects and sector-year fixed effects. Standard errors are clustered at the industry level.

Significance level: ++ = 11.3%; ** = 5%; *** = 1%.

De Loecker et al. (2016) observe panel data of Indian manufacturing firms over the period 1988–2012. In addition to standard firm-level production data, they observe product-level output prices and quantities. This allows them to obtain estimates of markups and marginal costs, in addition to efficiency, for each product-firm pair over the sample period. The interest of De Loecker et al. (2016) lies in analyzing the impact of the tariff changes, for both final and intermediate goods: that is, output and input tariffs. The main results are summarized in table A.2.

In column (1), the standard procompetitive effects from trade liberalization are confirmed: reduction in output tariffs implies, on average, lower output prices of Indian manufacturing products. However, this price effect masks the underlying dynamics of cost and pass-through. The lowering of output tariffs did not significantly affect the cost of production, which goes against the common wisdom of efficiency gains through X-inefficiency reductions—a popular narrative when describing measured productivity gains in the aftermath of a certain policy change (such as trade liberalization or deregulation). In fact, De Loecker et al. (2016) do not find any systematic impact on efficiency, as measured by TFPQ.

One of the major findings of this study is that input tariffs substantially lower marginal cost, by giving access to cheaper inputs, but the results in column (3) indicate that these cost savings are only partly passed on to consumers. This leads overall to only a modest price drop, and a negative association between markups and input tariffs: that is, as input tariffs fall, and intermediate input prices fall (relatively), Indian manufacturing firms see their variable profit margins (markups) increase.

Column (3) seems to go against standard economic theory and empirical evidence that increased competition in output markets does not affect markups. This specification is, however, not equipped to tease out this effect because cost and competition effects occur simultaneously. Therefore, in column (4), the authors condition on marginal cost of production, tracing out the pure procompetitive effects. And indeed, the fall in output tariffs leads to lower markups, holding fixed the cost of production.

In any event, the important insight from De Loecker et al.'s (2016) work for policy is that changes in tariffs or other trade policy instruments do not necessarily translate to proportional changes in prices, as typically assumed in the literature. In the presence of market power and variable markups, the response of prices and their components is substantially more complex. This insight has implications for the aggregate gains from trade, their distribution across consumers and producers, and the relative importance of static versus dynamic impacts.

Although this is an isolated study, and one of the first to decompose firm performance into price, cost, and markup effects, there is reason to believe these results will extend to other settings. Recent work by De Loecker, Van Biesebroeck, and Fuss (2016) follows a similar strategy to evaluate the impact of increased Chinese imports on Belgian manufacturing firm performance.

The results are qualitatively very similar: while output prices fall with increased imports from China, variable profit margins actually increase. The latter is precisely for the same reason as in India: producers have access to cheaper inputs. As a result, the marginal cost of production falls, but such savings are only partly passed on to consumers in the form of lower output prices.

De Loecker, Van Biesenbroeck, and Fuss (2016) delve deeper into the input market channel. They find that the reduction in intermediate input prices is not limited to firms that directly import, but the effect manifests itself through the entire input market. This suggests that the general equilibrium effects are important and suggests caution in applying the practice of preclassifying producers as importers when studying the role of imported intermediate inputs.

There are also other economic reasons that make the acknowledgment of demand factors embedded in the productivity residual relevant for economic policy. Lack of identification of demand and supply factors behind the residual can also lead to misleading conclusions regarding the sources of aggregate productivity growth. If variation in TFPR mainly reflects variations in markups instead of efficiency, then what appears to be a reallocation of activity toward more efficient firms (that is, allocative efficiency) may merely reflect a reallocation of activity and market shares toward firms with market power.

The identification of demand and supply factors is crucial to understanding the determinants of firm growth along a firm's life cycle. For decades economists have emphasized the role of efficiency to foster firm growth, but recent research shows that the demand component may play a more prominent role. Foster, Haltiwanger, and Syverson (2016) pioneered this demand versus supply debate by arguing that a firm's ability to increase its demand may be even more important to ensuring firm growth (profits, sales, employment) than is its ability to increase physical efficiency. By focusing on the accumulating process of the demand component in a particular homogeneous good sector, Foster, Haltiwanger, and Syverson (2016) argue that the observed slow U.S. firm growth comes about from the slow process of building up demand through different types of "soft" investments like advertising, marketing, and developing networks. This process is, certainly, very different from the process controlling efficiency, which occurs through "hard" investments like innovation, technology adoption, and managerial upgrading.

Recent work has focused on precisely decomposing the so-called TFPR residual, obtained from relating sales to inputs, into efficiency (TFPQ) and demand factors broadly defined. One of the first papers to discuss this issue at a theoretical and methodological level is Katayama, Liu, and Tybout 2009. However, the first empirical analysis, as far as we know, is by Foster, Haltiwanger, and Syverson (2008). They observe plant-level prices for a subset of 10 plausibly homogeneous goods U.S. manufacturing industries, including the ready-mixed concrete, sugar, and cardboard industries.

The main finding is that TFPR, the traditional productivity residual, is positively correlated with output prices, while efficiency (TFPQ) is negatively correlated with output prices. The latter is precisely what economic theory would predict: more efficient producers, all things equal, can set lower prices. A second major result is that when looking at the role of entrants in aggregate productivity, the distinction between TFPR and TFPQ becomes crucial yet again: entrants enter with higher TFPQ—that is, if anything, they enter with higher efficiency, which could reflect superior technology, management, or vintage of capital, but with lower TFPR. The latter suggests that entrants enter with lower demand, and therefore on average set lower prices.

These findings put the literature on productivity analysis in very different perspective and give very different policy prescriptions on the role of entry and, for example, the role of entry barriers or other entry frictions in markets. It also indicates that TFPR consists of two distinct economic variables of interest: demand (as reflected by prices) and efficiency. These variables also turn out to have very distinct time series patterns in the data. In a follow-up paper, Foster, Haltiwanger, and Syverson (2016) focus on the accumulating process of the demand component and argue that the slow growth comes about from the process of building up demand, through, say, building a customer list. This process is very different from the process controlling efficiency, which occurs through investment, innovation, and development.

In another study, De Loecker (2011) relies on a structural model of production and demand, without actually observing prices, but instead variables that affect them directly, in his application to the product-level quota for textile products in the European Union (EU), to do the same decomposition. Again, the distinction between demand and efficiency is found to be important. The trade liberalization episode in the EU textile market, through quota liberalization, largely affected the demand for domestic producers, and therefore negatively affected their prices, but did by and large not affect the efficiency of production. The immediate price effect is thus what is picked up in a productivity analysis, which again leads to a very different policy conclusion.

De Loecker (2011) also finds the demand component to be much more volatile than the efficiency component, which seems plausible given the cyclicality of tastes and fashion and competitive structures. This is in contrast to the more persistent process of technical efficiency, which moves much more slowly, with discrete jumps whenever firms invest in new technology or managerial practices.

Although many technical issues remain unresolved in the production function estimation literature, ranging from measurement error in inputs to the functional of production, the good news is that the discussion here leads to more interesting work to be done in terms of the economics of the problem, with the potential that we can learn more about the mechanism through which producers react to shocks. Topics that were previously not mentioned at all in the productivity literature now become central: price setting and pass-through, the role of input markets, market power, and how all these shapes the evolution of efficiency and aggregate outcomes through the allocation of resources.

Notes

1. This appendix summarizes the main methodological discussion presented by Cusolito, De Loecker, and Biondi (2018).
2. In what follows, we will omit subscripts of producers and time, and all variables are deflated with the appropriate industry-wide deflators. Moreover, we use the term "producer" to accommodate both plant and firm as units of observation in the data and analysis.
3. To simplify notation, we base our discussion on a (log) Cobb-Douglas production function, but our framework generalizes to any other functional form.
4. We refer to De Loecker and Scott 2016 for a detailed discussion of this issue; Ackerberg, Caves, and Frazer (2015) also discuss this in detail.
5. For treatment of capital measurement error, see De Loecker and Collard-Wexler 2015.
6. Other possible IVs are output prices, as long as the firm operates in competitive output markets. These instruments have been used less frequently, presumably because input markets are thought to be more likely to be competitive.
7. For empirical implementation, the user can use the following Stata command: ivreg.
8. For empirical implementation, the practitioner can use the following Stata command: xtreg, fe.
9. For empirical implementation, the practitioner can use *prodest*, a new and comprehensive Stata module for production function estimation based on the control function approach.
10. Under this setup, the control function and the dynamic panel data approach pioneered by Arellano and Bond (1991), and subsequent work by Blundell and Bond (1998), are closely related.
11. Under Leontief technology, the estimated parameters need to be adjusted by the intermediate-to-output ratio to obtain the correct output elasticities. See De Loecker and Scott 2016 for an application of this procedure.
12. Interestingly, this was clearly stated in footnote 3 of Olley and Pakes 1996.
13. This is precisely how Olley and Pakes (1996) proceed in their seminal paper.
14. See De Loecker and Goldberg 2014 for more details.
15. Identification here presumes that the change in the operating environment is exogenous with respect to an individual producer. This condition will, of course, not always be met. Additional work might be needed to guarantee a causal interpretation.

References

Ackerberg D., L. Benkard, S. Berry, and A. Pakes. 2007. "Econometric Tools for Analyzing Market Outcomes." In *The Handbook of Econometrics*, Vol. 6A, edited by J. Heckman and E. Learner, 4171–276. Amsterdam: North-Holland.

Ackerberg, D., K. Caves, and G. Frazer. 2015. "Identification Properties of Recent Production Function Estimators." *Econometrica* 83 (6, November): 2411–51.

Arellano, M., and S. Bond. 1991. "Some Tests of Specification for Panel Data: Monte Carlo Evidence and an Application to Employment Equations." *Review of Economic Studies* 58 (2): 277–97.

Blundell, R., and S. Bond. 1998. "Initial Conditions and Moment Restrictions in Dynamic Panel Data Models." *Journal of Econometrics* 87: 115–43.

Cusolito, A., J. De Loecker, and F. Biondi. 2018. "A Frontier Productivity Diagnostic for Micro and Macro Analysis and Country Engagement." World Bank, Washington, DC.

De Loecker. J. 2011 "Product Differentiation, Multi-Product Firms and Estimating the Impact of Trade Liberalization on Productivity." *Econometrica* 79 (5, September): 1407–51.

———. 2013. "Detecting Learning by Exporting." *American Economic Journal: Microeconomics* 5 (3, August): 1–21.

De Loecker, J., and A. Collard-Wexler. 2015. "Reallocation and Technology: Evidence from the US Steel Industry." *American Economic Review* 105 (1, January): 131–71.

De Loecker, J., and J. Eeckhout. 2018. "Global Market Power." http://www.janeeckhout.com/wp-content/uploads/Global.pdf.

De Loecker, J., and P. K. Goldberg. 2014. "Firm Performance in a Global Market." *Annual Review of Economics* 6 (1): 201–27.

De Loecker, J., P. Goldberg, A. Khandelwal, and N. Pavcnik. 2016. "Prices, Markups, and Trade Reform." *Econometrica* 84 (2): 445–510.

De Loecker, J., and P. T. Scott. 2016. "Estimating Market Power. Evidence from the US Brewing Industry." NBER Working Paper 22957, National Bureau of Economic Research, Cambridge, MA.

De Loecker, J., J. Van Biesebroeck, and J. Fuss. 2016. "International Competition and Firm-Level Adjustment in Markups and Production Efficiency." Working paper.

De Loecker, J., and F. Warzynski. 2012. "Markups and Firm-Level Export Status." *American Economic Review* 102 (6, October): 2437–71.

Doraszelski, U., and J. Jaumaundreu. 2013. "R&D and Productivity: Estimating Endogenous Productivity." *Review of Economic Studies* 80: 1338–83.

Ericson, R., and A. Pakes. 1995. "Markov-Perfect Industry Dynamics: A Framework for Empirical Work." *Review of Economic Studies* 62 (1): 53–82.

Foster, L., J. Haltiwanger, and C. Syverson. 2008. "Reallocation, Firm Turnover, and Efficiency: Selection on Productivity or Profitability?" *American Economic Review* 98 (1): 394–425.

———. 2016. "The Slow Growth of New Plants: Learning about Demand." *Economica* 83 (3289): 91–129.

Gandhi, A., S. Navarro, and D. Rivers. Forthcoming. "On the Identification of Gross Output Production Functions." *Journal of Political Economy*.

Gibrat, R. 1931. *Les inégalités économiques*. Paris: Sirey.

Katayama, H., S. Liu, and J. Tybout. 2009. "Why Plant-Level Productivity Studies Are Often Misleading, and an Alternative Approach to Inference." *International Journal of Industrial Organization* 27 (3): 403–13.

Klette, T. J., and Z. Griliches. 1996. "The Inconsistency of Common Scale Estimators When Output Prices Are Unobserved and Endogenous." *Journal of Applied Econometrics* 11 (4): 343–61.

Levinsohn, J., and A. Petrin. 2003. "Estimating Production Functions Using Inputs to Control for Unobservables." *Review of Economic Studies* 70: 317–40.

Olley, S. G., and A. Pakes. 1996. "The Dynamics of Productivity in the Telecommunications Equipment Industry." *Econometrica* 64 (6): 1263–97.

Pavcnik, N. 2002. "Trade Liberalization, Exit, and Productivity Improvement: Evidence from Chilean Plants." *Review of Economic Studies* 69: 245–76.

Syverson, C. 2004. "Market Structure and Productivity: A Concrete Example." *Journal of Political Economy* 112: 1181–222.